A NUT SHELL

We all emerge from our childhoods with psychological issues
that are out-of-order. No one escapes. With all the help and
information available today, it is simply up to us to resolve
these issues, and put ourselves in proper order. Our parents
were not perfect. Most grew up in a psychological blind era,
and raised amid circumstances beyond their control that
were no fault of their own. However, everyone is personally
responsible and accountable for their choices and behavior,
and ultimately, there comes a time when all accounts come
due, when we are charged with great interest to grow in an
upward direction.

APPROPRIATE QUOTES

"Great spirits always encounter violent opposition from mediocre minds. The mediocre mind is incapable of understanding the man who refuses to bow blindly to conventional prejudices, and chooses instead to express his opinions courageously and honestly."   Albert Einstein

* * *

"Never attribute to malice that which can adequately be explained by stupidity."   Hanlon's Razor: Robert J. Hanlon

* * *

"There are only two ways to live your life. One is as though nothing is a miracle. The other is as though everything is a miracle.   Albert Einstein

* * *

"It is not enough to learn. You must apply."   Bruce Lee

* * *

"Two things are infinite: The universe, and human stupidity; and I'm still wondering about the universe."   Albert Einstein

* * *

"Life is either a daring adventure, or it is nothing at all."   Helen Keller

* * *

"The only true source of knowledge is experience."   Albert Einstein

THE INAPPROPRIATE THERAPIST

Surviving the Dysfunctional Family
And Learning to Thrive

Valerie Lumley
Dysfunctional Family Survivor

April 2020 | Monterey, California

THE INAPPROPRIATE THERAPIST

COPYRIGHT 2020

ALL RIGHTS RESERVED - BY VALERIE LUMLEY

Visit author's website at valerielumley.com – to see Valerie's additional books; *Curing Chronic Fobromyalgia – Choosing What Works, and, The Grand Master And His Protégé – A Memoir Of Love, Courage, Endurance and Devotion.*

ISBN: 978-1-7349057-0-0

Printed in the United States
Cover art and interior design by Valerie Lumley.

CONTENTS

PUBLISHER'S NOTE

I have a special appreciation for what Valerie is addressing in this book, which is how to survive having lived in a dysfunctional family. Her experience seems like she grew up in a frighteningly vile cuckoo's nest. Most people have issues since they, almost by necessity, inherit behavioral traits from their parents who got them for their parents et cetera, because no one knew better. My early life was mostly wonderful – I was the son of a semi-Freudian psychoanalyst and a noted columnist and author – but I certainly came away with issues, and I've gotten great clarity on them reading this book.

There are very different degrees of dysfunction, but most aren't the horror story Valerie had to deal with into middle age. She no doubt had some of her personal demons in mind while researching to understand them and writing this book to expel them.

What she reveals about what she learned about narcissists and borderline personality disorder people provides particularly crucial information for those who unknowingly stumble across such people. To recognize these types early can save you considerable pain. Don't ask questions. Run, don't walk.

While there aren't many extreme narcissists and borderlines, the damage they can do is vastly greater than their numbers. Reading this book might awaken memories of such encounters, producing clarity on particular relationships, a better sense of self as more stable and decent, and deep sighs of relief at escaping them.

You will find some repetition in these pages, which is intended to benefit those in deeper struggle with these issues, and for those who are reading only certain chapters of this book.

You may find personal challenges in these pages, but they could certainly better your life.

Tony Seton
Carmel, California

PRAISE FOR THE INAPPROPRIATE THERAPIST

The Inappropriate Therapist is a unique book because it's partly memoir, and then evolves into presenting an overview of two primary personality disorders, and provides a strategy on how to extricate yourself from the inevitable chaos and various emotional entanglements that follow. In this case, the two disorders were Borderline Personality Disorder (BPD) and Narcissistic Personality Disorder (NPD), which are often comorbid with each other.

For those of you who may not know the difference between a personality disorder and less severe issues, personality disorders are pervasive, often lifelong patterns of cognition and behaviors that wreak havoc on loved ones, often leaving the family, friends or intimate partners feeling deceived, manipulated and hopeless.

When you live with someone or more than one person who is suffering from BPD/NPD, you can end up feeling as if all the energy has been sucked out of you. This is further complicated by feelings of confusion, guilt, unhealthy boundaries, codependent behaviors and grief. In other words, these kinds of disturbances are insidious, and the caretakers and enablers often end up in what often feels like "hell on earth." We all have tendencies toward unhealthy thoughts and behaviors, but in a full-blown personality disorder it disrupts life in major ways, often resulting in divorce, suicide attempts, addictions, and always lots of drama.

What is so unusual about Valerie Lumley is that she gives victims an internal perspective on what it's like to live in a family where more than one person is suffering with these types of problems. While describing an outside event in the manner of a reporter is relatively easy, bringing the internal hell to life in a way where you can peek inside a real loved ones profound confusion, shame and personal suffering, is rare. The author manages to do this very well, which is why this book reads like a good novel, especially the first half.

If you are living with someone with BPD/NPD, you won't be able to enter into any sort of shared reality. You also won't be able to reach them through logic, repetition, negotiation and so on. This is because they have a fragmented self-structure and inflexible ways of behaving that are largely conditioned, and often are extremely emotionally dysregulated in ways that interfere with just leading a normal life.

Perhaps the person with the disorder can present a good facade, but as a loved one, you are likely to feel betrayed and abandoned once the mask comes off. You can question your own sanity, and the whole situation seems surreal, because it is. The people you thought you knew are actually not at all what they seem, and what you thought was a meaningful, authentic shared history is really a fabricated situation, where you wanted to show up, but your compassion, love and commitment were taken advantage of. In brief, you feel used, emotionally raped, and even suicidal.

I wrote a lot of concepts above, but what you really need to understand about these disorders, and the spider web quality of the interactions, is what Valerie Lumley provides; A detailed history of the outer and inner events that lead to an "Alice in Wonderland" transformation that touches every area of your life on every level, including physical, emotional, mental, soul and spirit.

You don't see many books like this because most people don't want to share the tough stuff; it takes courage, empathy, and a strong sense of values. These are qualities that people with BPD/NPD so often lack, or that collapse under stress. This is because developmentally they may have gotten stuck on an emotional level in what many parents call the "terrible twos." There is a lot of black-and-white thinking, and life is about me, me and more me. This is appropriate in a two-year-old, but in an intelligent adult it's crazy-making.

Valerie gives you a bridge from personal history to a general understanding of the disorders, symptoms and defense mechanisms - and ultimately why your efforts to get through to the victims of these disorders fail. The short answer to why they can't change is they didn't develop enough of the capacities we take for granted, such as experiencing ourselves as having core values, empathy and a deep understanding of how social reciprocity works. Think again of a two-year-old: To them, something is either all "good" or "bad." They can't reconcile opposites, so they swing back and forth between extremes of shutdown. Where the self-structure should be, there is a deep sense of emptiness and/or core of shame.

After *The Inappropriate Therapist* looks at these disorders from the outside objectively, like a psychologist might do, the book then moves toward; how do I cope with this, extricate myself from the toxic person or people, and stop reflectively enabling the family member or loved ones locked into their own personal hell? This is even a challenge for a good psychologist treating these people. If you consider a psychologist's stance toward the nature of these problems, can you imagine what it's like for people who must spend the majority of their free time with them? It can suck you dry, and literally destroy you. This is exactly what Valerie makes land deeply through sharing her own internal and external struggles to arrive at taking her life back from the drama, the inauthentic love, and the manipulation – which is precisely due to having your best qualities, love and compassion, literally weaponized in all kinds of games. What you realize you don't have is a real relationship with the victim of these mental disorders.

By way of example, Valerie shows that what you must do is save yourself first. To one who is compassionate and sensitive, it could feel like you are betraying the person with the disorder. However, it's like being on a plane, where they tell you to put the mask on yourself first, and then assist others. You cannot possibly help the other person by jumping or being pulled into the rabbit hole of illusion along with them. That's where Valerie's thorough discussion of boundaries, understanding how to deconstruct emotional interactions, and make sense of them comes in. This entire area can be a book in itself, but Valerie Lumley gives you the survival skills and deep understanding you will need to make the often difficult decisions required to move on with your life. Trust me, you will need this information, and we can all benefit from hardening our boundaries and letting it sink in where our responsibility ends.

So, what are you getting when you purchase this book? A great story with all the complexities of a Russian novel, along with understanding why the characters act the way they do, what is keeping people (yourself) stuck, how the dynamics of interactions work so you can see deeper, and then the description and survival tools to go into the sort of tough decisions and action that are required to recover yourself and heal. That's a lot of ground to cover, and I find it difficult to do justice to the density of good material in this book.

In the final section of the book, more stories, anecdotes, and concrete examples are shared from the author's life, and you feel like you are accompanying her on her own inner transformation and healing. She will guide you to take back your life, and inspire you to break the trance and step into your own magnificence. This requires that you stand on firm ground in terms of clarifying your own values, where your responsibility begins and ends in crystal clear terms. You'll need the will to walk forward by a dialectic of deep inquiry alternating with taking meaningful action, back and forth toward a new vision. You will take that away from the sum of this book as it speaks to you on every level.

If you are in some sort of dysfunctional relationship, family bond, or even a bad work relationship, it likely evolved gradually and unnoticed over years. That's why you need to read this book; to learn all the things you may not find out in mere surface descriptions as if people are merely a case to be treated. If you suspect you may be in circumstances like Valerie describes, you need a map and to build a good support network. This book is your map, and Valerie is a loving tour guide.

On a personal note, my expertise is in biology, biochemistry, and psychology. I understand the neurotransmitters, drugs, developmental experiences and other things that help explain disorders and relationships from the outside. However, this alone can only assist someone in coping or transforming a "hellish" situation. I can explain the macro- and micro-economic and social issues to a starving person, but that won't fill their belly or get them through the day. If you are experiencing the emotional equivalent of this, you need to eat and drink from the deep well of Valerie Lumley's lived experience. Her journey in this book is a gift to all who may be suffering from overt and covert abuse, sexual exploitation, being caught in the nightmare of someone's acting out, and all the external forms that can take.

Valerie Lumley is a pioneer, and this a very good book. The Inappropriate Therapist is rather unique in presenting a coherent picture that real people can relate to. In terms of credibility, everyone is an authority on their own lived reality. When you write a book such as this, your first person truth-claims rest on your authenticity, and sharing that which at one time you may have been ashamed of. Valerie also has a good understanding of the BPD/NPD from an objective perspective, and presents the basics without all the unnecessary detail. That makes this work something that is accessible to everyone, and to be able to pull a feat like that off is really an achievement to be proud of. I'm sure this book will touch many lives, and bring comfort and healing.

Patrick D. Goonan, MA Psychology

THE LIONESS

Hale to the lioness —
who ventured into the jungle
and hunted down d'evil;
chased it out into the open
and roared the truth at it.

As she stood her ground
and weathered the fury of evil's hate-storms,
she felt the courage and strength
of her hard-fought convictions.
Afterward, she shook it all off
like stale desert dust,
and peaceably went along her way.

Valerie Lumley
March 1, 2020

TO LIVE DELIBERATELY

"I went to the woods because I wished to live deliberately,
to front only the essential facts of life,
and see if I could not learn what it had to teach,
and not when I come to die, discover that I had not lived.
I did not wish to live what was not life,
living is so dear;
nor did I wish to practice resignation
unless it was quite necessary."
"I wanted to live deep and suck out all the marrow of life,
to live so sturdily and Spartan-like
as to put to rout all that was not life,
to cut a broad swath and shave close,
to drive life into a corner,
and reduce it to its lowest terms,
and, if it proved to be mean, why then to get
the whole and genuine meanness of it,
and publish its meanness to the world;
or if it were sublime, to know it by experience,
and be able to give a true account of it
in my next excursion."

By Henry David Thoreau
Walden; or, Life in the Woods, pub. 1854

INTRODUCTION

This is a "telling" book, rather than a dry report, where I use my personal experiences to elucidate and demonstrate known facts about the various dysfunctions in family and personal relationships. I use the term inappropriate in the title because no therapist will ever share personal experience or information with a client. All they can ethically do is empathize, diagnose, treat, and educate.

Their methods may vary, and you are free to try one for a while, change therapists, or even take a break. They typically give out insights and information over time, while I am attempting to present vital information all at once, and provide a road map for choosing a healthier path in life. I feel we are all born into a family with a degree of dysfunction, and it is in this degree that they vary.

I was born into a wildly dysfunctional family full of self-oblivious narcissistic and borderline personalities, neurotic schizotypal sycophant personalities, codependents, and recluses. The cast of characters included one suicidal drug abuser, a macho man, a gambler, two alcoholics, two pedophiles, at least two philanderers, and a tragic deaf mute. Professionally, they were a singer/teacher, a landscape supply entrepreneur, a farmer/banker/mayor, a prostitute, several secretaries, a CEO, a stockbroker, and a judge.

There was the occasional incestuous advance toward the next generation of young females, numerous divorces and re-marriages, and several changes in religion. An aunt had a baby out of wedlock when she was young, and put it up for adoption; a father who disappeared for seven years and later returned occasionally; another who disappeared and later committed suicide with a rifle to his head; another died of alcoholism; and another died in a mental ward of collapsed lungs and heart failure. These men were all from my parents', aunts', and uncles' generation.

Among all the continuous evil behavior (that which is destructive) shenanigans and tom-foolery, on-going dramas, and chaotic crises, there was a degree of unexpressed love, and brief periods of jest and happiness. However, not nearly enough to compensate for the effects of the crazy, irrational, impetuous, childish, and yes, abusive behaviors that were chronically perpetuated among the dysfunctional relationships in my family. Fighting, grandstanding, bickering, raging, storming, sulking, feuding, drinking, pill-popping, withdrawing, disappearing, and so on, was the abnormal normal.

There were unsteady, eerie periods of peace that sometimes followed a perfect storm of clashing personality disorders and competitive power struggles. You never knew when the next shoe would drop, or when the next grenade would be launched. The psychological violence was nearly constant, insidious, and often horrific. One of my therapists said to me, "Honey, you spent your entire childhood trying to survive on the front lines of a war zone. You are a survivor, for sure!" Another said, "Don't worry, you'll never be like your mother. It is your greatest fear."

This book is not about my story. However, I use a number of my experiences as examples to show how I survived a dangerously dysfunctional family. I have created a road map for other survivors so they can find their way out of the morass of the lies, deceit, denial, manipulation, abuse, self-blindness and willful ignorance to become free from their unhealthy childhood survival adaptations, and learn to stop enabling and excusing evil, destructive behavior. My focus is on showing how to identify major offenders, and when and how to use internal and external boundaries. These are the tools for living healthier lives.

My life changed for the better as soon as I understood my unhealthy tolerance to destructive behavior, and chose to value myself enough to set boundaries of distance and time against the major offenders in my life who were chronically draining my energy, preventing me from living my own life and fully reaching my unique potential. As soon as I set much needed and long-overdue boundaries, I no longer needed to protect myself with my energy-draining "wall of humor" from the most dangerously insane people in my life: my own family. My energy began to improve, and I was able to discover a way to heal a chronic illness that forced me to face what I had to in order to get well.

The truth is: my family was a died-in-the-wool, self-oblivious clan that blindly passed down to their own children all of the aforementioned personality disorders. Their delusions of moral superiority are here to stay, and no amount of compassion, pity, anger, or frustration from trying to reach them to no avail, will ever change this fact. Sometimes the truth can be so harsh and tragic, it may seem like you will never be able to fully accept it, and may take years. I am very grateful that I have given up any hope of being in safe contact with even one of these unfortunate people, and I realize my hoping any of them will ever become healthier is a foolish pipe-dream I no longer need to fantasize.

My family has always personified the profound assertion that arrogance combined with willful ignorance equals psychological blindness. They never really were a family to me anyway, and represent the truth that our truest families are not always the ones we are born into. As for fully accepting the entirety of this tragedy, I am successful most of the time, and it has gotten easier as time goes by. Although I am grateful to have them out of my life, I truly wish them well.

I'd like to encourage other dysfunctional family survivors to enhance their view of life, and develop a clearer understanding of themselves and their relationships so their survival can be rewarded with health, wellbeing, and the energy and ability to reach their full potential. This is why I wrote this book: for all you survivors of dysfunctional families seeking healthier alternatives to the way you've experienced life so far. You deserve to enjoy peace, happiness, and the fulfillment of your own unique potential. You can discover that not only can you survive a dysfunctional family; you can learn to thrive as well!

Bear in mind that the process of healing a dysfunctional past and shedding unhealthy childhood adaptations requires work and commitment, a humble willingness to learn, and the ability to face facts honestly. Sadly, there will always be those with disordered personalities so serious they are prisoners of themselves; adult children who believe the lie their disorder tells them that they are the healthy ones, and others are the ones with the problem.

When I look back on my life now from a healthier, hard-earned perspective, I can see how evil forces from within my family, and from without, consistently tried to destroy me for most of it. Fortunately, I've never been afraid to stand up to evil, and thankfully had the courage to fight back, as depleting as it was.

Maybe my being born a sensitive empath made me a big enough threat to the evil around me – as I could always see beneath their "mask of sanity" – that I seemed an easy mark for being made the family scapegoat. And as the rebel, I was the most convenient one to ridicule and punish. I'll never really know for certain. What I can tell you with certainty about evil is that it subsists on fear, hate, and uncontrolled anger, and can only do harm when it is enabled, minimized, and excused. I've won my fight with evil and its enablers, and it no longer appears in my life. As far as what my family thinks about me now, well, I'm sure they discuss me from time to time, share their ignorance, judge me as crazy, still, and come away having protected their comfort zone and worldview. The rule, "what other people think of you is none of your business" applies here, as always.

The fact that I am not a licensed therapist permits me to freely express my perceptions that are based on combining my life experience with what I have gleaned from studying over 40 books on human psychology, including the DSM (Diagnostic and Statistical Manual of Mental Disorders) and countless extensive research articles. An informed layman's point of view can be extremely useful. Melody Beattie's wrote "Codependent No More" in 1986, which has been enormously useful to millions, and has stood the test of time. I hope my approach works for you as well.

LOVE IS SEPARATENESS

(God, the archer)

Your children are not your children.
They are the sons and daughters of life's longing for itself.
They come through you but not from you,
and though they are with you they belong not to you.
You may give them your love but not your thoughts,
for they have their own thoughts.
You may house their bodies but not their souls,
for their souls dwell in the house of tomorrow,
which you cannot visit, not even in your dreams.
You may strive to be like them,
but seek not to make them like you.
For life goes not backward, nor tarries with yesterday.
You are the bow from which your children,
as living arrows, are sent forth.
The archer sees the mark upon the path of the infinite,
and He bends you with His might that
His arrow may go swift and far.
Let your bending in the archer's hand be for gladness,
for even as He loves the arrow that flies,
so He loves also the bow that is stable.

Kahlil Gibran

ONE

DISTANCING DYSFUNCTIONAL RELATIONSHIPS
The pathway to healing begins with separateness

There was a therapist I knew that was skilled at cutting to the chase and summing up the truth in a nutshell for me. I think it was because she had a very popular radio show, and she was under a time crunch. At the end of our first session, she said to me, "After your parents' divorce, your father was still 50% responsible for raising you and keeping you safe. Yet, he ran off and left you in the hands of a lunatic without protection. As a result, you grew up on the front lines of a war zone, yet here you sit with your identity intact. You are one remarkably strong survivor, young woman!"

Although she was extremely successful, she took a lot of heat from her professional colleagues about her direct style. I liked her style because I've always preferred a direct approach. She was not concerned with feelings as much as she was with getting to the truth, and presenting useful suggestions and tools to people for handling it, all in only a few minutes. She had the same style when she gave lectures, which were widely attended. Most people liked her very much, but not all. Oh well, c'est la vie.

This book doesn't sum things up in a nutshell, but I do try to make it as simple as I think necessary to be most useful. I use myself as an example to illustrate the information I present, and I hope this approach is helpful. Like many people, I come from a severely dysfunctional biological family, full of the usual entitled egocentrics, intrusive drama-queens on wheels, and self-centered, self-oblivious neurotics. In other words: adult children.

I know from experience that dysfunctional families are exhausting and stressful. One day in my mid-forties, and after struggling for years from a life-threatening illness, I realized I had to eliminate all the unnecessary stress in my life in order to survive. This meant identifying the major stressors, setting some personal boundaries against the major offenders, and making some difficult changes and hard decisions.

1

For me, the starting place was distancing myself from my immediate family, with as much love, forgiveness, and compassion as possible at the time. Their overwhelming, toxic personality disorders were making my condition worse. Their predictable negative reactions to my entering therapy and setting the necessary boundaries were so intrusive and vicious, I had no choice other than to protect myself from them, and enlarge my boundaries of distance and time. A task so excruciating, I thought it would kill me, but ironically it was necessary to save my life.

Their arrogance, willful ignorance, and delusions of moral superiority was mind-blowing, especially when they failed to show me a modicum of concern for what I was suffering. They proved over and over again they were only concerned about themselves. I had to learn to understand the nature of the dysfunction in my family and in myself, in order to be at peace with my decisions, and move on with the business of healing my condition.

Dysfunctional relationships are wrought with crises and drama, and there are many clinical descriptions that identify the various individual dysfunctions. However, a simpler and more general description of the typical dysfunctional family can be that it is comprised of people who are emotionally and psychologically immature, unhealthy, and destructive to varying degrees for various reasons. Participants are usually bound together in codependency, share various degrees of "growing up" to do, and most likely live in a cooperative state of denial (a conspiracy of denial) about the nature of the family's overall health.

The unhealthy personality traits most pervasive in a dysfunctional family are: self-absorption, lack of personal responsibility, lack of personal boundaries, lack of respect for the boundaries of others, insecure egos, fearfulness, entitlement complexes, intrusiveness, judgmentalism, personal dishonesty, and tendency toward manipulation, lies, deceit. There is lack of expressed unselfish love, kindness, affection, and concern for others, and certain arrogance in defending their willful ignorance. In other words: they are impenetrable and impossible! Pervasive dysfunction is almost always unwittingly passed down as a legacy from previous generations, and represents a rule of thumb: where there is a sick child, there are usually sicker parents.

Very few people emerge from a dysfunctional family with an appropriate level of self-esteem, a clear sense of their individual identity, or knowledge or appreciation of boundaries, unless they find strong, healthy mentors or role models in childhood, usually outside the family unit. Low self-esteem and lack of boundaries are at the root of this immaturity. They are a natural result of the chronic abuse that takes place in a dysfunctional family system, and much of the time, it can be healed with work.

Anyone from a dysfunctional family who believes they are perfectly healthy, and do not have some work and growing up to do, is probably in denial about themselves and their family. I believe that in this denial, this lack of willingness or courage to humble themselves and look inward honestly, that people are vulnerable to developing lasting personality disorders over time, to different degrees. Some disorders are naturally more serious than others, hence the various types of disorders.

As I understand it, codependency is a natural reaction to being raised in an oppressive, dysfunctional environment. Codependency is more emotional than psychological in its disorder, and does not always occur with a more serious psychological disorder, although codependents are often emotionally enmeshed with complexly disordered people. I also believe there is a difference between a primarily emotional disorder and a deep-rooted psychological disorder, in that the latter is more severe, and a lot harder to get ahead of. In terms of recovery and severity, from the poorest prognosis to the better, there is what I call "an order to disorder."

In addition to exposure to outside positive role models, I believe a child growing up in a dysfunctional family can avoid becoming seriously disordered by experiencing an instinctive, constant inner conflict and disapproval about their family's behavior. I was very fortunate in that, although I grew up in a traumatic environment, I was born with a very strong and highly sensitive inner compass. One that caused me to conflict with, rail against, and finally reject the ways of my family. With time, I was able to consciously recognize and dislike the parts of myself that mimicked them. With this awareness, I was in constant inner conflict when I was around my family, which I naively thought was a normal state of being.

This inner conflict proved to be the gift that ultimately saved me. It was the burr under my saddle that kept me moving forward, albeit in an agitated state. I was the "rebel," the "difficult child," and the "troubled one with the problem," because there was so much to be troubled about. Ultimately, it brought me to understand the spiritual truth that I am the final source of my truth, and that I can choose my own spiritual family in my adult life. However, it took me until I was over 40 years old, stronger and more mature, before I was able to emotionally detach from my family so I could become healthy enough to truly be my own person.

Because of the onset of fibromyalgia at age 44 (I go into this later), I was referred to a trauma therapist who helped me discover the missing piece in the complex puzzle called my life. She told me that I was always right about my crazy family, and that I would never become like my mother, because it was my greatest fear. She said the only piece I was missing was simply that I didn't have to be there, struggling in my relationships with these people, and I had every right to live my life apart from them.

Freeing myself from entanglements with unhealthy and destructive people, and all those that enabled them at my expense, made it possible for me to leave the past behind with forgiveness, impersonal compassion, and detachment. Before arriving at this point, my desires to become healthy were "hands reaching beyond their grasp." I simply had to take charge of my life!

CUTTING THE TIES THAT BIND
Nelson Mandela said, "Judging without understanding in order to serve your own feelings is selfish thinking." Dysfunctional people are pervasively and unwittingly selfish, and what they think about you is always self-serving. When I first cut my family ties, the unhealthiest family members exhibited the most intense hostility and resistance, but I was met with resistance by all. In my family, the pot was constantly calling the kettle black, and what was good for the goose was never considered good for the gander.

The marbleized personality traits of a severely dysfunctional family that were unleashed on me in spades were: a total lack of boundaries, extreme intrusiveness into my private thoughts, feelings and choices, lack of respect, overt judgmentalism without

4

understanding, complete lack of personal responsibility for these behaviors, and outright trashing attacks. I made the foolish and detrimental mistake of trying to share my truth with the sickest member of my family, foolishly trying to shed light on my choices, and was called a "crazy liar."

I eventually learned these negative responses are common, predictable, and even natural in dysfunctional families. Interestingly, each family member displayed the degree of disregard for me that was in direct proportion to their emotional immaturity, willful ignorance, and unconscious denial. It was clear that they were experiencing my decision to distance myself from them as a serious threat to their own psychological balance. Throwing me under the bus was their easiest and most convenient way to preserve it.

Taking a step toward becoming healthier in a dysfunctional family represents a real threat to the individual and collective denial that supports the dysfunction. Denial enables the existence of the evil that arises from immature and disordered behavior. This evil is the byproduct of the family's dysfunction that no one wants to look at. I define evil simply as a destructive force. It was no surprise that my family played the victim role with me, and collectively believed that I was hurting *them*, when in truth, all I was doing was stopping them from hurting me with a boundary of distance and time. This, too, was predictable, *and* a sure sign I was on the right pathway.

When I first left my family, I had not the necessary support system in place to maintain my new position, and remain detached to complete the task of becoming healthier. After two years, I gave in to family pressures: their expressed disdain and disrespect, their emotional attacks, their guilt messages meant to manipulate me, and harsh judgments meant to cause me feelings of misguided loyalties and false obligations. I also gave into the naïve and unfounded hope that "maybe, if I tried even harder that this time, it would be different." Sadly, I returned to the fold.

Coincidentally, during this same time, I injured my neck exercising at home. This injury compounded an earlier neck injury from an auto accident over 22 years prior. The combined effects of these injuries triggered the onset of the devastating neuromuscular disease that would eventually consume my entire life called fibromyalgia syndrome (FMS).

Suddenly, the psychological stress I felt when around my family, that I had worked so hard to cope with throughout my life, caused a major exacerbation to my condition. One of my physicians advised me that it was critical that I get away from them, or I would have no chance of recovery. Numerous doctors and psychologists had said the same thing over the years. One psychologist said to me: "In the zoo, they keep the lions separated from the gazelles for good reason. It doesn't matter how much armor you acquire in the form of boundaries. When entering the lion's den, you will always get bit."

I very clearly saw that my condition would not allow me to further expose myself to any more unnecessary psychological stress. I had to face the fact that my family was so dangerous to me, I had to act in my own best interest, no matter how they reacted. Their reactions, after all, were their choice, and their problem, and were not my responsibility. I had to learn that my only responsibility was to myself, and my health.

The disease began to take over my life, forcing me to seek the help and support I needed to cut the ties to my family for as long as I needed to in order to get well. It forced me to educate myself so I could understand the seriousness and complexity of my family's mental illness, and to see each member as they really were apart from me.

Through this understanding, I acquired the compassion I needed that enabled me to authentically forgive my family for their failings without needing an apology I knew I would never receive, and the strength to detach from them emotionally. I also became free from an inappropriate feeling of responsibility for them, while taking responsibility for my condition, and myself. I accepted that identifying and assessing a person's behavior for health and safety is not judging. It is simply appropriate and responsible self-care. Like it or not, everyone is responsible and accountable for their behavior toward others, and in the end, all accounts come due.

STAY THE COURSE

Second Timothy 4:7-8 in the Bible says, "I have fought a good fight, I have finished my course, I have kept the faith, henceforth there is laid up for me a crown of righteousness, which the Lord, the righteous judge, shall give me at the day, but not to me only, but unto all them also that love his appearing." Because I have fought so hard for peace of mind through understanding, compassion, and forgiveness, and was willing to make the necessary changes and hard choices, my lifelong inner approach-avoidance conflict finally came to an end. What a relief!

Now I am free to fulfill my potential, and become who I was created to be through my own choices, unfettered by the distortions of my overly-adapted inner child. I have faith that what I feel and believe is right and true for me. I try to honor myself (one of the seven sacred truths, that correspond with the seven chakras of Hindu Kundalini). I stand up against all that is evil and do not enable it, and I stand for health and safety.

I no longer feel anger for my family, or for the harm they have caused me, simply because I cannot be angry at people with mental illness, or at the dysfunctional behavior I was once a part of. However, even though I knew that mental illness, and all the harm that arises from it is a tragedy, I could not go on enabling it. Given the choice between healing myself from an agonizing chronic illness, or coping with the stress of a severely dysfunctional family that made my symptoms worse, I naturally chose my own survival. If you are from a severely dysfunctional family that is draining your energy, preventing you from living your own life, or reaching your full potential, the pathway to freedom begins with emotionally detaching from them for as long as you may need, and that may be forever.

I now understand the importance of taking responsible care of myself, defining myself by my boundaries, and avoiding people incapable of respecting or honoring them. As a result, I am free to concentrate on the physical part of my healing process with great success, and am now feeling mentally and physically healthier than I have ever been. It has been a difficult journey, but well worth it. In spite of all the pain, I love the experience of learning, growing, and applying what I learn to my life. I hope to go on doing this for the rest of my days. I had to learn to develop a new, more informed view of my family, abandon the old one, and act accordingly. "Grin and bear it" no longer worked for me.

ADJUST YOUR POINT OF VIEW

To take charge of your physical life and mental health, you may have to adjust your point of view. Try to think of your family as the vehicle through which your soul entered into the material world, delivering it to its corporeal destination. The truth is that not every family is healthy, nurturing and loving. Love is defined by Morgan Scott Peck, MD, author of "People of the Lie," in its purest sense as an act of will: "A choice to extend oneself for the sake and betterment of another." I agree with him wholeheartedly.

Many biological parents are truly devoted to healthy nurturing of their children's growth and wellbeing, while others are present physically, but not there for their children emotionally or psychologically. These parents neglect their responsibilities to their children, and exist in their children's lives primarily as figureheads.

Some parents only see their children as an extension of themselves. In these cases, most of what these parents feel they have done for their child was unwittingly done for themselves at the expense of the child's rights and freedom to be who they are. These parents have no idea they are primarily meeting their own needs, while being unaware of the child's, assuming they were one in the same. Hence, the child's individual needs go unmet.

If the child complains or shows a lack of appreciation for this neglect, it can come as a great shock to the parent who may feel very hurt and betrayed, and see their child as exceedingly ungrateful. These are the traits of parental narcissism that embody a parent who is physically there, but is focused on and living life primarily for themselves. While I believe no sane parent wants to harm their children intentionally, child abuse and neglect occurs in dysfunctional families as a natural byproduct.

Society conditions us to "honor thy father and thy mother," and stick with our families through thick and thin, because we are told they are all we really have. Guilt, shame, false obligation, and misplaced responsibility are the misguided conditioning that unconsciously permeates dysfunctional families in so many ways.

These are the corrosive and illegitimate ties that bind us emotionally and psychologically to a dysfunctional relationship that might better be left behind. Although I fundamentally agree that honoring thy father and thy mother is a value not to be easily thrown aside, I believe our true father and mother is God, not our biological parents, that is the creator of our body, soul, and the universe we live in.

Our biological parents were simply the "means" through which we entered this world. They may or may not have met their parental responsibilities, or fully appreciated the privilege of caring for and nurturing one or more of God's creations, but this is nothing personal. The fact is that these "means," with all their abilities and limitations, would have done the best they could with what they had at the time, no matter who their children were. For better or for worse, the quality of their parenting skills and capacities for nurturing and loving were engrained in them long before you were born, and had little to do with you.

Some parents simply do not realize that their parenting skills are deficient, or that they can be improved upon. Others who know they are deficient deep down, may have no desire to improve due to an unhealthy ego, denial, cowardice, laziness, or selfishness. Even when they see that the family they have made is disordered and dysfunctional, and it becomes obvious to everyone else that improvement and growth are certainly indicated, some parents would rather maintain their status quo so they don't have to look at themselves. Grown children of dysfunctional parents are simply not responsible for their parents and family morals and personal standards, or their strengths and weaknesses of character. They are only responsible for their own.

Furthermore, I believe that whoever our parents and families happen to be, is somewhat irrelevant to the evolution of our own soul; however, what you learn by experiencing them is not. When you really look at life's lessons, they come to us from a vast variety of sources. Pragmatically speaking, our biological family can be seen simply as one of these sources. The dysfunctional family can be one of our most influential examples of how not to be, and what is unwholesome.

Therefore, what we learn from them, good or bad, becomes an important part of the perception of our life experience as a whole, and the way we choose to see our own reality. Finally, our family can be simply viewed as one of many stepping-stones on our path to enlightenment, self-realization, and fulfillment, rather than a necessary determining factor to our life's outcome. With this perspective, we can see them as a valuable means toward a higher good along an on-going path of spiritual evolution, and not as an end.

Our lives are not meant to be a stagnate microcosm defined by a group of people, or a familiar value system. Our lives are meant to be like the ever-expanding universe, moving outward and away from the previous positions of the past. Like the universe, and with the power of choice, we can expand outward into new positions, and better kinds of relationships.

Though the stars in the universe are forever grouped together within solar systems and galaxies, we on the other hand, can choose who surrounds us on our outward path, who gets to circle close to us, and who it is best to keep at a safe distance. We are never really stuck in our proximity to anyone else at any time.

When we feel our life force being sucked into a black hole by the gravity of false obligations and misplaced responsibilities, we have the ability to choose to pull away and redirect our course. We can move to different places, and see things from many different points of view. Like the universe, our lives are full of never-ending possibilities, and wonders beyond our human imagination.

Our lives are bigger than what took place in our past, or what is happening today. At the end, our lives are the sum total of the choices we are free to make along the way. Like the stars in our wondrous and mysterious universe, these choices are endless. A wise man once told me, "It's not how you start out, but where you end up, that counts."

EMBRACE THE MYSTERIOUS

Albert Einstein said, "The most beautiful thing we can experience is the mysterious." To me one of the great mysteries in the universe is love. Where does love come from, why are we so compelled to have it within us, and why do we need it for our very survival? The answer to these questions I believe has to do with the nature of the human spirit, and its eternal connection to creation. "God is love" is a well-known spiritual concept, widely accepted throughout the world. Perhaps as human beings who are physically separated from our creator through our biological confines, we simply require a continuous connection to Him in order to maintain a balance between our spiritual being and the physical realm into which we were born. Love serves as this vital connection. Without the guiding light of love, we are out of balance, vulnerable, and lost in darkness.

John Grey, author of "Men are from Mars – Women are From Venus" said, "When you can't get what you need from one source, and all you are getting is pain and disappointment, then stop looking there, and turn away and look somewhere else." I agree with him completely. When your family of origin is incapable of providing you what you need, find another source; someone else to take their place who is capable of being a healthy role model, and a nurturing source of love.

Your soul needs love and nurturing, and it does not matter who provides it. "A parent or family of choice" can provide the sense of healthy unity and caring respect that you may not be able to find within your own family. Furthermore, a biological connection to someone does not constitute a reason to maintain close ties, especially if that connection is an unhealthy and destructive drain on your energy. In a bigger and more evolved picture, family labels have no value.

LOSE THE LABELS

Believe it or not, we can reach a point in our spiritual maturity where the people in our families can appropriately lose their labels, and are simply seen as individuals that are subject to the same assessments of health and safety as everyone else. Family labels, adhering to a conditioned sense of duty and false obligations, misplaced responsibility, and illegitimate guilt and fear,

11

are all unhealthy shackles enslaving the soul, preventing it from expansion and fulfillment of its potential.

We can develop a detached form of compassion and love for our dysfunctional families, and feel this on a more impersonal level, as we would feel toward all the suffering souls in the world. I call this "living in loving detachment," and it has become one of my personal mottos. This healthy, detached form of compassion toward destructive people can simply be acquired through learning to appreciate a shared sense of spiritual creation and physical mortality, and not from the psychological enslavement of co-dependency, or an inappropriate sense of "obligation to" or "responsibility for" another person. In a healthy universe, you are only responsible "for" yourself.

The most important choice you make in this life is to "un-slave" your spirit through learning compassionate, loving detachment; freeing your spirit to soar into the unknown with courage and faith in yourself. The title of Susan Jeffers' book, "Feel the Fear and Do It Anyway" sums up the very essence of courage. It isn't courage if there exists no fear. Never become impeded when your taking appropriate action for your health and safety threatens those around you.

Fear can cause us to be careful, alert, and to pay attention to what is presented to us for our cognition, *without* allowing fear to control our decisions. In this way, appropriate, healthy fear is a loyal friend. Embrace your fear, and follow through with what you truly need for yourself, rather than live with an underlying fear of being too helpless to take charge of your own life. Growing in an upward direction is a choice, like all others, and the cost of making wise and sometimes painful choices in your best interest is a small fraction of the cost of choosing to be stuck in the same place for the rest of your life.

Einstein also said, "We cannot solve our problems by using the same kind of thinking we used when we created them." One definition of insanity is when we do the same thing over and over again, always expecting a different outcome. Learning to detach from a dysfunctional family, and cutting the ties that bind you to them, can be as simple as choosing to think in new and healthier ways that places responsibility where it is supposed to be, putting you in charge of yourself, your life, and your health. Einstein is also famous for his simple words, "Think differently!" Try to see the man on the moon as a profile, instead of the same old face. See partial participation or non-participation in your dysfunctional family system, as purely a choice for your own betterment.

STOP BEING A TEAM PLAYER

If you are still fully participating in a dysfunctional family system, you are being sapped of vital energy. Being a "team player," or even a bystander, requires building protective walls that require an exorbitant amount of energy to maintain. You never know when the next shoe will drop, or if it is going to drop on your head. Dysfunctional people are not safe to be around, and cannot be trusted. You cannot let your guard down for a second.

All my life, I had to build and maintain a protective "wall of humor" to protect myself when I was around my family, and believe me, it was exhausting. The enormous amount of energy required to build and maintain protective walls when you are involved with dysfunctional people, barely leaves you enough energy to live your own life. This protection comes at the expense of your personal growth, and also prevents you from reaching your full potential. If you are chronically ill, this outlay in energy is extremely detrimental to your chances of healing.

To truly heal illness and regain your mental and physical health, you need every bit of energy you can produce. You cannot afford to drive yourself into energy deficit by being exposed to abuse and unnecessary outside stressors that are beyond your control. Stress can actually block healing. Learn to protect the vulnerable core of your energetic being. This will mean unplugging from every possible source of unnecessary outside stress. This may include leaving a toxic job, a destructive marriage or friendship, and part or all of your dysfunctional family.

If you are enmeshed in a dysfunctional relationship, and choose to go on as you are, and not make the necessary changes to protect your life-force energy, you may never become healthier. I think the kinds of changes you need to make, and whether they must be partial or absolute, temporary or permanent, depend on a number of factors: how seriously or chronically something has been stressing you, how long your mental or physical health has been compromised, how seriously ill you have become, and how long it will take your mind and body to heal.

After you have been unplugged from your dysfunctional family for a while, and have made headway on your healing path, you will be able to tell who you are strong enough to be in contact with, how much contact is safe, and who you really need to stay away from a while longer, maybe even permanently. When you feel strong enough for trial contact, it will reveal much of what you need to know. You may have grown and changed, but others may have not. Trust your instincts, honor your feelings, and do not allow guilt, false obligations, loneliness, or inappropriate conditioning to sabotage you. Always do only what is best for you, and bear in mind why you had to detach in the first place.

YOU DESERVE A CHANCE
You deserve every chance to nurture your mental and physical health, and live your life in peace. You have every right to take charge of your life and choose to live it differently. It is your responsibility alone to do what you need to heal yourself. It is a real possibility that by the time you are healed, someone in your family may have passed on. You may not have gained enough strength in time to see them again. This may be a sad reality that is beyond your control, but a remission in your better health should not be jeopardized. However, your ability to assess safety in a family member will develop through the healing process. You will know when you are stronger just how close you can safely get to which members of your remaining family. When a family member will never be safe, it's time to let them go and move on.

Emerging from this process with your health, and a detached sense of compassion and forgiveness for your dysfunctional family, is a real possibility. Whether you choose to reconnect with a major offender, even in a very brief and detached way, is your decision. No one, especially someone of, or affiliated with, the dysfunctional family, has a right to interfere or influence you.

Wait and see how you feel after you are well, and try hard not to fall back into any old patterns of enabling destructive behavior if you choose to reconnect. Also, be wary of anyone with a seriously dysfunctional personality with whom you had a previous relationship. Your health matters the most. Keep yourself healthy and safe, keep detached, and do not reconnect with anyone until you feel strong enough and have gained basic understanding.

The last thing I want to say about detaching from a dysfunctional family is this: you must create a strong support system, and not tolerate any negativity or guilt trips from your family or others about your decision. As long as you understand what you need to do, you are under no obligation to converse, convince or persuade anyone. A decision as important as your choosing a safe way to become healthier and live a better life is never up for parlance or negotiation.

This is no one else's business, though you may choose to find a supportive therapist to help you through this transition. Safe discussion and feedback are very important when you are internalizing a fresh point of view. If you have a friend who is psychologically healthy enough to respect and support your decisions without judging you, this, of course, can be helpful too. Any form of nonjudgmental support will smoothen your transformation.

Distancing from stressful, destructive people, no matter who they are, may not be easy. But even so, life will always present challenges that we must rise to and face. Even if you have to clean house, and begin with all new friends, or pick a new spiritual family, you will attract a higher caliber of healthier people, capable of respecting you, honoring your boundaries, and behaving appropriately. The truth is, if you really desire to be healthy enough to fulfill your potential in life, you must avoid anyone who drains your energy by enduring their destructive, abusive behavior.

After I detached from my dysfunctional family, I fully grew to understand the importance of being true to myself, being defined by my boundaries, and honoring myself by staying away from people incapable of respecting them. I felt free to concentrate on the physical part of my healing process with great success. Over a ten-year period, I healed my illness and wrote the book "Curing Chronic Fibromyalgia – Choosing What Works" to help other FMS sufferers find their way out of the dark tunnel of despair they are thrown into by this horrific illness.

I appreciate that the experience of learning and growing is a natural, life-long process. And I so appreciate all those who have helped me along the way, as well as those who unexpectedly became my teachers. I hope with all my heart my experience inspires others to step onto their own healing path, take charge of their life and their mental and physical health, and discover the courage within themselves to make the necessary corrective choices.

THESE ARE MY WISHES FOR YOU

"May you always feel loved. May you find serenity and tranquility in a world you may not always understand. May the pain you have known and the conflict you have experienced give you the strength to walk through life facing each new situation with courage and optimism. Always know that there are those whose love and understanding will always be there, even when you feel most alone. May you discover enough goodness in others to believe in a world of peace. May a kind word, a reassuring touch, and a warm smile be yours every day of your life, and may you give these gifts as well as receive them. Remember the sunshine when the storm seems unending. Teach love to those who know hate, and let that love embrace you as you go into the world. May the teachings of those you admire become part of you, so that you may call upon them. Remember, those whose lives you have touched and who have touched yours are always a part of you, even if the encounters were less than you would have wished. It is the content of the encounter that is more important than it's form. May you not become too concerned with material matters, but instead place immeasurable value on the goodness in your heart. Find time in each day to see beauty and love in the world around you. Realize that each person has limitless abilities, but each of us is different in our own way. What you may feel you lack in one regard may be more than compensated for in another. What you feel you lack in the present may become one of your strengths in the future. May you see your future as one filled with promise and possibility. Learn to view everything as a worthwhile experience. May you find enough inner strength to determine your own worth by yourself, and not be dependent on another's judgment of your accomplishments. May you always feel loved."

Sandra Sturtz Hauss

TWO

UNDERSTANDING YOUR DYSFUNCTIONAL PAST
Remaining in the dark keeps you blind

Some say that the truth is like the sun. The harder you look at it, the fuzzier it gets. However, through education and personal experience, I have learned that family dysfunction is a state of chronic, unconscious deviation from the reality of spiritual morality and mental health that is self-sustaining, self-justifying, and is based on a system of denial that is fed by immaturity and selfish needs. Consequently, there is very little expression of healthy, unselfish love in a dysfunctional family system.

The overwhelming negative stress of this dysfunction can erode any hope of developing or maintaining a healthy balance between the mind, body, and spirit. The deprivation that occurs on all three levels can be devastating to a life. There is an old saying, "The only way out is through," and the only way through is by educating yourself, and most importantly, applying what you learn to your life. Your family legacy of dysfunction can stop with you. I finally hung an invisible sign at my front door to remind me that "The dysfunction stops here."

Learning to understand dysfunction means you will be taking off blinders you may have unknowingly worn most of your life. Once you remove them, you will see a 180-degree view of your life, and will no longer live partially in the dark. Seeing things illuminated for the first time means your eyes may need time to adjust before they can see clearly again, like walking out of a dimly lit room into full sunlight. But they will eventually adjust, you will eventually view things differently, and surprisingly, you will come to prefer it that way.

For me, I needed to learn to see each person in my family as they truly are, and understand what made them that way before I could understand myself. When I was first learning to understand my family, it was very hard and painful. It brought up suppressed feeling of frustrated rage, enormous grief, anxiety, and sadness. Seeing clearly the tragedy of what had been taking place in my family, and the effect it had on everyone, was agonizing. But I simply could not look away.

I had to look at it, work through my feelings, and accept what was really there. I felt sad for myself and everyone else in my family, and sad that the only person I could help was me. I knew helping myself was going to be hard enough, and even if I could perhaps have helped someone else, I did not have the strength to try. I also learned it would not even be appropriate, because it was simply not my job or responsibility. Getting myself well was going to take all that I had.

I had to take off blinders that had so often caused me to mislead my life. Though I often saw my family dysfunction more clearly than they did, I lacked sufficient understanding to relieve the anxiety about what was lurking in the dark shadows. There were scary gray areas, and mysterious black holes, and I could not see what was there until I stopped being blinded by my ignorance and childhood over-adaptations. I had to find help to heal the wounds of my past, and educate myself if I were ever to be freed by understanding. I needed the mysteries to be solved. The story had to be told, and it had to come to an end.

GETTING YOUR HISTORY STRAIGHT

The best way to begin healing the wounds from your past is by solving the mysteries, and telling and ending the story. The first step is getting your history straight. It is a very effective method for getting an accurate and balanced perspective of your life by mapping out events as they really happened based on true memories and known facts. Identifying the truth, and seeing it laid down in black and white, will set the past apart from your present, and help you connect the dots of the mysterious, blurry picture called your past.

This picture can be like a jumbled up jigsaw puzzle that can only be clearly seen and understood if you assemble it, and stand back far enough to view the picture as a whole all at once. Some of the mysteries will remain in gray areas, and may never be solved, but at least you'll know this, and can accept it. The rest of the mysteries can only be solved from your adult perspective, along with life-experience, and understanding you lacked as a child.

Remembering your past through the limitations of a child's perception only perpetuates unnecessary pain and uncertainty.

Taking a look at your past today through adult eyes will put things in their proper perspective. Then you can see the past as a story that can be understood, told, and ended. The story of your past does not define your life or who you are. It is merely a prelude to the choices you make in the present, and remains a stepping-stone for who you will continue to become. Knowing the clear truth about your past releases you from it, and empowers you to make wiser choices now, thus creating a better future. An important way to begin seeing this big picture is by assembling the puzzle of your past.

ASSEMBLING THE PUZZLE
(Standing back and viewing the big picture)
The best way to show you how to assemble the puzzle of your life is to tell my own story, clarifying my past history, and how I put together the giant jigsaw puzzle called my past. The easiest way to begin is making a chronological list of the year-to-year main events of your life. Briefly list the memories that stand out the most from that year and time, both negative and positive.

These memories should not be only the negative ones or the positive ones. Just be true to what is, and do not try to gloss things over or blow things up. Keep your most prominent memories of actual experiences as accurate as possible, and try to leave out any embellishments, exaggerations, minimizations, assumptions, excuses, or spins made by yourself or others as the years have gone by. Focus on your own true experiences, leaving nothing out.

Remember it is the truth that sets you free, not a distorted facsimile. The truth here is going to be your best and most powerful friend. It does not matter if anyone else remembers things the way you do. In every family each person has their own reality - their own individual experiences and memories - and they do not have to agree. You may clearly remember something that someone else swears never happened. This is of no importance, so allow others their reality. The safest thing to do is to keep this process private. Do not compare notes or share recollections with others outside your immediate support group, such as your spouse, trusted friends, or therapist, at this point in your healing.

There is no need to enter into a discussion with family members to prove anything, or convince anyone of what you remember. There is no harm in asking a few questions for the sake of checking the facts. However, do not explain what you are doing. Just say you would like to know, that's all. Later on when you establish who is safe and who is not, you can decide if you want to share some of what you have pieced together. Using my personal history as an example, I've summed up in order of occurrence, beginning with my birth to age forty-five, when I fell ill with FMS.

PUTT TOGETHER YOUR PERSONAL HISTORY
March 1, 1952 – I was born in Auburn, California to Warren and Norma Scott with one older brother born in Sacramento, California on July 2, 1950.
Age 6 months – I began wearing leg braces for 18 months on both legs to correct congenital hip dysplasia, discovered by my mother. I developed subsequent claustrophobia.
Ages 2 and 2-1/2 - My brother and I were playing unsupervised near a backyard swimming pool when he fell into the deep end. He was five. I ran into the house calling for help. My mother and grandmother ran out to find he had climbed out of the pool, and run into the garden shed to hide. Another incident during this time, my brother and I walked out into the orchard next to our house, and were charged by a Doberman Pinscher to the end of his chain by a guardhouse that ended only a few feet from us. We were so far out into the orchard we could not see our house. We ran back home, and by the time we arrived, the sun was setting. I also remember we had a fishpond in the front yard with goldfish and frogs in it.
Ages 3-4 – I remember being in my grandmother's house alone in the dark, playing with my dolls on the floor in a spot of streetlight. My mother and grandmother arrived home, and asked me what I was doing alone in the dark. I remember walking up the same street in play high-heels on a sunny day alone and unsupervised. I remember a family picnic held in my grandmother's back yard.
Age 5 – My parents divorced after 9 years of turbulent discord. I witnessed my mother's first suicide attempt, thwarted by my

father. I remember their fights, my mother's emotional upsets, and my father taking her to the hospital one night after she tried to commit suicide by taking an overdose of tranquilizers, confirmed by him years later. During the days I remember hiding and rocking myself in fear, wetting the bed every night, and leaving my body for short periods of time from stress. I remember my father being the one who put us to bed at night, and who gave us our baths.

Ages 6-9 – After the divorce, my mother moved us to Pacific Grove, California, where she secured a job as a music teacher in a local elementary school. She worked hard and was very tired on the weekends. I remember her hollering at us after we snuck downstairs to watch cartoons on Saturday mornings, "You god-damned little shit-asses! Keep that noise down! How am I supposed to get my sleep?" She began dating a man who lived in Carmel with his mother. My father disappeared for five years during this time. I only have one memory of seeing him briefly, arguing with my mother at the kitchen table, and afterward visiting with us on the front lawn of our Pacific Grove house. I grew up without guidance or affection, feeling unloved, unwanted, scared, and anxious. I developed allergies to house mold and mildew.

Age 10 - I visited my father alone for the first time since the divorce at my grandmother's house in Sacramento, CA. He was working as a California real estate agent. I spent a lot of time clinging to him in emotional shock. He took me to a parking lot in his VW bus, and showed me how to drive. Then he left, and I did not see or hear from him again for several more years.

Age 11 - My mother moved us to San Mateo, CA after breaking up with her boyfriend. She took another teaching job, and struggled to raise her kids alone. We stayed there for one year. I had become a chronic bed-wetter, and began developing bronchial asthma. Her boyfriend came to visit a few times.

Age 12 - We moved to Carmel, CA where my mother resumed her relationship with her boyfriend who was to become my stepfather. We all moved into a house together, and they were soon married. There was a lot of turbulence due to my stepfather's mother and crazy family. My mother's emotional upsets resumed. My mother tried to commit suicide again with tranquilizers, rescued by my stepfather. I do not remember seeing or hearing from my father during this time.

Age 13 - I had a skateboard that I became skilled with. I enjoyed riding horses at my step-grandparent's riding stables. My brother rode horses as well. My stepfather built us a home for my mother in Carmel next door to his parents. My brother worked on the house with the crew. We took our dogs for family walks on the beach after dinner in the evenings, and it seemed like a happier and more peaceful time.

Age 14 - We moved into the new house, and my stepfather landscaped the property through his new landscape supply business. His parents gave me a Morgan horse. I loved her very much, and rode her nearly every day. I was very active in school gymnastics, and track and field, swam on the water-ballet team, and participated in track and field events in the Junior Olympics in Sacramento, CA. My stepfather took me on a weekend "father-daughter" skiing trip, and tried to sleep with me. My heart was broken, yet I told no one.

Age 15 – I went to spend one week with my father in Winnemucca, Nevada that summer, and he took me on an adventure into the desert to find an old gold mine the last day of my visit. His truck's clutch burned out by mid-afternoon, and we were stranded at the base of the mountains 30 miles from the main road, and several miles from the nearest ranch. He hadn't told anyone where we were going, had no cell phone, no coats or blankets, no food, and no water.

I spent the night in the truck's cab, turning the engine off and on to keep semi-warm, while my father slept in the back of the truck covered with a couple old, moldy curtains, snoring all night long. I got so cold I got out of the cab, and gathered up an enormous pile of dried tumbleweed. Since there were no matches, I curled up the only Kleenex I had, and lit it with the cigarette lighter on the dash. I carefully walked out to the pile and lit it on fire. The blaze was so huge, you could have seen it for miles, and warmed me up for about 20 minutes. My father woke up, and said to me, "Don't light another fire, honey, because there are old miners in the hills who would come down and kill us for the truck."

When morning light rose dimly over the mountains, it was around 5:00 am. We began walking on the dirt road toward the nearest ranch right away before the desert heat began to climb. About 10:00 am, the temperature was around 90 degrees. I was so tired from no sleep I couldn't go on. My father sat me down on the side of the road near a ditch, and handed me a loaded 45 Magnum pistol. He told me to rest, and he'd go get some help from the ranchers down the road, and be back as soon as possible, and walked off into the haze.

Suddenly, after about an hour, a stream of water came slowly running down the ditch toward me, as run-off from nearby irrigation, I thought. I quickly took off my shoes and socks, and drenched my feet, pants, shirt, and head with the cool, brown water. I drank a little, but it was nasty. Then I put back on my socks and shoes. Not long afterward, I noticed off in the distance, and in the opposite direction from where my father headed, there was a cloud of dust moving along the base of the mountains in a steady line. As it grew nearer, I could see it was a truck with two men in the cab, approaching me slowly.

I stood up so they could see me, and waited for them to arrive. When they saw me standing there, soaking wet, and with a large, long-barreled gun in one hand, they looked shocked and amazed, and a little confused. The man by the passenger window said to me, "What the hell? What's a young girl doing all the way out here, soaking wet in 100 degree heat, with a gun in her hand?" I promptly explained my situation, and after they quietly exchanged some private words, the same man said, "Well, I guess we can give you a ride, but you'll have to climb in the back, and keep that gun of yours pointed downwards!" I thanked them, and climbed up over the sides of the bed into the back of their pick-up truck that was full of giant old tires. I made it to the top of the pile, and held on for dear life as they drove on down the bumpy, dusty, dirt road. Clouds of dust surrounded me, and stuck to my wet face, clothes, and all throughout my hair. When we got to the first ranch, about 15 minutes after my father did, I was a dark, dirty brown.

The ranchers gave my father and me a ride to the next ranch who were friends of my father's, and they lent us a jeep. It had a hoist on it, but Dad's truck had no attachment. By the time we made it back to his truck, it was noon, and over 100 degrees. My father tied the two vehicles together with a four-foot rope. He pulled his truck with the jeep, and I rode in the truck, tapping the breaks all the way to his friends' ranch. By the time we got back, it was after 1:00 pm, and the rancher's wife had cooked us up a huge, country style lunch. There was fried chicken, green beans, macaroni salad, sweet corn on the cob, mashed potatoes and biscuits and gravy, iced tea, milk, and chocolate cake for desert! It was unbelievable!

After we washed our hands, we sat down with the family for the feast, and it was like we'd died and gone to heaven. We had to eat up, because there was no time to waste. I had a flight out of Reno that afternoon for home. The rancher loaned my father a car, and he drove me straight back to Winnemucca, and I only had time enough to grab my ticket. From there we made a beeline for the airport. It was a two-hour drive. We ran to the gate, and I made it within minutes of take-off. The plane was literally loaded. We said our goodbyes while the stewardess called the captain to hold the plane for a minute, explaining there was one more passenger. I ran down the tube and onto the plane. As I walked down the aisle, out of breath, to my seat at the very back, everyone was looking at me like I was a runaway hillbilly. My knotted and disheveled hair was filthy with dust, my face, neck, arms, and clothes were dirty brown also, and I stank like desert dust and sweat. I didn't say a word to the two people I sat between. I fell asleep until the plain landed with a thud back in San Jose where my stepfather was waiting to take me home. He said when he saw me, "What the hell happened to you?" I didn't tell him the whole story.

I didn't tell anyone until it was time for the eulogy at my father's memorial service many years later, and I stood before the gathering in the church and told the whole story. There are many "adventures" with my father that won't be told in this book, that were just as bizarre and harrowing, involving having tea with local Madams and prostitutes at a house of ill repute, going spelunking with strippers in the mountain caves by the great salt lakes, and one or two more episodes of getting stranded in the desert after exploring old, abandoned mine shafts and towns. No one had a father like mine, and none of my friends from broken homes had these kinds of stories to share after visiting their father's. No one!

Ages 15 to 16 – Family feuds broke out within my stepfather's family. My mother gave my beloved horse back to my step-grandparents, who promptly sold her, and I was permanently barred from the stables. This broke my heart, and created a very deep wound. My mother bought me my first guitar, and I took lessons and taught myself to play and sing folk songs. My mother took another overdose of pills, rescued once again by my stepfather. This was her third suicide attempt to my knowledge. I convinced my brother to talk to her with me, to plead with her to get some help, because I was afraid we were going to be abandoned again. She responded, and soon seemed less overwhelmed.

Age 16 – My parents let me have a big birthday party with lots of friends sleeping over. My stepfather filled his topsoil hauling truck with hay, and we all rode down Carmel hill to our beach party, and afterward rode home through town. All the squealing girls attracted a line of boys in cars a couple blocks long that followed us home. My stepfather stood in the driveway, and directed them on their way. That night he scared us all wearing a white sheet in the dark outside the living room windows where we were all sleeping. I saw he wasn't all bad.

Later that year I unintentionally lost my virginity with a stranger that I met hitchhiking with a friend on a dare. I was under the influence of marijuana and alcohol, and told no one. I began smoking marijuana with my friends during and after school.

I also began to date my first serious boyfriend, and became infatuated. My parents liked him at first, but later grew to dislike him intensely because he was a championship racecar driver. When they forbade me to see him, I still saw him whenever I could. My brother went away to college at University of California at Santa Barbara, CA, and I road the bus to visit him frequently on weekends.

Three months before my 17th birthday, I met a man 20 years my senior who became the most influential person in my entire life. He was the great American baritone, James Tippey, who was soloing in *The Creation* along side my mother at the Carmel Mission Basilica. He instantly became my life-long guiding light. He was the first person who recognized me for the old soul that I was, perceptive beyond my years, and thought so much of me, he came back for me when I was 19. We made a deep and profound, connection that lasted a lifetime, and I grew to love him very much. Forty years later he became my surrogate father and voice teacher. Our story is told in my book, *"The Grand Master And His Protégé: A memoir of love, courage, endurance and devotion."*

Age 17 - My racecar driver boyfriend moved with his family to New York, and soon afterward, I accepted his invitation to visit him and his parents. I graduated high school mid-year, and left to visit him as soon as I turned 18. My mother was so angry, she said, "You can go to your boyfriend, and if he doesn't want you, you can go to your father, and if he doesn't want you, you can go straight to hell!" I wanted to get away from my family's drama, my abusive mother, and my stepfather's covert sexual harassment. I returned from New York two weeks later, and began working as a waitress in a local pancake house. I bought my first car, began composing songs on my guitar, and performing in local coffee shops. I adopted a Beagle mix puppy from the SPCA I named Dante. He was so joyful and loving, and so incredibly wonderful, he made me very happy.

Age 18 – My brother was killed in an auto accident at UCSB on May 25, 1970, two months after my 18th birthday. My mother went to bed in shock, and was on heavy medication much of the time for an entire year, and I received no help from anyone. We took in a foreign exchange student from Australia for one year. I began searching for my brother in my male friends.

While my mother was absent, my stepfather threw me out of the house, saying, "We don't want to deal with your problems any longer. You are a zero, and we don't want you around anymore. You have three days to leave the house." He was clearly trying to destroy me because I was keeping his secret of his having tried to sleep with me when I was 14. My mother left me an electric blanket on my bed with a note that read, "It's a cold world out there, you'll need this! Mom." I continued working as a waitress, and rented a room from a kindly alcoholic lady. My boyfriend at the time gave me a kitten I named Zerilda.

I developed female problems and had a therapeutic diagnostic curettage through the Welfare program. I became very ill with bronchitis, and after my landlady notified my parents, they visited me and decided to allow me to move back home if I went back to school.

I agreed, and signed up for a two-year Medical Assisting course I planned to complete in one year at the local college, beginning after the coming summer. While living in my brother's room, I continued working and saving money for a college abroad trip through Europe that summer. My boyfriend took my cat for one year, and my parents took care of my dog while I was traveling on tour. My stepfather helped me buy a new car.

Age 19 - In May of that year in 1971, two months after I turned 19, James Tippey returned into my life. He was singing the lead role in *The Elijah* with the Monterey Symphony, and I was singing the part of the youth. He wanted to connect with me again when I was of age, and was out of school. However, I felt unworthy this time, when before I would have run away with him when I was

16. We went our separate ways. However, he kept track of me over the coming years through my mother.

Age 20 – In the summer of 1971, I went on a seven-week college abroad tour to visit six countries in Europe, and I dove into each adventure. I returned home to attend the college course. My father sent me a monthly check for $65. My mother said it was back child support he never paid. When the semester began in the Fall, I went to school from 8:00 am to 5:00 pm five days a week, night school from 7:00 pm to 10:00 pm two nights a week, and studied between classes and all day on the weekends. I graduated from the course with a B average, and my certificate in hand. After I became a certified medical assistant, my stepfather threw me out of the house again for staying out a little past my 10:00 pm curfew, sitting in the driveway talking with a boy he did not like. Again, my mother was absent. I had to leave my dog, Dante, with them for the time being. I began taking drugs again, continued working as a waitress, and shared a duplex with friends, first in Carmel, and then in Pacific Grove. My parents had a family miniature poodle named Jacque. One day, my stepfather took Dante and Jacque to work with him, and put them on his tractor's seat by his side while he was working. Jacque fell off the seat, and was run over by one of the huge tractor wheels, and killed. After that, my mother got a Spaniel puppy. One morning, she let him out the front door to go into the front yard unsupervised. The puppy wandered down onto the street, and was run over by a car, and killed. It's a miracle we survived our childhood at all. I wouldn't trust these people with a fish!

I met my first husband at a drug party. I was on LSD, and had been dating a drug dealer, and taking whatever I could get my hands on. I weighed 135 pound at 5'10" tall. We soon moved in together, he got me off drugs, and most likely saved my life. I collected my dog from my parents, and got a job working for an ophthalmology group in Monterey, CA. My mother became so irate at me for "shacking up" with my boyfriend, I had to detach from her for a year, move to a secret location, and have an unlisted number.

Age 21 - We got married in Reno, NV, and I kept working for the ophthalmologists. My possessive husband became violent, and I was battered and threatened for the next five years. During that time I sustained injuries to the face, ribs, head, right jaw, and mouth. I left my body frequently, as I did as a child under similar stress. I had to place Dante in a new home because my landlord would not let me keep him. This broke my heart. I only went to visit him once because his new owner said he cried all that night after I left. I saw that he had a really loving home with another dog to play with, and was grateful for this. I was able to keep my cat.

Age 22 - I began working in a one-girl ophthalmology office for a kindly semi-retired doctor from San Francisco. I was in a serious auto accident in Los Angeles, CA where I suffered whiplash and a head injury on the right side, which I seemed to recover from. I resumed song composition, and singing with my guitar.

Age 23 - My husband and I bought our first house. We remodeled it, and then sold it after one year. We adopted a Labrador puppy I named Onna, and a kitten I named Lacy. I still had my cat Zerilda. My animal friends brought me joy.

Age 24 - My husband and I bought another house on Del Monte Beach in Monterey, CA. We remodeled it, and filled it with auction antiques. We put in a large hot tub in the back patio, and a huge succulent garden in the front yard. My husband had a house painting business. He also started a furniture stripping business, and sold it after one of his managers was knifed to death behind the store, and the other employee died after losing consciousness over the stripping vat. I continued working for the kindly ophthalmologist. My maternal grandmother passed away.

Age 25 - I quit my job and developed a private medical insurance billing system and started my own business in what was then an unknown field. I was the second person in California to begin such a business, and was contacted by the other business for training and consultation. I published an operations manual, obtained a national trademark, and a CA copyright for my business. I began taking piano lessons and studying voice locally with a kindly old voice teacher for the next two and a half years, against my husband's wishes.

Age 26 - The physical abuse from my husband began to escalate. I became depressed for much of the time. I remember leaving my body in frequent episodes when he would scream and threaten me. I developed a female bleeding disorder for 8 months, and after another diagnostic curettage, I eventually found a doctor who cured me with birth-control pills. I planned an escape from my husband for two years, and secretly saved money. A neighbor gave me a poodle puppy that I named Gigot, and he made me very happy. My animals were my salvation and sanity.

Age 27 - My husband became even more violent, and nearly killed me. I escaped under his death threat while he went skiing over a weekend with some friends and his mistress. I took my one-year-old poodle, Gigot, and my eight-year-old cat, Zerilda, with me. Lacy had been killed by a car that year, and I had to leave Onna, my black lab, behind. This, again, broke my heart. I told no one I was leaving, or where I was going. Only an aunt knew where I was because she allowed my pets and me to secretly stay in her condo in Monterey. I kept my business going from the room I occupied, and took care of my pets and myself. I learned how to handle my own divorce with help from the local library. I was awarded a fair settlement.

Age 28 – Six months later, my parents discovered I was alone, sold me a condo in the same neighborhood my mother had bought with her inheritance from her mother, and gave me a part time job in their business for one year. My mother sold me the condo with no money down for a price above current market value, and carried a second loan with me for the difference to be paid "on demand," even though my stepfather wanted to sell it to me for the original purchase price. My controlling mother wanted to hold a big note over my head. Eventually, she began to forgive the note she held on my condo at $10,000 per year until it was gone, for which I was very grateful. I continued studying voice, and working in my business.

Age 29 - I lived alone, operated my business in my home-office, and saved money. I was active in tennis and swimming, continued studying voice with my dear teacher, and began giving local recitals. I studied with her until she stopped teaching, due to arthritis. She was 84, and I was the last student of her life after a distinguished career in voice and teaching. I loved her very much. She called me her virtuoso and protégé.

Age 30 - I went on a tour to Egypt and Greece, which would be the first of a series of world trips over the next 7 years. My dear voice teacher passed away. I became a soloist for the Monterey Methodist Church, and continued to sing in programs.

Age 31 - I dated a young man from Austria. I traveled, worked, played tennis, sang in church, and joined a voice performance class at the local college.

Age 32 - I traveled abroad with a friend to Italy, and broke up with the Austrian. My business continued to thrive, and I continued singing and performing locally.

Age 33 - My stepfather died in the mental ward of the local hospital of collapsed lungs after many years of asthma and mental illness. I forgave him for everything.

Age 34 - I started dating my second husband, and continued to travel and work. I moved my office downtown to a professional building above a local savings and loan.

Age 35 - I married a second time to what turned out to be another disordered man. I had it annulled after six months. I moved my business to an office I found in a professional complex with all women-run businesses. I continued with the vocal class at night at the college, and studied locally with a beautiful, retired opera singer. I began soloing again. Life was getting more stable and secure.

Age 36 - I continued operating my business downtown. In September of 1988, my beloved teacher died of cancer at age 54, and I sang at her memorial service at the Carmel Mission. I continued to give recitals and do solo work.

Age 37 - I became a principal singer with Cabrillo College opera project under their director. I met my third husband who became the love of my life. I continued operating my very lucrative and successful business, and performing frequently.

Age 38 - I continued singing with the opera project, studying voice, and singing in recitals. My husband moved in with me on March 17, 1990. His three children began visitation with us regularly. I kept performing and my business continued to thrive.

Age 39 - Times were stressed by problems with visitation with my husband's three children. In addition to singing with the Cabrillo College, I soloed in concert with Burlingame Opera Company, and began coaching with their conductor. Business was still good.

Age 40 – My husband, Ron, and I got married on May 16, 1992. I added a music room below my condo, and we were very happy. His children visited regularly. I sang as guest soloist with the local symphony, and others. I moved my office back home to take care of my aging little Poodle, Gigot, because he was becoming frail.

Age 41 - I detached from my mother a second time for two years to overcome my intense anger with her. I suffered from separation anxiety, and Post Traumatic Stress Disorder (PTSD). I began vocal lessons with a new and wonderful teacher, and began soloing with Monterey Opera Association in Gala concerts. I guest soloed with Monterey County Symphony where former astronaut Alan Shepard heard me sing, and afterward told me he loved my voice.

I injured my neck at home doing sit-ups improperly on November 14, 1993, which triggered the onset of chronic FMS. I soloed in a concert of *The Messiah* at Christmas time. I was in a lot of pain, and getting physical therapy. I began swimming for water therapy, and seeing a chiropractor.

Age 42 - The disease was worsening steadily with increasing pain in my back, neck, and the right side of my body. I could only work three to four hours a day in my business until the pain stopped me. I continued to work toward my long awaited debut in a supporting role in the operetta *Hansel and Gretel* in September of 1994. A deeply disordered family member became so intensely threatened by me detaching from my mother, she blind-sided me with intrusive, vicious attacks, siding with my mother. She was too immature and dysfunctional to mind her own business. Due to my own immaturity and lack of boundaries at the time, I fought for two days to "make her understand" but could not get through to her. I remembered hating her when I was growing up because I could not stand the fantasy world she lived in, and how oblivious she was to our abusive and terrifying circumstances.

Her suppressed, unconscious anger for me became evident. These attacks hurt me so deeply, I was physically ill for two months, which happened to be the running time of the operetta, and I had to perform my long-awaited debut performance physically compromised. All this stress exacerbated the FMS symptoms to a point where I was in constant pain. To punish me for detaching from my mother, she tried to psychologically destroy me, and had become so dangerous to me, I finally had to set tough boundaries of distance and time with her, and let her go. She proved to be impervious to anyone else's reality outside her own, and was unlikely to ever change. She was clearly and irrevocably damaged and disordered.

Age 43 - In February of 1995, I struggled on to perform in another musical in a supporting role in the musical *The Sound of Music*. I gave in to family pressure, and resumed my relationship with my mother foolishly hoping things would be different. In May I sang in another operatic recital with other opera singers. In June I sang in an Opera Gala concert with Monterey Opera Association. On August 26, 1995, the day I sang in another opera concert as one of four principal soloists, I had to put down my beloved little dog, Gigot, that morning. In September of 1995 I played the role of Glenda in *The Wizard of Oz* at a local theater with my twin stepdaughters, who played darling little munchkins. My health continued to deteriorate, and I could only work in short blocks of time measured by an egg timer.

Age 44 - In February of 1996, I debuted in my first lead role as Josephine in the operetta *HMS Pinafore* in a seven-week run of 21 performances. Although I received rave reviews in all the local papers, I was re-injured in the show, was still struggling with constant pain, seeing a chiropractor regularly, and working part time out of my home. I soloed in an *Opera Pops* concert with Monterey Opera Association in May, and in August I soloed with the Monterey County Symphony. I was then offered and accepted the lead role in Monterey Opera's production of the operetta *The Merry Widow*, which opened in November of 1996 for seven performances. Although it was sold out all seven performances, and I received rave reviews, I was in so much pain I could hardly walk, I had to be helped on and off the stage, and took a lot of pain medications during each of the performances. None of the medical doctors knew what was wrong with me. When the operetta closed in December, I suffered an emotional and physical collapse, and became bedridden most of the time for two years, and housebound for the next ten. I could no longer sing.

Age 45 - The syndrome had progressed to such an advanced stage, my biological systems began shutting down, and it became clear I was dying. I had peptic ulcer disease, and could not keep food down, so I went on a baby-food diet. I could not walk or even move, was too weak to talk, and in so much pain I could not mentally combine words into sentences. My husband had to help me to the bathroom, and hold me up in the shower. I was also constipated, could barely urinate, could not sleep more than a few minutes at a time, and could hardly breathe. The muscles in my back were so tight they pulled out five ribs chronically, and I was having six to seven migraine headaches per month.

I was referred to an osteopath who wanted to admit me into the hospital immediately, but I refused. He then referred me to a Homeopath who was the first to offer me a near diagnosis of my condition. The two worked together, and I was put on a few medications, began osteopathy treatments, and classic homeopathy. I slowly began to turn around, but remained bed-ridden and completely disabled. I was eventually referred to a psychologist who specialized in helping trauma patients and PTSD. When I called my mother and told her that my new doctor said I wasn't going to die, she said, "I can't talk to you now, honey. I'm expecting an important call." and she hung up on me. All along, she had expected me to fight for my life, and make it easy for her at the same time.

The rest of my story from this point forward is found in my book *Curing Chronic Fibromyalgia - Choosing What Works,* and has a happy ending! During these nightmare years, not one single person in my self-absorbed, narcissistic family called me once to ask me how I was. When they eventually called a couple times, it was only to attack me, berate me, and call me a crazy liar. When I later asked one family member why she did not ever call to see how I was, she said, "I don't call any body. That's just the way I am." Such is the behavior of those with serious personality disorders.

PUTT TOGETHER YOUR HEALTH HISTORY
(Map of the body and mind)
After you've completed listing your personal history, it is also helpful to put your health record in order. This may help you see a progressive pattern, and give you an idea about when you began to exhibit symptoms, both physically and mentally. Again, the best way to show you how to do this is to give you an example of how I did it. Keep it as simple and as accurate as possible with respect to your age, and the health issues you had at that age. Physical manifestations of health issues have a pattern of their own. You will begin to see this pattern when you outline your health history. Using mine as an example, go back as far as you can remember, and try to list each condition in a brief one-line description, if possible.

MY HEALTH HISTORY
Congenital hip dysplasia from birth, which was corrected by leg braces in 18 months
Claustrophobia from age 2 through early adulthood
Panic attacks resulting in leaving my body throughout childhood
Asthma until age 12, and a few times in adulthood
Bed wetting until age 14
Cystic acne from age 15 through 30, treated with cortisone injections, and finally was cured with prescription Accutaine
Female hormone disorders from age 17 through age 26
Had a therapeutic curettage at age 18

Peptic ulcer disease from age 19 to late 20's
Hypoglycemia diagnosed at age 20 at 135 pounds
Head and neck injury from an auto accident with whiplash and 3"
lacerations at the back of my head at age 23
Second therapeutic curettage at age 26
Mild nervous breakdown at age 30 from inner conflicts about my
mother's chronic psychological violence
Esophageal constriction disorder for 30+ years since auto accident
at age 23
Had temporal-mandible joint dysfunction (TMJ) right side of jaw
for 30+ years ever since the auto accident at age 23
Another neck injury during home exercise accident, causing an
atlas subluxation (C-1) that triggered FMS at age 41
Post-traumatic stress disorder diagnosed at age 41
Chronic fatigue syndrome, onset at age 42
Recurrence of peptic ulcer disease at age 44
Chronic body-wide pain, causing a narcotic addiction to painkillers
at age 45, and fully disabled by FMS

Finally, full-blown fibromyalgia syndrome (FMS) caused a physical
and mental breakdown, forced me to become bedridden for the
next 2 years from pain, and mostly housebound for the next 10
years. It was not diagnosed until I was 45, 4 years after the second
neck injury. I had been suffering with chronic pain syndrome,
chronic fatigue syndrome, chronic migraine syndrome, and
misalignment of the atlas (cervical vertebra-1), which eventually
caused early degenerative disc disease in my neck between C-4, 5,
and 6.

The syndrome had completely taken over my life, and changed it
forever. It came into my life like a thief in the night, and made off
with my hopes, my dreams and my future as a professional
classical singer. As the years went by, the disease in my body
became deeper, and more widely manifested. I believe that the
various conditions up to the auto accident at age 23 in 1975 were
mostly related to my life stress and the emotional and
psychological abuse from all the dysfunctional people in my life.
However, after the injuries from the auto accident, the older I got
the less strength and vitality I had to maintain the barely functional
level of health I once could when I was younger.

And so at age 41, 18 years after a major auto accident, chronic FMS was triggered by a minor compounding exercise injury to my neck that caused an Atlas subluxation on November 23, 1993. This hallmarked a "last straw injury" that broke the proverbial camel's back. FMS was triggered and exacerbated by stress, and by age 45 had became full-blown and fully disabling. As I became weaker, I could no longer hold back the grief and frustrated rage from the psychological violence from my morally bankrupt family, that I had spent a lifetime suppressing. It began flowing out of me in a torrent psychological sorrow.

It then became important for me to solve the unsolved mysteries that seem inextricably connected to the out-pouring of all this erupting pain and suffering. As soon as I realized I needed help, I got it.

SOLVE THE UNSOLVED MYSTERIES
(Seeing things through new eyes)
The last step in putting together the puzzle of your past is analyzing and reconciling consequential unsolved mysteries, and bring them to their nearest, most logical conclusion. I would like to share a handy road map I have come up with a to assist you.

Pick the mysteries that seem to be linked with the on-going themes in your life that have come up the most. Your life-themes may or may not be the same as others in your family, and when they are shared, they are most likely linked in a major way. What affected others may have indirectly affected you as well, and visa versa. Think back and recall the comments made by others about these issues, and then think about what you actually remember. What you were told and what you remember can be woven into a tapestry of sorts, and you can stand back and look at it through new eyes, with the understanding of the adult you are now, and apply the common sense and wisdom that you lacked a child.

Ask questions about absolute judgments that were made by others that you may have accepted as fact. Leave open all possibilities when you look back on things now. Lay them out in order, and then decide what is most likely, knowing the people involved the way you do now. Most of the time you can assess the past by the present. Patterns rarely change in people, especially in dysfunctional families, and behaviors can be predictable and consistent to a point. It is always admirable to give the benefit of the doubt, but not when what is in doubt has very little history of a benefit. Be consistent with reality, and with your truest recollections.

There are two issues most relevant to my life-themes. They are old inappropriate feelings of low self-esteem and worthlessness, and an old intense fear of abandonment. I believe these are based on a few unsolved mysteries, the ghosts that have haunted me for much of my life. At this point, I have resolved them sufficiently and have let them go. But for the purpose of showing you a clear example of how to tackle the job of solving your own unsolved mysteries, I will go through mine with you from the questions, to what I have accepted to be the best answers I will most likely ever have.

The first question relevant to my life themes is, "Why did my parents get divorced?" The second question is, " What happened to my father after the divorce, and where was my father during all those years when we heard nothing from him?" And the third question is, "Did he or did he not pay child support?"

To answer these important questions, I listed all my relevant memories, along with all of the remarks I could remember over the years made to me by my parents and others. I concentrated on the remarks that seemed to align with events and felt closest to the truth, and I listed them in an order according to their relevancy to each question. These memories and remarks told a story that I was eventually able to assemble.

TELLING AND ENDING THE STORY
(Telling the story solves many mysteries)
Before assembling a story from these questions, I first had to bear in mind the natures of the people involved, and the credibility of their testimony. As do some people in our society today, both of my parents suffered from Narcissistic Personality Disorder, which is hallmarked by a compulsion toward veiling the truth out of fear of psychological humiliation through the exposure of a less than perfect self-image.

So when I recall the remarks made to me by each of them, I have to remember that, although both of them were damaged by their childhoods, it would still be unfair to automatically discount all they have said, and deem it as untrue. There can occur what is called a "window of truth" where, in one moment a truth that has gone veiled thus far is honestly seen and admitted, and in the next moment the window closes, and the denial returns. This can be very confusing, which is the aim of the veil to begin with, but it is important to remember that in those moments of unveiled truth, no matter how inconsistent to the status quo it may seem, insights into your past can be revealed with a profound clarity.

It then becomes necessary to compare and combine these various remarks with your actual memories, along with the remarks of other people, to establish their relative truthfulness and meaning. Pay closest attention to the remarks that were made by your parents and family members that feel like those told through a "window of truth," and trust your instincts.

To begin with, I know my parents were very much in love when they married, and their immediate problems were related to conflicting goals, priorities, and values, as well as a shared chronic immaturity and disorder. My father grew up on a cattle ranch in North Dakota, and once told me that when he met my mother she was very beautiful, intelligent, and very talented. He said he considered her to be good breeding stock, but that he later saw he had married her for all the wrong reasons.

While my father was in the Navy, my mother graduated from Northwestern University in Illinois with a Master's degree in music. My mother grew up in poverty in Newcastle, Indiana. She was a young, talented soprano with a beautiful voice, and a kindly towns lady who recognized her potential paid for her classical music education. My father and mother met through a mutual friend at my mother's college. They wrote to each other for a year until my father got out of the Navy.

Afterward, they got married, moved to California, and had a family. She once told me how handsome he was in his uniform, and how romantic their year of love-letter correspondence had been while he was in the Navy. I remember my mother saying to me that she was so dumb when she got married, she didn't even know she would get pregnant. They began married life living in small country towns in California where my father worked first in his own dairy farm, and then later on, became a banker.

As the years unfolded following the birth of their last child, my mother wanted to return to her pursuit of a singing career. My father wanted her to stay at home with us kids through our formative years and be a nurturing mother, and then return to her singing after we were both in school. My mother always said, "Your father once joked he wanted to keep me barefoot and pregnant." Postponing her singing career to be a mother was unacceptable to her, and my father said she did as she pleased, and joined a local classical singing group.

My father once told me, "Your mother would go out each night to her singing group, and leave me with you kids. I wanted her to tuck you kids in, and read you bedtime stories, and be a mother, but she would not listen to me, so I stopped trying to talk to her. Once I got so mad I tore up her music. Your mother told me each month for the last two years of our marriage, that if I did not let her sing and do what ever she pleased, she would divorce me and take you kids away, and I would never see you again."

He said, "She would stay out late at night all the time, and one night she stayed out until morning. When she came home (I didn't know where she had been) I told her I was not going to permit her to do that because it made me late for work. I could not leave you kids alone, and I could not lose my job. We fought, and I slapped her once, and said, "OK, you can have your damned divorce. She fell down on the bed crying, and acted like I was going to kill her. After I left for work, she went down to the police station and told them I beat her. They did not see any signs of this, as there were no red marks or bruises etc., so they did nothing about it. And that was the only time I ever hit her." I remembered that we were all living in Madera, California at the time.

My mother once said to me, "Your father beat me, and he tore up my music, and was very abusive." Another time she said, "The more he would forbid me to sing, the more I wanted to go out and sing just to spite him." and, "I could never get through to your father. He would just stop talking for days at a time. It was awful." In 1998, I told my mother that my father said he never minded her singing. He just wanted her first to be a mother to us kids during our formative years, and wait until after we were in school before she resumed her singing. She said, "Well, I was there all day! What more could he want?"

My father also told me once, "She was a cold, unaffectionate, and uninterested mother. She never read you stories at night, or bathed you, or tucked you in. She let you kids run around all day in dirty clothes." I remember wetting my pants frequently during the day, and wearing them wet for hours. I also remember my mother venting her frustration with me while I was playing alone in the front yard as she screamed at me from the front door, "You can just sit in your urine! I've run out of clean pants for you to wear, and I'm sick of washing them!"

Once my mother said to me on the phone after I got with FMS, "I was a lousy mother. I never did any teaching, and there was never any affection or anything. I was always too wrapped up in my own problems." I told her she always did the best she knew how, but it was not entirely true. After I got sick, there was another time when my mother took me to a lab for blood tests when I was withdrawing from a Vicodin and Valium addiction. She saw me being held down on a table by two technicians because I was having strong convulsions, while a third drew blood. She closed her eyes, and left the room.

Afterward, in the car on the way home, she said, "You know, you kids were terribly neglected when you were small. I neglected you." I said, "It's OK Mom, you did the best you could with what you had." Her reflection made me very sad for her. I felt the heavy weight of her regret. I thought to myself what parent does not have regrets? Hers must weigh a ton.

When I was four and five, I remember my parent's fighting at night after my mother got home from singing. Once in particular was when my mother locked herself in the bathroom crying and wailing, while my father paced up and down the hall, and had to break down the door to get in. It was the first time to my knowledge she tried to commit suicide with an overdose of tranquilizers. My father had to take her and us kids to the hospital in the middle of the night to have her stomach pumped. This memory was confirmed a few decades later when I told my father about two incidences that I distinctly remembered when my mother overdosed on tranquilizers while married to my stepfather. After her second attempt, I remember my mother saying to me, "I'd have killed myself years ago if it weren't for you kids."

I remember my mother was indeed gone most nights when I was little, and I remember my father bathing us and tucking us in bed. He was unhappy and distant, and otherwise kept to himself. I do not remember any expressed love or affection from my mother, and very little from my father. Neither of them seemed able to put the emotional needs of their children first. My parent's conflict escalated until the tension and discord between them was unbearable.

When I was four and five, I also remember my mother fuming around the house during the day, consumed in anger toward my father. I frequently wet my pants and left my body from fear and anxiety. I sometimes hid during the day, and held and rocked myself for what seemed like hours. Rocking myself to self-comfort under extreme stress became a habit I carried well into my adulthood.

When my parents divorced, I was six and my brother was seven. I barely remember my brother during this time. We were taken to my father's parents' northern California cattle ranch during the divorce proceedings. I remember climbing high, unsupervised, to the top of a tall fence, and looking down into a large corral full of huge Texas long-horned cattle, and my grandfather riding a large red horse he called Big Red.

I remember my grandmother cooking in the kitchen, and seeing her false teeth in a glass by the bathroom sink at night. I do not remember much more from that time. The next thing I remember was my mother and us kids living in a house in Pacific Grove, CA. I could not understand at the time why my father was absent. No one had explained any of these events to me. My parents were clearly suffering a great deal, along with us kids. Now I can more clearly see why my parents got a divorce, and why my brother and I were neglected. Both of my parents were emotionally immature and psychologically disordered at the time, and doing the best they could with what they had.

Unfortunately, their best was seriously deficient. Like so many young marriages that end in divorce, my parents' youthful selfishness, irresponsibility, and basic differences, along with their mental disorders, caused them to fall far short of providing a loving and nurturing atmosphere for their children. Fifty years later, my father said to me, "If I'd been gentler with your mother, I may not have lost her. We were both very immature then."

My mother once said, "Your father was so harsh and cruel. I couldn't take it." The neglect I experienced as a child explains where my feelings of low self-esteem and worthlessness came from, but what about my fear of abandonment that controlled my behavior with men for so much of my life? This brings up the next question. What happened to my father after the divorce, and where was he all those years when we did not hear from him?

My father once told me, "When we divorced, your mother persuaded her sister to come into court at the custody hearing, and tell the judge I beat your mother regularly, so the judge denied me joint custody and visitation rights. Your mother was awarded sole custody, and if I were to see you kids, it was to be at her discretion.

Your mother was awarded the car, and I did not have enough money to buy another one. When she left me, she took the car and moved you all to Pacific Grove. I was left in Madera with a $400 per month bank job, $1,700 worth of bills, and no car. I lived on oatmeal for a long time. I only had enough money for one bus ticket to Pacific Grove per month, which took all day to get there."

"I saw you kids for one hour that evening, and one hour in the morning, and then I rode six hours on the bus to get home. I was trying to keep my job, pay child support, pay off all the bills, and I had no money for an attorney. The judge told me there wasn't anything I could do without hiring an attorney, which would have cost $1,500, and I just didn't have it." He said he came to see us a few times, visited with us for a couple hours, and then stopped coming. He said it was just too hard all round, and it was easier to stay away. He said, "I finally got so frustrated I wrote your mother a letter, and told her if she did not let you kids come and see me, I would cut off the child support."

I only remember my father visiting us at the house in Pacific Grove once. My brother and I were told to stay in the downstairs bedroom, but I peeked out the door into the dining room. He was standing over my mother at the kitchen table while she was polishing her nails. They were arguing, and my mother's jaw was very rigid. He left without speaking to us or saying goodbye.

I have no memory of his visiting us a few times under the conditions he described. I do remember feeling he had abandoned me, and I grew up feeling unwanted and unloved by him. There were never any birthday cards or Christmas gifts from him. This easily explains my intense fear of abandonment that affected me into adult life, especially since I had felt closer to him than my mother up until the divorce.

A few years ago my aunt said to me, "In those days you had to prove in court why you should be granted a divorce, and I had to testify against your Dad. I was asked questions by her attorney, and I had to say 'Yes, Jean was unhappy' and 'Yes, Warren hit Jean', etc. I always felt bad for your Dad." Decades later, in a conversation with my father about the court outcome, he told me that two months prior to our conversation, the same aunt had called him to apologize for lying to the judge for my mother.

She told him my mother had put her up to it, and she had been so sorry all her life, especially after the way it affected all of us kids. My father told my aunt they were all young at the time, and that he forgave her long ago. He told me a year before he died, after I shared with him more about my hardships in life, "If it hadn't been for that unfair judge, none of this would have happened.

I remember a time long ago my mother said to me on the phone, "I always felt guilty about taking you kids away from your father the way I did." I also remember her mother, my grandmother, saying, "If your mother hadn't taken you kids away from your father the way she did, you'd be married to some man who worked in the street wearing a hard hat, and packing him sacked lunches every day, with a bunch of screaming kids hanging on you. She gave you a better life." Now, when think of that remark, I say to myself, "What would be wrong with my mother marrying a blue-color worker? Actually, she eventually did! And was our life really better?"

I can see why the family always said that it was a very bitter divorce, but why did so many years go by until I saw my father again? What kept him away for so long, and where was he all that time? I remember my father's mother saying to me once, "Your Dad disappeared for two years after the divorce, and none of us knew where he was. We were all terribly worried about him." Decades later, a friend of my father's visited me, and said my father was on the run from my mother's lawyers, and tried to make a living as a professional gambler for a while.

As far back as I could remember my mother said repeatedly, "Your father never paid one red cent of child support!" I do remember when we all lived in Pacific Grove after the divorce, my mother was teaching music in the local elementary school, and had hired a sweet old woman to be a housekeeper and babysitter in the afternoons. How could she support us all, and hire a housekeeper on a teacher's salary alone? She was also dating my stepfather, and I remember she once said, "I told him that if he wanted to see me, he had to bring groceries when he came," and I do remember him bringing in sacks of groceries. This shows she must have been struggling, but that alone was not an answer.

As I mentioned, my father told me he threatened to cut off the child support out of frustration over not seeing us. He also said years later, "I did cut off the child support for one year, and she took the letter I once wrote her to an attorney, and dragged me into court. I paid my child support after that, and didn't miss a payment. I had a file of cancelled checks for years until recently, and when I moved I saw no reason to keep them any longer, so I threw them out."

Another time he told me that he only stopped paying child support for one summer. He seemed a bit inconsistent in his accounting of how long he stopped paying, but he did admit he had stopped for a time. I remember when I returned home for a year to go back to school after being thrown out of the house the first time at age 18, my mother had my father send a check directly to me in the amount of $65 a month for that entire year. She said this was to make up for the support he never paid. The period of one year coincides with his first account.

So did he or did he not pay child support? This question was a puzzlement for me all of my life. I remember my mother saying, "Your father never paid a red cent in child support, and I finally had to take him to court. It was after I was married to your stepfather, and your Dad told the judge that he was not going to pay another man to raise his kids. The judge got mad, he hit the gavel, and sentenced him to 90 days in jail for contempt, and he still didn't pay! I do not know why you are so devoted to him. He has never done a thing for you kids, and he doesn't deserve it!"

I also remember someone saying that the judge also ordered my father out of the state of California. He always hated California after that. He'd say now and then, "California is the land of fruits, nuts and flakes, with a tree-hugging, pot-smoking, faggot for a governor!" The fact remains, if he had indeed paid all his child support, then why was he prosecuted in this way?

My father eventually told me that, "During the custody hearing, the judge asked your mother at one point if she wanted him to give me 90 days in jail, and she said yes. I could not believe she could do that to me!" If he spent 90 days in jail, how could he pay child-support during this time – which would be one summer and coincide with his second account - hence my mother's statement, "He still didn't pay!" On the other hand, why would any judge ask my mother to be the one who made this decision?

When I was 13 or 14, my brother and I began to take the bus to Nevada to visit my father. I also remember the first time I visited my father alone without my brother. My father was living in a seedy apartment next to a railroad track across from an all night bar that had neon lights flashing through his living room window

45

blinds. It was obvious, even to me that he was struggling. The train would come by every few hours throughout the night, and make a lot of track-racket.

There was no TV, and I slept on a worn out couch in the living room. The apartment was sparsely furnished, and had no amenities. So I went out during the day while he was at work and bought him some plastic flowers and a vase for the living room, and some kitchen supplies at the local dime store with my saved allowance from home. I remember he only took me out to a restaurant for sodas while he drank coffee. He was always pinching pennies and never had any money.

When I told my mother about the way he lived, she said, "He has always been a big martyr, always crying poor-mouth. I don't know what he's been doing with all his money. Maybe he's been keeping another woman, or gambling, or something! He wants you to feel sorry for him!" In 1994, after I had become ill, I again asked my father outright about the child support, and I told him it has always been very confusing because of the conflicting stories.

My mother was still telling everyone that, "Warren was a dead-beat Dad." My father said to me, "I paid my child support, all except for one year when I was trying to save money to hire an attorney to fight your mother for visitation rights to see you kids, and that's the truth! I even paid a couple extra years for you when you were in college." I was really only in college for one year, and I knew he paid me monthly for that year, but I knew nothing about any second year, nor did I receive anything from him.

He could not look me in the eye when he said he paid all his support, and seemed understandably uncomfortable about being asked again. He looked down, smirking, and said, "Yah know honey, I'm just a dumb cowboy." I could not tell how much truth there was in what he said any more than I could when I talked to my mother. One day when I was out to lunch with my mother, I told her what he said, and she got so angry she got up and left. If he had paid it all but one year, why was she still so livid? There had to be a reason.

So the answer to the question - did he or did he not pay all his child support? Well, it seems he paid it some of the time, but not all of the time, and that is the best conclusion that can be made. My mother recently said, "I never knew what happened to all his money. He never paid child support, and after I married your stepfather, I just let it go." What possible reason could she have for misrepresenting the situation so many years afterward? In any case, I no longer associate my self-worth and security to the answer to this question, or why he disappeared for so many years.

I feel that all the earlier bitterness between my parents, that was fueled over this controversy for so many years, was rooted in the deeper issue of their different beliefs about family values and parental responsibilities, and that neither of them could let go of the rancor from the way they separated until many years later. But they did let it go, they did forgive each other, and they made peace with the past, for which I greatly admire them both.

My father once said to me, "It breaks a man's heart to lose his kids. Looking back now, I guess I should have tried harder to get an attorney." It was something that was always with him. I do not feel this is being a martyr. I see it as being human to feel a deep loss for a lifetime. My mother once said to me tearfully after she had been married to my stepfather for over a decade, "I loved your Dad so much, you don't ever get over a love like that."

I appreciate now that the true answer to the question of child support resides in my parents' hearts. It is not for anyone else to know or understand, and it should probably remain this way. The whole truth about all that happened between them, although it adversely affected their children's lives, is between them. After all, they are the ones who had to live with their choices, as we all do, and their choices do not have to define me, nor do they determine my self-worth or sense of security.

I realize now that I do not have to go through life being haunted by someone else's ghosts that never had anything to do with me to begin with. As an adult, I am responsible for determining my self-worth, my truth determines who I am, and what I choose to do or not do is my business, and no one else's. Once my parents made a choice to get married and have a family. The rest of their choices created what happened after that.

I can understand my father's emphasis on family values, and I can also see why my mother would need to return to utilizing her well-cultivated talent. Who could blame either one. What they lacked was a mutually agreed upon plan, designed to meld their dynamically different backgrounds into a family unit that could work to their mutual benefit. They were simply too young, naïve, and immature to realize it at the time. Opposites do attract, but they do not always meld naturally. Mental illness certainly adds greatly to the challenge.

When I think of my parents now, my father, the handsome, home-spun cowboy who joined the Navy, and son of a cattle rancher who had made and lost two fortunes in his lifetime, and my mother, the poor, beautiful little Hoosier girl, who was given the chance to become educated and cultivate her amazing talent, I marvel at what each one of them accomplished throughout their lives, in spite of their humble beginnings and their psychological damage. My father became a banker and mayor, and a well-known public servant in his community. My mother became an accomplished classical singer, a well-known artistic figure, and eventual philanthropist in her community.

I see them both now with the compassion, understanding, and forgiveness of an adult, and no longer with the grief of a child. I try to always remember everyone is doing the best they can with what they have at the time, based on what they got in childhood, and based on their awareness of the choices that were within their power to make. Whether or not people use this power in a constructive or destructive way is something they alone are responsible for.

Not everyone realizes that life is a series of choices, and although we cannot always control what happens, we can always control how we choose to respond. When people suffer from mental illnesses as serious as Narcissistic and Borderline Personality Disorders, their choices are always self-serving at the expense of those around them, and this is a tragedy for everyone concerned.

We are all either limited or freed by our awareness of the power of choice, and sadly so many people are prisoners of themselves due to their own willful ignorance. The only way out of this prison is to choose to expand your understanding, apply what you learn to your life, and make new and wiser choices one day at a time. I could easily choose to judge my mother for seeming to care more about a singing career than she did her husband and children, or my father for giving up too easily and cutting off contact for seven years, and not supplying sufficient support for a time.

However, I truly believe the best choice I can make at this point is to say goodbye to the past, and let it go as if it were a school I once attended and graduated from, although I would never have wanted to learn what I had to. I can take what I learned and move forward in life with my head held high, with a clear and peaceful mind, a warm whole heart, and greater understanding of myself and others. The wisdom I have gained from viewing the past as an informed adult with more confident intuition, will guide me until it is my turn to leave this world.

My father never remarried. After retiring from banking and local public office in a small town in Nevada, he moved from a medium sized trailer in the middle of the desert, 20 miles outside of Winnemucca, to a one room cabin back in town. He always loved the peace and quiet of the open spaces. He kept himself safe by living a solitary life, and never again committed to an intimate relationship.

My mother lived in a town near to me, and was remarried for the third time. Her husband was a wealthy man, and made all of her material dreams come true. She traveled extensively with him, and was a known figure in high society as she always wanted to be. Both of my parents were exactly where they wanted to be in life. Before each of them died, I considered them good friends.

I am also where I want to be, on the path of maintaining my health and recovery, and I no longer want my past to have the power to drain my energy, or disrupt my serenity and happiness in the present. The past can be like a giant suction hose attached to a powerful vacuum cleaner. When you maintain a close connection with it, it can suck your life-force energy right down its long, unyielding tube into the bottom of a dark bag full of debris and bacteria, where nothing from the present can live. Detaching from this hose will reconnect you to the vital energy you didn't know you were missing, energy that you must have if you are going to be healthy in a well-rounded way. The farther away I get from my past, the more energy I have for healing in the present.

I heard Dr. Carolyn Myss, PhD, a known medical intuit and healer, say in one of her PBS-TV lectures, "If you want to heal, you must chart a course far away from the past, and into the future." The past no longer has any living reality for me. Only the present is real, and in the present I am very blessed. My many blessings are my husband, his kids, my amazing pets, and my loving friends, all who are my family of choice. I know that not all of life's mysteries are meant to be solved. Some are simply there for us to observe, and be a part of for a time, and exist only for us to learn to live within life's mysteries as gracefully as possible.

Life can really be as simple as that. From what I have experienced and learned so far, I now look out the windows of my here and now, and I marvel at how wonderful life can be when you make the right choices. In his book *The Power of Now,* the wonderful modern-day spiritual leader and teacher, Eckhart Tolle, says, "The only sane way to live is in complete acceptance of what is, and know that it is neither good nor bad, but a part of a higher good, the higher good that has no opposite. The conflict within you ceases when the demands and expectations of your mind no longer clash with what is. Accept what is. Do what you have to do, but accept what is."

So, go ahead and do what you have to do to heal yourself, and accept everything else as a part of a greater good for you, your spiritual growth, and your life. Start by educating yourself in all that you need to understand, so you can free yourself from your past and gain the wisdom to handle the future in a way that allows you to evolve and thrive. You will use this information for the rest of your life, and you will never be sorry you acquired it.

SERENITY PRAYER

God grant me the serenity
to accept the things I cannot change,
the courage to change the things I can,
and the wisdom to know the difference.

And God, grant me the courage
not to give up on what I think is right,
even when I think it is hopeless.

Reinhold Niebuhr

THREE

TWO EXAMPLES OF DESTRUCTIVE PERSONALITIES
The Narcissist and the Borderline
Behind the mask hide their crippled inner child

In the field of psychology, there has been extensive study and research into personality disorders that adversely effect or relationships and society. The Narcissist, Borderline, Anti-social, and Histrionic Personality Disorders are among the heaviest hitters of the top-ten most toxic and destructive conditions in the field of psychology, and fall under the sub-category called "the dramatic cluster." I will only be focusing on the two that I am most familiar with: the narcissist and borderline personalities.

It can be simply said that the narcissist is someone who had one or both parents who was a narcissist: a parent who was so obsessed with the child as their extension, that the child became obsessed with itself. It can also be simply said that the borderline is someone who was hurt so deeply as a child, that his or her nervous system became stuck in fight-or-flight mode.

One thing can be said with near certainty: people are not born with a personality disorder. They developed one through the process of surviving destructive and dangerous people and circumstances beyond their control to no fault of their own. The following profiles represent these two forms of personality disorders in their pathological states. Both disorders frequently occur with other personality disorders. This is not to say that they are "multiple personalities," as this is a separate diagnosis.

THE NARCISSIST
(The mighty narcissist: the biggest contender among the most toxic and destructive known personality disorders under the dramatic cluster)
"Why do I feel so bad?" Because that's what the narcissist does. They are masters of making you doubt yourself or feel crazy, when all you are doing is having a rational response to their insanity. When someone says that when their mother, father, aunt, uncle, or whoever, sucks the air right out of the room, they are

52

talking about the narcissist. Narcissists are so self-absorbed and self-oblivious, they are among psychology's hardest nuts to crack. Talk therapy is ineffective in reaching them, and drug therapy helps very little. There's a saying from Texas Democrat Sam Rayburn, "There's no education in the second kick of the mule." Well, with the narcissist, the first kick doesn't faze them, as they automatically dismiss any evidence that there is something wrong with them. Researchers have come to understand why. Narcissists may be self-absorbed, but they jolly well believe they are entitled to be.

It is difficult to persuade them to see a therapist, and even more difficult when they deny there is a problem at all, and proclaim they are perfectly healthy. Narcissists are involved in many of society's ills: divorce, child abuse, and psychological and physical violence. Estimates for the prevalence Narcissistic Personality Disorder is up to 16% of identified patients in the clinical population, and 1% in the general population. Narcissism is considered to be rare, but I disagree. I feel it is safe to say that, since the narcissist does not go into therapy, thus becoming an identified patient, the actual number of them is likely much higher.

DIAGNOSTIC CRITERIA
Diagnostic criteria for Narcissistic Personality Disorder are a generally pervasive pattern of grandiosity (in fantasy or behavior), an insatiable need for admiration, and lack of empathy, all beginning by early adulthood, and present in a variety of contexts. The narcissistic personality, described in the DSM under the diagnostic code of #301.81, is summarized as having the following specific characteristics: an inflated sense of self-importance; fantasies of unlimited success, fame, power, beauty, and "ideal love" (an uncritical adoration); exhibitionism (a need to be looked at and admired), a tendency to feel rage with little objective cause; a readiness to treat people with cool indifference as punishment for offensive treatment, or as an indication of the fact they have no current use for the person; a tendency toward severe feelings of inferiority, shame, and emptiness; a sense of entitlement accompanied by the tendency to exploit; a tendency to over-idealize or devalue people based largely on a narrow focus; and an inability to empathize.

The ego of the narcissist can also be described in another way: an oblivious, erotic obsession with oneself; inability to see anyone or recognize anything that is not perceived as an extension of themselves; as a parent, an unconscious need to set out and destroy the individual identity of the child who becomes the focus of their narcissistic obsession, only allowing a perceived extension of themselves to exist; inability to have true interpersonal relationships, other than with fans or slave type people (sycophants); parasitic in their nature, entering into your world attempting to consume your individual identity; readily using threats, insults, gifts, or promises to seduce you and keep you in their narcissistic range of control; they are chronically and overpoweringly intrusive; they believe the lie the illness tells them that there is nothing wrong with them. They are oblivious to the effect they have on others; developmentally, they are emotionally frozen between ages two and five. They are extremely toxic, and psychologically, emotionally, and spiritually dangerous. Prognosis: incurable lifelong disorder with minimal potential for improvement. In later years they may exhibit paranoid behavior and psychosis.

KEY ASPECTS

The narcissist is typically cheap with others, while being very generous with themselves. While being insensitive to the feelings of others, they are hypersensitive to their own feelings. They do not "see" or "hear" others, and make no attempt to remember other's boundaries, likes, or dislikes. They laugh at, resent, or ignore the boundaries of others, and typically manipulate around them, or bulldoze right over them without a thought. They are able to easily justify cruel and abusive behavior toward others, and are incapable of mature love. As parents, they can only see their children as an extension of themselves.

Although narcissistic disorder is a conditioned mental illness, we are all born 100% narcissistic in order to survive. By age five, we have discovered that the world outside ourselves has limits, and we become resigned to this reality. From this point on, with the proper amount of love and nurturing, we begin to outgrow our narcissism naturally. The narcissist, due to lack of love and nurturing during their formative years, becomes emotionally stuck between ages two and five; a case of arrested development.

Although they are able to mature physically and intellectually, they do not mature emotionally beyond this point. They learn to dupe people into thinking that they are normal, healthy adults with their mask of sanity because their self-image of perfection demands it.

However, as soon as someone crosses them or confronts them with their toxic, inappropriate behavior, they give themselves away by their intense, and sometimes violent, angry reaction, revealing their true nature hidden behind a well-polished mask. Then their reaction is one of a spoiled, enraged child, who feels something they are entitled to was unjustly taken away.

Although a degree of narcissism is inherent in all of us from birth, a healthy conscience and intact personal integrity are all that is needed to keep this in check. Because narcissists are entirely devoid of the ability to be honest with themselves in any lasting way, they are blindly unaware their narcissism has gone out of control, and has become a mental illness. This is when their narcissism has become "marbleized" throughout their personality; hence, their entire personality has become disordered.

TOP TEN TELL-TALE SIGNS
1) Responds immediately with defensive rage and denial at the slightest hint of criticism, no matter how justified or constructive.
2) Interpersonally exploitive, and routinely takes advantage of others to meet their covert ego needs, means, and ends.
3) Experiences feelings of self-grandiosity, and is preoccupied with feelings of unlimited success, and expects to be recognized as superior, even without commensurate achievements.
4) Has a constant sense of inexorable power, accompanied by an indomitable will.
5) Has a constant sense of entitlement, unreasonable expectations of especially favorable treatment, and automatic, unchallenged compliance with, and acceptance of, his or her wishes, desires and behaviors. What they have is never enough.
6) Unquenchable thirst to be associated with, identified with, and move within the circles of the rich and powerful. A belief that he or she is "special" and unique, and can only be understood and appreciated by, or should only associate with, others they

perceive to be special or associated with high-status institutions.

7) Lack of human empathy, and are unwilling and incapable of recognizing and identifying with the feelings and needs of others.

8) Obsessed with self-gratification at any cost, showing an arrogant, haughty behavior or attitude, i.e. the "Prima-Donna." They believe, "My needs and pure motives are all important, and nothing else matters." They feel no responsibility for the effect their harmful actions and/or behaviors have on others.

9) Require constant and excessive admiration, adulation, and attention.

10) They are often envious of others, or believe that others are envious of them.

If someone consistently exhibits five or more of these traits, they are suffering from Narcissistic Personality Disorder. The prognosis for a cure is poor, because there is no known treatment that has yet proven effective since the narcissist sincerely believes there is nothing wrong with them. They are emotionally, psychologically, and spiritually destructive to anyone who attempts an intimate relationship with them.

They are an energetic black hole: the more effort you put into your relationship, the more energy they pull out of you. Giving back little or nothing of themselves in return, they leave you barely enough energy to live your own life. Over time, they can deplete your life-force energy to such an extent that they prevent you from reaching your individual life potential. Healthy, self-respecting people will not allow themselves to be sacrificed in this way, and will naturally pull away from, or entirely reject the narcissist.

THE SLAVE: SCHIZOTYPAL-SYCOPHANT PERSONALITY
(The narcissist primary enablers)
It was famed suffragette organizer, Emmeline Pankhurst, during 1903-1928 Britain, who said at one of her rallies, "I'd rather be a rebel than a slave." Between 1903 and 1914 she was imprisoned 13 times, and ridiculed and persecuted by traditionalist men and women for her belief in a woman's right to vote. Her indomitable spirit brought about worldwide change in women's rights becoming human rights in finally winning the women's vote

through her movement in 1928. It took effort and sacrifice to chance the injustices of spiritual suppression, and it took being a rebel, not a slave, to accomplish what she did. She knew that what you ignore, you enable, and her high integrity would not allow her be a sycophant.

The only people who will remain close to a narcissist are either other narcissists, or the classic sycophant who suffers from such low self-esteem that they do not value themselves enough to reject destructive and suppressive behaviors, and instead enables and comforts those who should be made uncomfortable.

The sycophant behaves so obsequiously, they may not even recognize that the narcissist's behavior as abusive, and may have become so overly adapted from their childhood traumas that they misperceive neglect and abuse as love. These people tend to live life on the surface, never seeing more than a superficial meaning to the behavior of others, and prefer taking things at face value. To them, their willful ignorance is truly their bliss.

The narcissist uses people who are ignorant, naïve, or blinded by their childhood maladaptations to enable and excuse their incessant ego-feeding behaviors, and make excuses for the evil they do as a result of their mental illness. These enablers unwittingly perpetuate their own mental illness in the process of maintaining their emotional attachment with the narcissist.

Schizotypal-sycophant personalities are people who perceive life through what I call a "cult-bubble mentality" and are a willfully ignorant segment of our society that is entirely self-oblivious and has no identity of their own, other than the one given to them by a role or label. These unfortunate, maladapted lost souls are the followers of egomaniacs and cult leaders everywhere. They are so self-oblivious, their mental illness is not even known to them. In addition, with regard to the slave's willful ignorance, it's helpful to remember Robert J. Hanlon's Razor: "Never attribute to malice that which can be adequately explained by stupidity."

Furthermore, there are important distinctions between stupidity, ignorance, and willful ignorance. Stupidity is when a person is too slow to process unfamiliar incoming data, or does not possess the capacity to understand it. Ignorance is when a person possesses the capacity to understand, but is not aware of information outside their known reality. Willful ignorance is when a person is capable and aware of the information, but refuses to consider it for selfish, ego-feeding reasons to protect their worldview.

KEY ASPSECTS (The cult-bubble mentality)
Schizotypal Personality Disorder is uncommon, but the disorder is not difficult to spot. Self-worth is extremely low, and personal identity is non-existent. These unfortunate souls are the primary targets of prey of radical cult and religious leaders everywhere.
1) They are loners. Because they are uncomfortable being close to others, they lack close friends outside of the immediate family, prefer to be alone during times of crises and handle life's challenges in a solitary manner, rarely asking for help.
2) They prefer to occupy their time with solitary pursuits, and choose occupations where they can work alone.
3) They do not experience appropriate emotional responses to disturbing events, and are noticeably "flat" or unemotional in their reactions. They are often seen as "developmentally disabled" or "slow."
4) They are insecure in social situations, and often feel persistent and/or acute anxiety, causing them to act in ways that make them appear schizophrenic.
5) They interpret events incorrectly, and assign incorrect meaning, often taking innocent events personally as being harmful.
6) Their thinking is peculiar, and displays unusual beliefs and mannerisms, like picking their nose in public, or snorting when they laugh out loud, acting silly and child-like in social situations.
7) They are neurotic, suspicious and paranoid, and constantly doubt others.
8) They dress in peculiar ways, and look childlike in appearance.
9) They have a peculiar style of speech, using childlike terminology throughout their adulthood, like "more better."
10) They cannot easily discern the difference between reality and their distorted thinking patterns.
11) Their parents suffered from severe personality disorders, such as narcissistic and/or borderline personalities.

The interesting thing about a slave personality is that they are the opposite side of the narcissist coin, and at any point in their life,

58

when they become sufficiently disillusioned, they can flip into the mindset of the narcissist, and can even flip back into slave mode again. Either way, they are lost to their true self, and not authentic in their representation of who they are.

One major distinguishing characteristic used in discriminating the narcissist from other similarly destructive disorders, such as the Borderline, the Histrionic, and the Anti-social personalities, is their sense of apparent grandiosity and superiority. Other distinguishing characteristics are the relative stability in the narcissist's inflated self-image, their lack of abandonment concerns, their lack of emotional displays of affection, their disdain for the sensitivities of others, and their specific need for full attention and constant admiration.

Because the narcissist consciously believes they have achieved perfection, they live in unconscious fear that the truth about their imperfections may at some time be revealed. Many highly successful individuals display personality traits that might be considered narcissistic. Only when these traits are inflexible, maladaptive, persisting, and cause significant functional impairment or subjective distress, do they constitute Narcissistic Personality Disorder. In other words, a person can exhibit random, periodic narcissistic traits without them being marbleized throughout their personality as a disorder.

In Scott Peck's book "People of the Lie" he quotes a wise old priest, saying about human evil, "It is not only a disease; it is the ultimate disease." A description of the classification called "the evil," as a variant of Narcissistic Personality Disorder, is called Malignant Narcissistic Disorder. Evil behavior, or evil as a predilection, simply means that which is destructive; that which tears down and destroys.

The sicker the patient, the more dishonest they are in their behavior, the more distorted they are in their thinking, and the less able they are to be helped with any modicum of success. Since "the evil" refuses to assume any personal responsibility for their behavior, or even acknowledge their deficit or the effect they have on others, and thus are never repentant, and are not successfully treatable by any means yet known, saying things like, "I know you want me to apologize, but I wouldn't even want to. I never took responsibility for anything!"

A cure for the malignant narcissist has gone unstudied because 1) the evil do not want to be studied, and 2) psychologists are rarely strong enough, psychologically and spiritually, to enter into the lion's den without being consumed by the labyrinth of lies, twisted motives, and distorted communication, into which they would be drawn in an attempt to help them. In other words, not only would the therapist be unsuccessful in their attempts to pull the narcissist out of the morass of their sickness, they may become lost in it themselves. Malignant narcissists can be described as a regular narcissist whose classic symptoms have been hugely magnified.

Choosing to remain uninformed, or naïve about evil, enables it. Jumping to forgive it fails to acknowledge it, or place appropriate responsibility for the damage done out of mental illness, and is a form of denial in an effort to avoid facing it. Enabling is cowardice, plain and simple. Do not accept destructive behavior, do not excuse it, and try to eventually forgive it for your own sake, while at the same time removing yourself from it.

The needs of the ego are selfish and unloving, yet the soul's only need is to grow and evolve with love. Those who are engulfed by their egos through self-absorption and delusions of moral superiority are doomed to live out their lives as tragic cases of the un-evolved soul, lost in darkness, and devoid of love and joy.

This is the saddest fate of all. When you consider the tragedy of the life of the narcissist, it becomes easier to have compassion for them. Their mental illness takes away from them any chance of experiencing true peace within themselves. Denial is the closest form of peace they will ever achieve, but denial does not comfort them from their profound loneliness. My heart goes out to them.

As I said, narcissists were not born to be this way, and were made this way through the pain and suffering, brought upon them as a child from circumstances beyond their control through no fault of their own. It is best to forgive them, feel detached compassion for them, and keep your distance.

WHEN THE NARCISSIST MARRIES A NARCISSIST

When one narcissist marries another narcissist, they match themselves with someone who they innocently perceive as understanding and simpatico, who will support them in their sick, ego-feeding ways. Someone they perceive as willing to share their same views and values, and is unchallenging to their modus operandi, and feels these modi are natural and normal. The narcissist will choose someone who can be symbiotic in a process of ongoing counter-ego gratifications; you scratch my ego needs, and I'll scratch yours. Someone who will not only enable and support the abusive way their partner treats anyone who crosses them, but who will contribute to it as well. This is called "chiming in" with destructive behavior. These marriages can end in bitter self-righteous indignation, as soon as one narcissist crosses another. Some of the most bitter of divorces occur between narcissists who can no longer use each other as a self-sustaining, ego-feeding support system, perceiving this as ultimate betrayal.

WHEN THE NARCISSIST MARRIES A SLAVE

When the narcissist marries a slave (their sycophant and primary enabler), they match themselves with someone they perceive as self-oblivious, naïve, impressionable, easy to control, with no identity of their own. These are the people who enter into cults, and are willing to sacrifice their own life to worship its leader. They are people who were abused in childhood that have been preconditioned to be overly accommodating (the doormat), and need to hide from reality in a relationship with an egotist they can worship. In adulthood, they choose to remain willfully ignorant and do not recognize oppression, neglect, or destructive behavior, as being abusive, unhealthy, or unnatural. They often misinterpret abuse as love, can become addicted to it, tragically lack the appropriate self-esteem to say no to it, and even worse, believes it is their responsibility to adapt to it.

The narcissist will pick a partner who has no sense of their own identity who does not even realize they matter. Someone who thinks so little about themselves, they can actually put another person on a pedestal, and live their entire life in a fantasy world based on the lie of an illusion. In other words, narcissists prey on children of other narcissists who have been conditioned to be slaves, already programmed to believe exploitation and disregard is an acceptable form of love.

These marriages can last a lifetime, because the slave often molds their entire life around the narcissist, and has no life of their own. These marriages can dissolve when the slave is expected to sacrifice themselves in a way that is traumatic enough to wake them up to the true nature of their relationship, such as being expected to tolerate a severe betrayal. The slave can then work to get healthier through talk therapy and guided education. This can only work if the slave can acknowledge their deficit, retain what they learn, apply and incorporate it into their life, and not revert back into fantasy and denial. They also have to stay away from narcissistic people, just as a recovering alcoholic has to stay out of bars, to avoid their "slave trigger."

WHEN THE NARCISSIST IS A PARENT

When the narcissist is a parent, it all started at the beginning when every narcissist was once a rejected and neglected child. Like their parent, or parents before them, the narcissistic parent sought to destroy the individual identity of their child to clone them into a replica of themselves. To grow up into a wholesome person, an infant must experience genuine acknowledgment, stability in acceptance through its formative years, and be seen as perfect in their parents' eyes. Through parental acceptance, they learn they merit love, have worth, and matter as much as anyone else.

The forming narcissist is neglected, does not receive parental acceptance, and is not seen or loved for themselves. So they turn away from a world that is perceived as being devoid of love and nurturing. To protect themselves from intense feelings of worthlessness, they withdraw into fantasies of grandiosity as pathetic compensation for experiencing no true parental love and acceptance. The only way the child of a narcissist can be seen is when it mimics the self-obsessed behavior of the parent, tragically causing the child's own identity to be sacrificed. Thus, behold the birth of the narcissist.

This parent unwittingly commits a most devastating crime of all against their child: the crime of non-recognition and acceptance, when the child is not seen as they are apart from the parent.

Furthermore, the narcissist is often more demanding, deforming, and damaging to the child they most intensely identify with. This tragic child inherits rejection as a birthright.

The Groucho Marx syndrome, "I will not join any club that will have me as a member," is unconsciously translated by the narcissist into, "I will not love any child that would have me as parent." Consciously the narcissist will only recognize and accept traits in their child that replicate those of the narcissist, projecting onto them their own motives, beliefs, values, feelings, likes, and dislikes, so their children grow up not knowing who they are.

When these parents die, the child who stood up to them in life to maintain their own identity, is typically punished from the grave by being cut out of their will. This happened to me with both my biological parents who left all they had to another. It was my stepfather who set up an irrevocable trust in which I was given 42.5%. However, my father and mother named a grasping schizotypal sycophant as their trustee, who by "honoring" their evil wishes, hid behind their punishing wills to conceal her true motives of greed, jealousy, envy, and hate. She convinced herself and others that she was simply doing what was morally correct. I had to legally fight for my rightful inheritance for two years, and won. I only wanted what was mine.

However, her named co-trustee was a young attorney who failed his bar exam in California, and was forced to seek his license in Oregon where the test was less stringent, where he is now practicing. During a meeting with myself, my husband, this co-trustee, and the overseeing trust attorney, the co-trustee informed me he would only be representing named trustee's clan, and not my interest as a major beneficiary, which was unethical. He then suggested I get my own attorney. Although this co-trustee could not practice law in California, he then called me directly on behalf of the trustee's clan — outside of the active legal dispute proceedings — which was highly unethical, in an attempt to swindle me out of a large portion of my trust. He tried to bully me into selling my rightful 42.5% of the total trust value to the trustee's clan for less than half its actually worth, and threatened that they would not sign any final release papers unless I responded to him directly and outside of the trust's attorney's legal communications regarding the formal active dispute, which was heinously unethical. He was foolish enough to send me an email outlining their demands and conditions, adding they would not pay one penny more than their calculated offer. I forwarded his email to my attorney, who forwarded it to the overseeing attorney. I had already made them a buy-out offer prior to my initiating the legal dispute that was less than what I finally received after inheritance tax, but they had refused it.

By then, my attorney could not believe the behavior of this clan of disordered people; their fervent attempts at my character assassination, their constant bullying, and overall lack of ethics and morality. She expressed to me her astonishment at how sane and healthy I was in contrast. After I had won the dispute and received my full trust value, and placed my trust under the management of a reputable bank, their own overseeing trust attorney called mine to sympathize with my disappointment in his clients. I am reminded here of Hanlon's razor: "Never attribute to malice that which can be adequately explained by stupidity." Knowing these people, and the disrespectful, willfully ignorant and entitled way they have always treated me, I believe it was equal parts of stupidity, malice, and mental illness. Such is the behavior of the psychologically disordered.

WHEN THE NARCISSIST IS A MOTHER
When the narcissist is a mother, the primary caregiver, and the one who is forming the child in their developmental years, she can be paradoxically cold, and at the same time overly protective. She will ruthlessly and incessantly invade her child's autonomy with overwhelming intrusiveness, and be unyielding in her criticism and manipulation of the child to conform it to her self-image. Mothers who are autistically narcissistic in their endeavor to completely engulf the child they most identify with, are unconsciously devoted to destroying its individuality to create a parasitic coupling. Because she rejects any expression of individuality from her child that differentiates it from her self-image, the child lives in constant fear of rejection, or withdrawal of love.

Her withdrawal of love causes intense negative feelings in the child that are beyond its ability to cope with, because any expression of these feelings may threaten the betrayal-bond between the child and the narcissistic mother it depends on for survival. The chronic pressure of this dilemma can cause the total collapse of any autonomous identity the child would have otherwise developed, resulting in a child that has no sense of self. The child can then misinterpret this evil as being within themselves, and believe they are somehow the cause of the rejection. This is where the tragic, negative self-image of being deserving of this kind of treatment is formed.

The bright and vibrant individual self the child was born with has been brutally destroyed by the intense ego of the narcissistic mother. Even before birth, this mother's toxic energy can have a negative effect on the child's development. The burning candle of individualism is insidiously snuffed out, and not even a flicker of the original flame remains. There is no more "self" left to value, protect, or uphold. Their life will never be their own, and they are unlikely to ever know who they are, and why. They did not possess the spiritual strength to prevail against the power of the mighty narcissistic ego. This unlucky child's original ego completely collapses into utter compliancy. Behold the birth of the sycophant/slave.

The lucky child of the narcissistic mother is born with enough spiritual strength to fight for its own identity, against the oppressive and destructive forces of the evil narcissistic ego. They consequently spend their entire childhood in a battle for self. This battle is like trying to throw off a giant octopus with its many powerful tentacles that latch onto the child to smother and engulf its identity. In this battle, each time the child succeeds in throwing off a tentacle, another one comes swinging down and latches on, each time draining a little more of the child's life-force energy. It takes an incredibly strong child to endure and sustain this battle.

Eventually the child's energy can become depleted to a point where even the strongest spirit can no longer withstand the draining effects of this giant, over-powering octopus. Battle weary, it is not uncommon for this child to eventually experience some degree of collapse of the identity they have so long and valiantly fought for. This collapse can manifest in illness, either physical, mental, or both. Children are rarely strong enough to match a relentless adult will. At this point, the child's identity may or may not be vanquished. In some rare cases, the child's natural spiritual strength may be strong enough to prevail with the loving care of someone other than the narcissistic parent, someone usually outside the family unit.

After the compounding neck injury that triggered chronic FMS in me in 1993, I became so weakened from the illness, on top of a 40-plus year battle for self with my narcissistic mother, my sense of self began to collapse. However, my illness forced me to save myself. With the help of a wonderful guiding therapist, and the support of my husband, I was able to win my battle for self, and gain the strength I needed to leave the care of the medical profession, distance myself from my dangerously crazy family, and find the right healing combination for my illness. I slowly, but steadily, began turning around, and after twelve years of struggle and continued search, I discovered the cause and the cure for FMS. As a result, I felt a spiritual debt of gratitude that compelled me to share my experience in my book *Curing Chronic Fibromyalgia,* in a way I hope will lead others out of the dark and frightening jungle of this dreadful, disabling disease.

People often marry someone just like their dominant parent, because they unconsciously pick someone with the traits they are used to adapting to, and because they pick the relationship they unconsciously believe will provide them the opportunity to solve and heal the problems and deprivations of their childhood. In this scenario, people look for approval, and to be valued, accepted, and seen by someone who may not be capable of satisfying these needs.

If you suspect that one or both your parents are narcissists, there is a chance you are married to one. My first husband was an abusive narcissist. Not only can you choose to free yourself from the power of the narcissistic ego, you can learn enough to see yourself and your life in an entirely anew. If you apply what you learn to your life, you can reap the benefits of the best possible gift you could ever receive: your true self.

When you look at the characteristics of the narcissist, it is easy to see why they are so hard to reach, because these characteristics are marbleized throughout their entire personality. There is simply no way to reach them. They are impervious, impenetrable, unreachable, unreasonable, unloving, unconcerned, unrepentant, and uninterested in anything that does not serve to feed and reinforce their egoic outer shell: their self-image of perfection, and that of their children. This is all unconscious of course, and they are not the least bit aware they have these destructive traits.

The narcissist's outer shell is so hard because it has to be in order to hide the soft and vulnerable inner core of their unconscious insecurity, inferiority, and self-loathing. Their outward show of compensative grandiosity is in direct proportion to their inward feelings of intense unconscious fear: the fear that their secret weaknesses and imperfections may be revealed. In other words, the bigger they feel on the outside, the smaller they feel on the inside. This is very sad, and a real human tragedy, and they cannot help themselves.

If I wanted to live secretly in hell on earth, I would be a narcissist. In all honesty, I cannot hate them because in reality, they are very lost human beings, who deep down already hate themselves. They suffer enough to grow and learn and evolve, but they don't because their illness prevents them from doing so. They literally imprison and torture themselves.

It is predictable for a parent-narcissist to retaliate against any child that crosses them, or sets boundaries against their toxicity and intrusiveness. They even promise and hold over the child what they will leave them, and what they can take away after they die, in an attempt to control their child's life. If they are unsuccessful, the evil narcissist uses their Last Will And Testament as a weapon to punish their deviant child from the grave. They always rely on a dutiful attorney, and/or a sycophant offspring to deliver the punishment in a legal way to hide their true motives. Sycophants have no spiritual morality of their own, other than what supports their denial and the fantasy world they live in.

The message here is: don't buy into it! Your health is much more valuable than anything someone could ever leave you at their time of death. And you know what? The boundaries I set against my toxic parents and family worked! I was able to discover the cause and a cure for FMS, and have been symptom free ever since. Lord knows, if I didn't keep them away for all those few years, I would have never gotten well. Being around them always made me much worse.

A relatively healthy person suffers to degrees in cycles, resulting in sustained expansion, growth, and learning, with breaks in between. When the narcissist suffers, they simply become smaller inwardly, compensate outwardly in their delusions of grandeur, and the suffering never ends for them. As I said before, this is unconscious, and they would be the first to deny they suffer at all. In any case, the narcissist is a tragic and lonely byproduct of the inequities of their formative years.

Unless you have the unlikely capacity to understand, forgive, and love them unconditionally without sacrificing yourself in any way, they are best left to themselves to exist in the only way they know how: thinking primarily of themselves, and finding people who think so little of themselves they will enable and take care of them. Remember that not even a trained and experienced professional therapist wants to take on a narcissist.

Although every narcissist is a child of a narcissist, not every child of a narcissist becomes one. Some become slaves (sycophants), and some make it to adulthood being relatively healthy, depending on their spiritual strength and their exposure to positive role models, love, and acceptance received from outside sources. If you believe you are a child of a narcissist, are married to a narcissist, or exhibit slave-like or narcissistic tendencies, I strongly recommend that you read *Trapped in the Mirror - for adult children of narcissists in their struggle for self* by Dr. Elan Golomb. It is an inspiring and enlightening read, and provides hope where it may seem like none exists.

In the final analysis, and not to be construed as redeeming, the narcissist is as innocently self-oblivious as a very small child. Even so, it is impossible, and extremely inappropriate, for a healthy adult to try having a mature relationship with a child. Furthermore, although they are generally devoid of empathy and compassion for the feelings of others, they are at the same time excessively self-sensitive, and over-react dramatically with vile anger whenever they are confronted with their constant misbehaviors and misdeeds as a small child would, and honestly do not understand what all the fuss is about.

This is all very confusing to the children of the narcissist, but it can all become clear to their children when they grow up, provided they educate themselves about the nature of the disorder. Learn to develop a will of your own that introduces you to your "true self." Put as many boundaries or as much distance and time between yourself and the narcissist in your life for as long as you need to accomplish this. Emotionally detach and disengage in an effort to reach an understanding with them, stop needing anything from them, and stop focusing on them. Focus on learning to understand yourself, and then chart a course as far away from the past and into the future as you can.

Over time, learn to understand – and forgive for your own sake – the people who have hurt you. Place them into a detached and impersonal category with "all the other suffering souls in the world." If you can, develop a detached and impersonal loving compassion for them. As I said before, I call this "living in loving detachment." Begin to live in the present, and practice letting go of the past. The past is only useful as a reference for making wiser decisions in the present, while learning to live life in new and healthier ways: ways that keep you safe, and allow you to discover the unique gifts within you that have been sacrificed to the gigantic, evil ego of the mighty, yet small and tragic, narcissist.

THE BORDERLINE PERSONALITY
(Among the masters of denial, the borderline is equally toxic and destructive as the narcissist)
Out of the four personality disorders subcategorized under the "dramatic cluster"- the borderline is the one who gives doctors and family members the most headaches. People with Borderline Personality Disorder establish highly volatile relationships, whipping back and forth from idealizing family and friends, to completely trashing them as worthless or hateful. They are extremely afraid of being abandoned, but react so savagely when a loved one disappoints them, that they often bring abandonment upon themselves. When they are pushed into therapy, the same dynamics take place. In the beginning the therapist is their best friend, and in a very short time the therapist becomes their worst

enemy. The pendulum continually swings with an inexhaustible fervor.

A Norwegian study published in 2000, found that the borderline personality had an estimated 69% level in heritability, confirming what some doctors in the field have observed; higher rates of personality disorders among descendants of personality disorder sufferers. Their conclusion was that there are multiple genes involved in predisposing people to personality disorders. However, research also shows that borderline personality disorder affects more women than men, and that up to 70% of borderline women were sexually or physically abused, or suffered severe psychological abuse of equal intensity at some point in their childhood. It is hard to blame genes for that kind of mistreatment! Abuse and disorder, breeds more abuse and disorder.

This principle can just as easily apply here, and has nothing to do with genes. When children are raised in the environment of a severely dysfunctional family that does not provide consistent and clear boundaries, and is thus wrought with chaos and instability, they do not know where their limits are, and as a result, they do not feel safe. The chronic anxiety these children live with 24/7, along with abuse they suffer from their disordered parents, causes their sensitive, developing nervous systems to become stuck in fight-or-flight mode. Life is a chronically stressful experience for the child of a borderline, and the world is perceived as a scary and unsafe place. When a child cannot feel the safety of consistent boundaries, nor can they feel safe in their home environment, they become so overwhelmed with anxiety, they scream things like, "I hate you!" to their parents, and tragically become dramatically disordered psychologically. Behold the birth of the borderline.

DIAGNOSTIC CRITERIA
Diagnostic criteria for Borderline Personality Disorder are pervasive patterns of intensity and instability of interpersonal relationships and self-image, and a marked impulsivity beginning by early adulthood, that is present in a variety of contexts. Borderline Personality Disorder is described in the DSM, as having the perception of impending separation or rejection, or loss of external structure, that can lead to profound changes in self-image, cognition, and behavior; sensitivity to environmental

circumstances; intense abandonment fears; inappropriate anger when faced with realistic time-limited separation or an unavoidable change in plans; intolerance of being alone with a need to have other people with them; and frantic efforts to avoid abandonment that may include impulsive actions of self-mutilation or suicidal behavior.

Further patterns are: the tendency to idealize people at first meeting, demanding to spend a lot of time together, share the most intimate detail early in a relationship, and then switch quickly from idealizing to devaluing the other person when their own needs are not met; can nurture and love others, but only when their unreasonable expectations, needs, and demands that the other person "be there" for them, are always met; prone to sudden and dramatic shifts in their view of others who are alternately seen as beneficent support or as being cruelly punitive.

Other criteria include identity disturbances, characterized by markedly and persistently unstable self-image and sense of self that show as shifting goals, values, and vocational aspirations; suddenly changes from the role of a needy supplicant for help, to a righteous avenger of past mistreatment. In addition to having a self-image based on being bad or evil, they may feel that they do not exist at all from feeling a lack of meaningful relationships; display impulsivity in at least two areas that are potentially self-damaging – gambling, spending money irresponsibly, binge eating, bulimia, and abusing substance, etc.; recurrent suicidal behavior, gestures, or threats that are usually precipitated by a threat of separation or rejection, or by the expectation that they assume more personal responsibility. Successful suicides occur in 8%-10% of these individuals.

Further criteria include: a marked reactivity of mood, such as intense irritability and anxiety, usually lasting a few hours, that is often disrupted by periods of anger, panic attacks, or despair, and is rarely relieved by periods of well-being or satisfaction; troubled by chronic feelings of emptiness, they are easily bored, and constantly seeking something to do; frequently express inappropriate, intense anger, and has difficulty controlling their anger; may display extreme sarcasm, enduring bitterness, or verbally abusive outbursts of moral superiority.

During periods of extreme stress, transient paranoid or dissociative symptoms (staring off into space) may occur, that tend to last minutes or hours, and occur as a response to real or imagined abandonment; displays a pattern of undermining themselves at the moment a goal is about to be realized; may develop psychotic-like symptoms during times of stress; feel more secure with transitional objects, such as a pet or inanimate possession, than in interpersonal relationships.

The borderline personality has a common history of recurrent job losses, interrupted education, and broken marriages. Symptoms of physical and sexual abuse, neglect, hostile conflict, intense psychological abuse, and early parental loss or separation, are common in their early childhood history. Common accompanying disorders further include post-traumatic stress disorder (PTSD), attention deficit/hyperactivity disorder, and substance-related disorders.

The prevalence of Borderline Personality Disorder is estimated to be about 2% of the general population, about 10% among individuals seen in outpatient mental health clinics, and about 20% among psychiatric inpatients. It ranges from 30% to 60% among clinical populations with personality disorders, per se. The course of the borderline is variable, and the most common pattern is chronic instability in early adulthood, with episodes of serious affective and impulsive lack of behavioral control, and high-level use of health and mental resources.

The impairments from this disorder, and the risk of suicide, are greatest in the young-adult years, and gradually wane with advancing age. During their thirties and forties, the majority of these individuals attain greater stability in their relationships and vocational functioning. What distinguishes the borderline from the narcissist is, while the borderline may also be characterized by an angry reaction to minor stimuli, and outright displays of rage when confronted just like the narcissist, the relative stability of the narcissist's inflated self-image, relative lack of impulsivity, lack of self-destructiveness, and lack of abandonment concerns and fears that are prevalent in the narcissist, are not prevalent in the borderline.

The borderline personality, whose interactive style is respectively coquettish, callous, and intensely needy, can be described another way. They are extremely dramatic, all-or-nothing people; they quickly run from hot to cold; can exude a "sicky-sweet" toxic honey; they are extremely manipulative in their use of the "con of niceness and charm" and in their use of toxic guilt and shame in an effort to make other people feel responsible for their well-being and happiness; they are consistently unwilling to take personal responsibility for their destructive behaviors.

They are always in a "pity-pot" – thinking everything is about them; they use extreme negative control through judging, punishing, raging, and/or rejection; they often use fixed delusional systems in certain areas involving delusions of moral superiority, entitlement and intrusiveness, which can prompt psychotic episodes with no memory of them when these delusions are thwarted; they are extremely abusive and destructive to those who try to be in a close, interpersonal relationship with them.

The borderline uses and abuses people with no conscience or remorse of any kind. ("I'm not sorry for what I said!") Neither do they have any regard for the humanity of the people they exploit, or the lives they damage. They are easily able to rationalize and justify anything they do because their actions are characteristically self-serving. They do not consciously believe that there is anything wrong with them, and are rarely capable of self-awareness. The insidious nature of their covert manipulation and deception, and their calculating use of their mask of sanity can make them difficult to detect. With surgical precision, they can quickly reject in an "off with their head" gesture. A diagnosis of Borderline Personality Disorder can be made if five or more symptoms apply.

KEY ASPECTS
1) Frantic efforts to avoid real or imagined abandonment, including suicide attempts, or threats.
2) A pattern of unstable and intense interpersonal relationships, characterized by alternating between extremes of idealization, and devaluation (worshiping to trashing a person).
3) Identity disturbances with markedly persistent unstable self-image or sense-of-self, unconsciously believing they are bad or evil.

4) Impulsivity in at least two areas that are potentially self-damaging (spending, sex, substance abuse, reckless driving, binge eating, or bulimia).
5) Recurrent suicidal behavior, gestures, or threats, and/or self-mutilating behavior.
6) Affective instability due to a marked reactivity of mood: intense episodes of feeling acutely hopeless, uncomfortable, and unhappy; feelings of irritability or anxiety, usually lasting a few hours to a few days.
7) Chronic feelings of emptiness.
8) Inappropriately intense anger, or difficulty controlling anger with no remorse.
9) Transient stress-related paranoid ideation, or severe dissociative symptoms.

The prognosis for curing this disorder is very poor. It is considered in some cases to be terminal and life-long. Intelligent borderlines are the most dangerous, because they are masters of denial and can easily conceal their disorder at times with a mask of sanity. However, the intense complexity of their projected inner darkness is impossible to deflect. Another dead giveaway is their preoccupation with deep thought, or wide-eyed, unconscious stares deep into themselves. Sometimes improvement in these individuals can be made with talk therapy, and a lot of hard work over time. But sadly, the borderline is prone to turning against their therapist, telling themselves things like, "They only tell you what you want to hear" thereby discrediting the entire profession.

For a highly sensitive person, it is necessary to employ an immutable wall at all times to protect against the dark projections and the unpredictable instability of the borderline while in their company. A wall of this nature takes a tremendous amount of energy to maintain, and is extremely draining energetically. But it's the only way to avoid being emotionally poisoned or traumatized by them.

With their intense drama, their indiscriminate theatrics, their entitled intrusiveness, their covert manipulation and deceit, their unpredictable swings from worshiping to trashing others, and their periodic use of the confusing mask of sanity, the borderline controls the emotional atmosphere of the entire family. No one can ever relax, or let down their guard for a second, because the home of a borderline parent is a perpetual war zone, and everyone is always walking along the front lines trying to avoid setting off a landmine.

Periodic breaks from their insanity, temporary shows of normalcy with brief gestures of limited, conditional love and nurturing, do not compensate for the degree of damage and devastation the borderline can inflict in one fell swoop on those around them. Ironically, and not so ironically, because borderlines are people who have been hurt so deeply during their formative years, they are also fearful and on maximum alert most of the time. Their nervous systems are literally stuck in fight-or-flight mode, and their entire life is seen through the lens of drama and trauma. For the borderline, in all their constant anxiety, there can be very little lasting peace and stability.

Conversely, for the children of the borderline, there are literally no boundaries, and therefore there is very little peace, stability, safety, or security, no sustained expression of genuine love, acceptance, or nurturing, and no chance of natural development. Their only chance of surviving psychologically and emotionally without becoming entirely immobilized by fear, is to adapt in some way (childhood maladaptations, i.e. the overly adapted child), such as repelling the borderline parent through detachment and/or constant rebellion, or by creating a fantasy world to escape into, and staying out of the borderline's way.

With the help of outside influences, exposure to healthier role models, and unconditional love from relationship other than the borderline parent – i.e. the child that hangs out at the neighbors – the child has a chance to reach adulthood without being severely disordered themselves, or may only be damaged in ways that can be healed with the help of the right therapist.

Because borderlines commonly suffer from other disorders at the same time, such as narcissism and/or codependency, they are not usually interested in being loving and nurturing parents in healthy ways, nor are they equipped to handle the responsibility of raising children. Of course they do the best they can with what they have at the time, in spite of their mental disorder, like everyone else.

But what they have tragically falls far short of what is needed to be a barely adequate parent.

For me, as a child of a narcissistic borderline, it took two failed marriages to narcissistic men, and emotionally detaching myself from my family before I could learn to become psychologically healthy myself. My hard work earned me a third and happy 30-year marriage with a loving and devoted husband with three terrific stepchildren. I feel a responsibility to guard my life like a momma lion against any force that would threaten the wellbeing and serenity of my chosen family. It took me over 40 years to realize that I have every right to do just that!

I realize there are a lot of jokes about being in therapy, and blaming your parents, but therapy is not about blame. It is about understanding yourself, your past, and the people in it, so you can take responsibility for your life, and learn to take better care of yourself and the people you love now. This kind of control only comes from healing the wounds of the past through the emotional and intellectual adventure of psychotherapy and guided education. Pervasive patterns of destructiveness and abuse are not due to ignorance. They are due to a mental illness that requires willful ignorance as its life's blood.

When I first entered into therapy, I did not even know what the word narcissist meant or anything about borderline personality disorder. After two years of therapy, and reading over 40 books on human psychology and appropriate educational materials in a timely manner, I grew to understand enough to free myself from the past, put responsibility in all the appropriate places, and gain the tools I lacked to create and protect the healthy life I've always wanted. I chose to apply what I learned to my life.

Now, I rarely visit the past except in referencing it to make wise decisions in the present. I have sufficiently processed it all out of me, and let it all go. When I feel a pang of sadness, it is for the tragedy of the sense of family I never had, and for the children my parent's never really saw, knew, appreciated, or truly experienced. I will live with this for the rest of my life. My compassion for my family spreads over my life like a healing salve, and is merged into my generalized, detached compassion for all the suffering souls on the planet, who in their developmental years needed love, nurturing, and acceptance, and did not received it.

The Bible says a lot of things that apply to standing up to what is evil (that which is destructive). The representative Christ so famously said, "Get thee behind me Satan!" and Satan was dispelled. Evil only exists when people enable it. When you stand up to evil, it shrinks and dissipates. When you excuse it for any reason, be it by self-serving willful ignorance, or cowardice, it grows and takes hold. When you pay evil too much attention, it flourishes, because it feeds on creating fear, confusion, and control over others. When you stand up to it, turn your back on it, remove it from your life by the use of healthy boundaries, it starves, shrivels and shrinks, and loses its power over you.

Excusing destructive behavior enables it, guarantees its existence, perpetuates it, and is equal to collaborating with it. It is spiritually and morally bankrupt, and psychologically inappropriate to justify any refusal to take personal responsibility for destructive behavior with the use of the "nobody's perfect" abuse excuse. Anyone who is not diagnosed as being developmentally disabled or completely psychotic is personally responsible for their behavior, regardless of their history. We must all take responsibility for facing and correcting the errors within us, and actively try to do no harm.

The Bible, under Saint Luke 11:15, also says, "Ye are they which justify yourselves before men; but God knoweth your hearts; for that which is highly esteemed among men is an abomination in the sight of God." The God who resides within us all sees into our hearts and knows our true motives and aspirations. Recognize and acknowledge evil, and do not excuse it. Forgive your parents and your family, but hold them responsible for their behavior, and hold yourself responsible for yours, while guarding and protecting your health, safety, and serenity.

I survived a childhood with a narcissist, absentee father who abandoned me with a narcissist/borderline mother with no protection. Among my other family members, I was the lucky one. I was born with an old soul, wise and perceptive beyond my years. I was also born a sensitive empath who feels the energy of others in my body when my energetic aura comes in contact with theirs. I can feel who to stay away from and who is safe. I have always been able to walk into a room full of people, and intuit the safe zone in the room. The emotional aura is said to radiate from you in a circular field of around 6 to 10 feet. The psychological aura is said to radiate from you in a field of around 2 to 4 feet.

My empathic sensitivity has always been very difficult to live with, but it became a great friend to me later in life, and has taught me a great deal about sensing who is safe and who is not, just by being in their general proximity. This empathic ability always instinctively alerted me to keep my mother at a distance. This caused her a great deal of frustration, anger, and pain because she desperately needed to have a parasitic coupling with me, as the child she most identified with. I also had the spiritual strength to fight for, and hold on to, my identity.

Even when I gave in to my need to be acknowledged by my mother, and mimicked her prima-donna behavior at times just to feel "seen" by her, it was never worth it. I always felt sick and empty afterward, especially when she praised me whenever she saw herself in me. It just made me feel more alone in the world than ever. I then quickly resumed the fight for self, and went back to being "the difficult child" in my rebellion of her pressure to be like her. I was nothing like her, and she never even saw me or knew who I was. All she saw was my wall of humor, and her projected glimpses of herself.

My mother's primary enabler in the family, who spent most of her life worshiping, enabling, and excusing evil behavior, arrogantly and sanctimoniously accused me for years of holding on to the past, and not letting go of my issues with my mother, as they continued to be recreated in the present. She repeatedly bragged about how she lived in the present, while living nowhere near the rest of our family. She consistently called me as a crazy liar for being honest about my perceptions of my experiences with my family's drama.

My ability to identify and call out the evil behavior in my mother and family was always a mortal threat to her, and contradicted the narcissistic bubble she had constructed over her life to protect her comfort zone and her worldview. Even when the rest of the family thought her developmentally disabled while she was growing up, and always called her "slow," my father told me during our final conversations before his death that he felt her dysfunction was due to all those years she spent in a cult. I responded by saying, "Dad, she's always lived in denial and fantasy. You just weren't around often enough to see it." He then said, "Well, maybe so. It must be due to a deep hurt early in life that she never overcame."

He went on to tell me about the lack of boundaries, lack of consequences, lack of respect, and the abuse prevalent in her family's behavior that he witnessed over the years on his bi-annual visits, and that he was very disappointed and disturbed at what he saw. I always felt her obvious dysfunctions were from unconscious maladaptations to childhood traumas that she carried into adulthood, traumas she buried deep inside.

The behavior of my family was chronically entitled, intrusive, disrespectful, and willfully ignorant in their judgementalism, all behaviors indicative of people who only care about themselves. For example, after I separated from my disordered mother for a decade for health reasons, her primary enabler in the family became so deeply threatened, she called me to attack, berate, judge, condemn, and scorn me for "doing this to my mother." When I told her that it was none of her business, and that she had no right to speak to me this way, she replied with cold self-righteous indignation, and while chewing on some food, "Well, I know you want me to apologize, but I wouldn't even want to!" These were the words of a selfish, narcissist child.

Then she proceeded to launch a calculated character assassination in a 30-year hate campaign against me, and told anyone who would listen to her that I was a crazy liar. She was obviously so deeply threatened that she felt uncontrollably compelled and entitled to slander me to her own family, her children, and others to ensure her self-image and worldview would be unmarred.

She had succeeded to poison her children so deeply against me, that one of them, a college student, called me to attack me, and demanded answers to my private boundaries with my mother, and other things that were absolutely none of her business. When I tried to answer one of this child's questions, she called me a liar. When I refused to comply with any more of her demands, saying none of this was any of her business, she said, "Well, I'm making it my business, and if you won't answer my questions, I'll call Ron and his kids and make them tell me!"

She then bragged about how intelligent she was, called me a narcissist, and demanded my husband's cell number! Her own mother had told me that this girl had been diagnosed with Borderline Personality Disorder, was bulimic and suicidal throughout her teens, that her life was wrought with chaos and drama, and that she was highly unpredictable and undependable.

Furthermore, the same family member who launched the hate campaign against me, enjoyed saying to me with her usual sanctimonious condescension, "I've always been the healthy one, and you have always been the one with the problem! I've never had any need to read all those books you read, or any need to search for answers like you have. I've just been happily living my dream life." This struck me as being ironic.

I could easily have said, "Of course I always had a problem with what went on in the family, because there were so many horrible things happening all the time. It was naturally very disturbing to me, and kept me in an uproar. And what does it say about you that you didn't have a problem with any of it, or that you admittedly don't even remember ten years of your childhood? You walked around in a fantasy world we all called "la-la land," with a smile pasted on your face, and peeping not a word? How can you continue claiming to have had a happy childhood?"

I also could have easily said, "Oh, really? What about the fact you entered into a cult and were brainwashed for the better part of a decade, worshiping the evil egomaniac that called himself "the prophet of the age," while working your way up to the position of your cult-leader's bookkeeper? You actually believed yourself to be superior to those outside the cult, looking down your nose and smirking at them, while calling yourself "it". Then you married the man who drew you into the cult, had four children with him, and unwittingly passed on generations of the family's mental illnesses. How does any of this make you the healthy one?"

During another of her attacks, when I again told her to mind her own business about my boundaries with my mother, she angrily replied, "I have had to go through all this with her, and I have every right to involve myself!" Thus, she felt narcissistically entitled to continue attacking and judging me with her arrogant, willful ignorance, call me anything she wanted to, and slander me to anyone she needed to. Her persistent delusions of moral superiority were still paramount in her behavior toward me. People like this are incapable of taking personal responsibility for their behavior, nor do they remember or care about the things they say or do to others.

Again, I could have easily responded, "I went through all your years in that cult with her as well, but I never once interfered or judged you. I was simply concerned about you. In fact, I was the one who supported you when you left, gave you a place to live, helped you find a car, a job, and an apartment, and never attacked you once!" I did not want to respond to people like this in kind, or allow someone else's abhorrent dysfunctional behavior to push me off the rails. I had already inappropriately tried to reach this particular individual in the past in an effort to keep my relationship with them, fighting over the phone for hours to no avail, and even sent truthful, heart-felt letters, but this only threatened, upset, and enraged them further.

I had to learn that you cannot reach people who do not want to be reached, especially people who have spent their life turning a blind eye to what they didn't want to see. I knew that anything I said would continue to fall on deaf ears, and I didn't want to behave toward them the way they had behaved toward me, by judging, attacking, and slandering me. There is no justification for returning evil behavior.

After separating from my family, and hearing from numerous sources about the person who was skulking around behind my back, telling people I was crazy, it was easy for me to understand their self-serving motivation and agenda. My leaving the family had not only threatened them to their core, they must have felt deep, extreme anger that I had the courage to save myself, and they did not. Everyone who knew my mother understood completely why I had to get away from her, and I received tremendous support and understanding without even soliciting it. It was easy to see that this person believed that if they convinced others that I was crazy for leaving, they would appear more norma; and sane for staying. They had no idea that this strategy had the opposite result. By this person's behavior, they were already leaning toward extreme narcissism after having been a schizotypal sycophant for most of their life, as these disorders are opposite sides of the same coin. Their underlying, extreme low self-esteem will always show itself in their prevalent, compensative delusions of moral superiority, combined with their neurotic insecurity and compulsion to control an outside reality they are not capable of fully connecting with or comprehending.

Their inappropriately flat non-responsiveness to evil, and their perpetual, well-polished mask of overt, sicky sweetness-and-light (toxic honey), is extremely controlling and manipulative, and meant to hide the darkness deep within them that they refuses to look at, or heal. Not only is this persona entirely artificial, it is also extremely toxic and confusing for the offspring. Children can sense falsehood.

I think it is human nature to avoid looking inward honestly to some extent. My heart goes out to people like these – prisoners of themselves – with a detached feeling of compassion. In my view, there is nothing more tragic than a life lived without self-honesty, with no real understanding of the true meaning of healthy, mature love, empathy and compassion, or the experience of true intimacy in relationship to another. How can anyone reach their full, unique potential without these? I truly wish my family peace and happiness in whatever form they perceive it to be, but I do so from a distance!

My mother's pressure for me to abandon my identity, and become her clone was endless, until one day I was forced by illness to reckon with this psychological abuse, and distance myself from my family, and the most unwittingly evil and destructive force in my life; my own mother.

I finally came to realize that the family members who judged me the harshest for leaving, were the ones who had been serving as my mother's primary enablers, and were nothing more than willfully-ignorant and disingenuous cowards, unwilling to look at and see the way things really were between my mother and me.

The ones who did see confessed to me years later how concerned they always were about me being abused and picked on relentlessly by my mother, and admitted they were too worried about retaliation from her to stick up for me. Truthfully, I don't believe anyone in my family really cared enough about me to help me anyway. They only cared about themselves.

My mother's psychological control over the family was absolute, and their denial was self-serving at my expense, and this never had anything to do with me. Yes, I was the lucky one. I finally got away and saved myself, but this did not mean I missed having a mother and a real family I never had. So what else was I to do but free myself with understanding, learn to become my own mother, make older friends who could substitute in this role to some extent, and make friends my own age who were like-minded, which I did, all of whom have become my surrogate family. This has worked out very well for me, and I consider my personal experiences with the narcissist and borderline to be valuable lessons on what is evil and destructive in human relationships.

To sum up, the family we are born into is not always the healthiest for us. Finding healthier people to substitute in surrogate roles can work well as a family of choice. Being mistreated by disordered people can leave scars that may fade in time with work, guidance and support, but no one is worth sacrificing your health, serenity, and ability to reach your full potential in life. We are not here to be victims of the pathologies of others. It is best to learn to assess who is safe and who isn't, set boundaries of distance and time between you and your major offenders, forgive them for the sake of your own sake, and move on.

COMES THE DAWN

After a while you learn the subtle difference
Between holding a hand and chaining a soul,
And you learn that love doesn't mean leaning
And company doesn't mean security,
And you begin to learn that kisses aren't contracts
And presents aren't promises,
And you begin to accept your defeats
With your head up and your eyes open
With the grace of a woman, not the grief of a child,
And you learn to build all your roads on today
Because tomorrow's ground is too uncertain for plans.
And futures have a way of falling down in midflight.
After a while you learn
That even sunshine burns if you get too much.
So you plant your own garden and decorate your own soul,
Instead of waiting for someone to bring you flowers.
And you learn that you really can endure ....
That you really are strong,
And you really do have worth.
And you learn and learn ....
With every goodbye, you learn.

Virginia Shopstall

FOUR

CODEPENDENCY
A natural response to unnatural oppression

Codependency, or Dependent Personality Disorder, is not uncommon. Many people are codependent due to a certain degree of dysfunction in their families. But in a sane, nurturing environment, the tendency toward codependency is avoided as children are allowed to develop their own identity. As children become more self-confident, self-sufficient, and autonomous, they learn to define themselves by their boundaries. But when a child emerges from their upbringing with no boundaries defining who they are, has low self-esteem, and lacks confidence, there is no way to dodge this bullet.

Codependency is only considered a disorder when it becomes a maladaptive pattern throughout adult life. Furthermore, when codependency becomes marbleized throughout a child's personality, he or she does not develop into well-rounded, functional adult. Codependents expect to "rely on the kindness of strangers" for the majority of their life, and are unaware of the boundaries that are necessary for appropriate autonomy and self-care. They believe others are responsible for their wellbeing, and that they are responsible for the wellbeing of others. Codependents have it all upside down and backward.

A codependent is anyone who is raised in an emotionally oppressive, dysfunctional environment, i.e. a family with one or more alcoholic or substance abusers as parents, for instance, or with one or more parent with a personality disorder. Codependency can be a standalone condition, or it can occur with other personality disorders.

Recovery from codependency requires the willingness to acquire an understanding of what is healthy and what is not, along with the skills to set boundaries, and a clear understanding where responsibility lies. Remaining willfully ignorant is equal to choosing to remain in a state of immaturity and non-recovery that can make a person susceptible to becoming disordered as well.

Diagnostic features for codependency are listed in the DSM under diagnosis code #301.6 as Dependent Personality Disorder. It is described as a pervasive and excessive need to be taken care of, and told what to think and do that leads to submissive and clinging behavior, and fears of separation. This pattern begins in early childhood and is present in a variety of contexts.

The neurotic, dependent and submissive behaviors are designed to elicit caretaking behavior from others, and arise from a self-perception of being unable to function adequately on their own. There is great difficulty in making everyday decisions without an excessive amount of advice and reassurance from others.

DIAGNOSTIC CRITERIA FOR THE DEPENDENT PERSONALITY - The codependent has:
1) A tendency to be passive and allow others to take the initiative in major areas of their lives. They also blame others for the consequences of their own decisions.
2) Their need for others to assume responsibility for them goes beyond age-appropriate and situation-appropriate requests. Because they fear losing support or approval, they often have difficulty expressing disagreement with others, especially those on whom they are dependent.
3) An inability to express their reality in moderation, experience appropriate anger, or address their issues around needing and wanting, often doing things they feel are wrong out of fear of alienating themselves from the person they are dependent on for support and guidance.
4) A lack of self-confidence in initiating tasks independently, and presents oneself as inept and requiring constant assistance. They fear appearing to be competent because they believe it may lead to abandonment, and go to excessive lengths to obtain nurturance and support from others.
5) An inability to set functional boundaries with others, with a willingness to submit to what others want, even when their demands are unreasonable, and may make extraordinary self-sacrifice or tolerate abuse because of an excessive discomfort in being alone.
6) A willingness to "tag along" with others to avoid being alone, even when they are not interested or involved with what is

happening. When a close relationship ends, they may urgently seek another to provide the care and support they need.

7) Inability to "own" or understand their reality, believing they are unable to function alone, they will become quickly and indiscriminately attached to another person without boundaries for fear of being left to care for themselves.

8) Inability to experience appropriate levels of self-esteem, and view themselves as so dependent on others, they experience excessive fear of abandonment without grounds to justify it.

People who suffer from codependency are so full of self-doubt, they are characteristically pessimistic, and see themselves as "stupid" even when they are not. Their view of themselves is so low that they are extremely sensitive to criticism and disapproval, and take it as proof of their worthlessness. They may even seek to be overprotected and dominated by others. Codependency is among the most prevalently reported personality disorders encountered in mental health clinics. Codependency commonly occurs with other disorders, but is not always diagnosed when it occurs simultaneously with severe and disabling physical illnesses when dependency is a natural result.

CAREGIVER VERSUS CARETAKER

Here are some healthy guidelines that clearly distinguish the difference between mature, *interdependent* adults, and persons suffering from codependency. These guidelines clarify the differences between what I call the "caregiver" representing mature, autonomous adults, and the "caretaker" representing immature codependents. Caregivers give care in appropriate ways that allow personal responsibility to be placed where it should be. Caretakers take care in inappropriate ways that take the personal responsibility of others onto themselves.

Caregivers respect people's right to have their own feelings and thoughts, even when they don't understand them. They allow others to own their problems, do not offer unsolicited advice, and do not meddle in the affairs of others. They are capable of healthy, intimate relationships based on respect, where love can grow, deepen, and thrive. They do not over-share, they keep their own counsel, and they take personal responsibility for solving their own problems. They make safe listeners (without rescuing gestures), which allow others to open up and feel comfortable sharing who they are. They understand that it is appropriate to set healthy boundaries in our daily interactions with all persons, and doing so, attract mature, healthy partners and weed out disordered people. They are often called crazy by unhealthy people for simply taking good care of themselves.

Caretakers dismiss and devalue the feelings and thoughts of others. They are intrusive and controlling, feel entitled to pry and meddle in the affairs of others, and to offer unsolicited advice based on their personal feelings, needs, and desires. By presenting themselves as trying to be helpful, they prevent others from taking responsibility for their own problems. By concentrating on the problems of others, they often remain blind to their own. They have intimacy problems due to their neediness, where love is stifled, suffocated, and eventually dies. They are often abandoned abruptly, and take no personal responsibility for their thoughts, feelings, and behaviors. When they are confronted with their inappropriate behavior, they blame it on others, saying things like, "You made me do, feel, or act this way,"

Caretakers may seem caring and well-meaning, but they believe that sacrificing themselves needlessly is the correct way to behave, and expect others to do the same. They make unsafe listeners, and make others feel so uncomfortable and guarded that they do not share who they are. They are often referred to as smothering, stifling, and meddlesome. As a result, caretakers often do not know who others are. They do not set healthy boundaries for themselves, often because they are not aware they need to, and they run all over the boundaries of others without realizing it. They attract other immature, disordered people who make unhealthy partners, and repel potentially healthy ones. Like attracts like. They do not know how to behave appropriately, yet they tell others how they should behave.

Healthy adults see a severely codependent person as being something like a large, psychological spider. Needy and lost, this spider approaches with its eight legs, each with dozens of sticky hairs, ready to grab onto the first person that pays it any attention. This spider then attempts to capture its prey with an over-dose of charm, and then spin a web of obligation and guilt around them so their prey cannot escape. A healthy person's first instinct is to run away, or set boundaries to keep a safe distance. Unfortunately, the codependent usually chooses to ignore the polite, and not so polite resistance they receive from the healthier person they are trying to ensnare, and will usually ignore any boundary set against their codependent behavior.

Since the codependent cannot recognize when they are being inappropriately intrusive, they can't see that they are trampling on others' rights and freedoms with their caretaking gestures. The codependent believes that all they are doing is being "helpful" while trying to elicit help of others. This backward mindset comes from growing up with an unnatural, unhealthy attachment to their primary caregiver. This usually means the child did not received appropriate amount of love and nurturing that adjusted to the child's age throughout its developmental years, through adolescence, and into adulthood.

People who are healthy grew up with a natural, healthy attachment to their primary caregiver, and received the appropriate amount of love and nurturing that adjusted with their age. Codependency is a natural response to an unnatural attachment to a primary caregiver, created from either too much attention (from obsession and/or fear), or too little attention (from neglect and/or abandonment). When this kind of imbalanced attention does not adjust and correct throughout the child's developmental years, the codependent response can be carried into adulthood. Recovery is extremely important to alleviate the internal approach-avoidance conflict with the parent that gave the wrong kind of attention to the child.

RECOVERING FROM CODEPENDENCY
Healthy adult's "live and let live." They are generally at peace with themselves and the world most of the time, and able to feel their joy. A codependent's motto is "here, let me fix you, help you, rescue you, and yes, tell you what you should do and control you." Life for the codependent is "something you have to get through." This causes a tremendous amount of anxiety and creates the shackles of constant worry and obsessive fear-based thinking that burdens the daily life of the codependent.

Recovery from codependency is therefore a daily goal, and is accomplished one step at a time. Many people are a little bit codependent, and all they need to do is "keep it in check" by tuning in to what feels good and what feels bad, and setting the appropriate boundaries around these feelings. There are three basic strategies for recovering from codependency, and they involve developing external and internal boundaries.

THREE STRATEGIES FOR RECOVERY
1) BECOME A SAFE LISTENER
One of the first things you can do to recover from codependency is become a safe listener, and only confide in a safe listener when you need one. Everyone needs some support and someone safe to talk to, and finding a safe listener is sometimes all you need to get yourself on track. When something in your life is causing you distress, and you are having difficulty sorting things out, finding a safe listener to confide in can be very helpful. This can be a friend, spouse, or counselor you feel safe sharing with. A safe listener is a neutral, non-rescuing listener, who will allow you to air your concerns and have whatever feelings you are having, while remaining neutral.

Most of the time the best thing a friend can do for another friend is to be a safe listener. This allows a person to get things out in the open. To hear themselves without their head being cluttered up by another person's thoughts, needs, opinions, and fears, helps a person put things into perspective so they can figure out what they need to do. Your guiding inner voice is not drowned out or contaminated by the content of someone else's head that is based on their experiences. Unsafe listeners block personal evolution, and do not allow others to proceed on their own path. Codependents do not give others a chance to take responsibility for themselves.

What a safe listener can do is give feedback, like repeating what a person has just said to them, or saying things like, "sounds like you are very upset about this" (or mad, sad, scared, etc.). You can simply say supportive things, like, "I know you'll figure out what you need to do. I believe in you." You can also ask a simple question such as, "What do you plan to do about it?" in a loving and neutral way. Supportive comments that do not trample on a person's reality respect their process as being strictly between themselves and God or their better angels. Offering to be a safe listener can be the best gift you can give your friends, and if they ask you for your advice or opinion, you can offer that too, but think moderation.

What we learn from our dysfunctional families, and from society, is the codependent triangle of the three classic positions of victim, rescuer, and judge/prosecutor. Healthy relationships lie outside of this triangle, and ask others to take responsibility for their behavior, while you take responsibility for yours. Move all of your relationships out of this controlling triangle, and stop participating in unsafe listening.

In her book "Codependent No More" Melody Beattie said, "In order to find yourself, you need to sever your connection with the people who control you." I highly recommend this book to those in or affiliated with codependent relationships. Meanwhile, give some thought to defining a new way of being by adopting the strategy of becoming a safe listener. Another strategy for a new way of being is to define a new personal policy.

2) DEFINE A NEW PERSONAL POLICY
Christopher Reeves said, "Hope is based on information, and the future projection of the outcome of that information." There is every reason to hope for healthy relationships. All you need to do is educate yourself, apply what you learn to your life, and see what happens. Bruce Lee said, "It is not enough to learn; you must apply!" Begin by writing out a contract with yourself that defines and outlines a new and healthier way of interacting with others appropriately, using healthy guidelines. The contract I wrote for myself called, "My new personal policy."

MY NEW PERSONAL POLICY
My new personal policy is a *hands-off* approach in all my relationships. This means that I take full responsibility for what I choose to think and feel as a self-governing adult, as I take care of myself, and my private business. This includes my health, my marriage, my family, my friendships, my relationship to doctors, my career, etc. When I am offered unsolicited advice, my responses will simply be; "Thanks anyway, but if I need any advice, I'll let you

know" or "Thanks, but I prefer to take care of myself," and so on, in a polite and respectful way. When someone refuses to honor my boundary, I will set a boundary of distance and time between them and me.

When I can, without sacrificing my energy or serenity, I will offer myself to others as a safe listener. However, I will not offer support that will enable anyone to stay in an unhealthy pattern, because I do not want to be used as an enabler. I am committed to healthy growth, learning, and moving forward with the understanding that I am solely responsible for everything I choose to think and feel. I also understand that I have the power to learn to control what I think and feel for the most part, if I choose to do so. In my conversations with my friends and others regarding my personal business, I will welcome questions such as; "How is it going?" or "What are you doing these days?" or "How are you and the family?" and so on.

What I share is my choice, and I am not obligated to answer questions or reveal anything I do not feel comfortable revealing. Any intrusive questioning will be considered "prying into my private life" and will not be appreciated. An appropriate response will be given, such as, "I'm sorry, but that's personal" or "I'm afraid that's private" or if the person is persistent and rude, "I'm sorry, but no, I am not going to answer that. It's simply none of your business.

When I do share something personal, it will be in moderation to someone safe. I will only air my concerns to help me put things into perspective to figure out what I want to do. My sharing is not a request for an opinion or help, unless I specifically ask for it. When I am airing my concerns, I will welcome the following non-advisory responses; "I here what you are saying" or "I'm sorry that your are hurting" or "What are your plans, if any?" etc. However, there are people I have come to respect enough to allow them some leeway, and am occasionally open to the benefit of their unsolicited wisdom and experience, and this is my decision.

I will become a more private person for a reason. I do not want to allow my natural path toward enlightenment to become blocked by allowing my mind to be cluttered or contaminated by other people's judgments, speculations, opinions, and fears. I want to have a clear and open mind to receive my inner wisdom. I believe this will be the answer to guiding myself to be healthier. When I make my most important decisions, I will make them in private, and then share with whom I choose, if at all.

I also hope to attract like-minded people, as I detach from those who do not treat me with kindness and respect, understanding that they too have a right to choose how they want to be. This position also includes saying no to the intrusion of "well-intentioned" analysis and judgments of others regarding my life choices, especially with regard to the path I am taking for my better health. I will dwell in the present, and not the past, and only reference the past to help make decisions in the present. Maintaining this position in my relationships with others is my new goal."

Once you have composed your new personal policy, keep it handy to read any time you need a reminder of what you have decided. John Quincy Adams said, "Patience and perseverance have a magical effect before which difficulties disappear and obstacles vanish." Be patient with yourself, and pursue your goal of mental health with self-love and dedication. If you feel you have codependent tendencies in your relationships with others, or are involved in a relationship with someone who is codependent, then become aware of this on a regular basis, and practice more appropriate behavior.

Learning how to set boundaries and establishing a new way of being only takes practice, like learning how to play a new musical instrument. Learn to be the key-master of your life choices, and the gatekeeper of your safety and wellbeing. Protect yourself from toxic, intrusive people, and leave the stress with the stressful. Do not allow anyone to intrude on your autonomy, or disrupt your hard earned serenity. Do this with the use of healthy boundaries.

3) SET HEALTHY BOUNDARIES
The process of recovering from codependency requires a boundary strategy; i.e., "When you are an alcoholic, you stay out of bars!" This also applies to codependent relationships. The way you stay out of them is to begin setting healthy boundaries. This

does not mean that you should build protective walls around you, or become hyper-vigilant about what you say. It just means you need to pay more attention to what is transpiring in your transactions with others, and when you notice the conversation slipping into codependency mode, back off and start again, or leave the situation. It may help to have a few handy tips (tools) for strengthening your boundary setting abilities.

SOME HANDY TIPS

1) When you feel that a boundary (limit) needs to be set with someone, set it in as few words as possible, set it clearly; and preferably without anger. Avoid explaining, justifying, rationalizing, or apologizing. Offer a brief explanation only when it makes sense to do so. When you are setting a boundary in an intimate relationship, it makes more sense to share how you feel only when it's safe. Remember, the most important person to notify of your boundary first is you. Then make it clear to others. In some cases, you don't need to explain what you're doing, just do it. Actions speak louder – and sometimes more clearly – than words.

2) Remember that when you set a personal boundary to take care of yourself, it is impossible to take care of the feelings of others at the same time. Nor is it appropriate. The two acts are mutually exclusive, and you are only responsible for the manner in which you set the boundary. Try to be kind, but not at your own expense.

3) When learning to set boundaries, you will most likely feel shame and fear, but do not let this prevent you from setting them. People do not always know they are trespassing or intruding on you personally, and no one respects a person who allows themselves to be used as a doormat. People only use people that can be used, and they respect people that cannot. Healthy boundaries benefit everyone. Both children and adults feel more comfortable around people who have clear boundaries.

4) If you are experiencing anger or rage, or find yourself whining and complaining about something, this indicates that a boundary is screaming to be set. It is natural to feel anger when you do not like the way you are being treated. It is simply not natural to ignore your feelings, or suffer in silence. Anger is an indicator of a problem that needs to be addressed, like a

flashing red light on a car dashboard. Other indicators may be the feeling of being threatened, suffocated, or manipulated. While it may be necessary to get angry at times to set a boundary, it is never appropriate to become abusive, or feel resentment about having to set boundaries. Setting boundaries is what healthy adults do for self-care, and they can say no as easily and naturally as they can say yes.

5) Remember to plan on your boundaries being tested, especially when you did not routinely set them before. Be ready to enforce them. You do not need to convince anyone but yourself of your boundaries. Once you really know what your limits are, others will sense when you have reached them, and will not be hard to persuade. In this way, you will stop attracting intrusive boundary invaders and violators. Immature and ill-behaved people naturally fall out of your life, and this leaves room for healthier, like-minded people to enter.

6) Be congruent with your boundaries. Your behavior (what you do and say) needs to match the limits you set. Boundaries can be enforced by ultimatums and consequences, and if they are not enforced they are not yet boundaries. Remember that we set boundaries to take care of ourselves, and not to control others. However, those who are referred to in modern-day parlance as "control freaks," will play the victim and accuse you of trying to control them. This is because they have always felt entitled to be intrusive, etc., and have their values upside-down and backward. If you live with an alcoholic, and you set a boundary that says they either stop drinking or they move out, it is because you will not permit yourself to live with an alcoholic, and not that you want to force someone to stop drinking, or control them in any way.

7) There are plenty of people who will be happy to honor and respect your boundaries with no problem. Others, especially people who are accustomed to using you or controlling you, or accustomed to you taking care of them by sacrificing yourself, will most likely become angry, and even be baffled, by your boundaries, when before you had few or none. Allow them their discomfort, and change things anyway. For you, feel the fear, and do it anyway. They need to grow up and take responsibility for themselves, and their behavior. Remember, you are not trying to control their life, as they might suggest, but only your own.

8) Setting boundaries is a part of your personal growth process, and you will do it in your own time. Remember, things will change when you are truly ready for them to, and not before. It is simply a matter of choice, and is your sole responsibility.

9) Learning to establish limits by setting boundaries may require a support system, especially if there is an excessive amount of inappropriate fear and shame involved, and especially when you are setting boundaries against a major offender. Yes, you are taking action when before you didn't, but with apologies to Confucius, You would be making a second mistake by not correcting a first. Building healthy self-esteem, self-respect, and confidence in one's own worth and abilities, is a one-day-at-a-time process. Feedback can be very helpful in becoming clear about what is and is not right for you.

10) The positive side of learning to set boundaries is discovering who you are. By identifying what you do not like (what hurts you and feels bad) you begin to identify what you do like (what brings you pleasure and feels good). The best way to remain connected to your spiritual path to enlightenment is to pay attention to your likes and dislikes, and set boundaries around them. The more you risk being true to yourself, the more you move into the abundant good in your life. Setting boundaries is an ongoing process of listening and showing respect to yourself, understanding your basic human rights and freedoms to be self-governed, and understanding your responsibility to take good care of yourself.

11) When setting boundaries, strive for a healthy balance between flexibility, and a sense of self. Healthy living includes giving in to people from time to time, but remember, there is a difference between giving in a little, and being robbed.

12) Finally, understand that there is a reason for the way others behave, but that reasons are not excuses! Don't be a coward, a martyr, or an enabler. Hold others reasonably accountable for their behavior, and set needed boundaries on a daily basis. Enabling codependent or inappropriate behavior will chip away at your self-esteem and self-respect, and cause an enormous amount of inner conflict and turmoil that will drain your energy, prevent you from being your best self, and also prevent you from reaching your full potential as a unique human being.

Although these tips may be helpful, we all have our own guide within us. To begin recovering from codependency, all that you need to develop your boundary skills is to continue working at them every day. You will eventually become stronger in your boundary setting abilities, and sensitive enough to listen to the feelings that register in your body, and the messages they are sending to your mind. You will learn to love and respect yourself enough to set good boundaries, and keep yourself safe and healthy. Stay tuned in to what hurts and what feels good.

If you are at risk, uncomfortable, or in a painful relationship, set limits to stop it. Become clear about what is, and is not, your responsibility. Decide what is appropriate and healthy, and evaluate what you are willing to lose and not lose when you set limits. The fact is, you may not have any ground to give up, and you may not find any middle ground either. There are times when your differences are simply too cut and dried to ignore.

When you are recovering from codependency, begin to ask yourself questions like: "Is someone in my life using me, being intrusive or disrespectful, or not treating me appropriately?" "Am I complaining, upset, or angry about something that is going on in my life, or with someone I am in a relationship with?" "What do I think will happen if I identify a problem, and set up a healthy boundary?" "What do I think will happen if I do not?" It might be a starting point for you if you are too afraid to ask someone to turn down the music for you, and are likely to give in to codependency by taking care of them and sacrificing yourself.

Also, begin to pay attention to how you feel around people who have healthy limits, and see if you feel comfortable with them. Do you feel that there are too many restrictions? Pay attention to how you feel around people who have too few boundaries, or none at all. Do you feel awkward, uncertain, or at loose ends? Are you compelled to take care of them, or go along with whatever they want? Then ask yourself the final and most telling questions: "In the past, what have I been willing to lose or give up for the sake of a particular relationship, and what am I willing to lose or give up now?" Conversely, "What am I not willing to lose, or give up now?" Finally, "How much do I value my psychological health and serenity?"

This kind of self-examination will help you understand more about where your boundaries are weak and need work, and where they are non-existent and need to be established. To better judge this with yourself, it is helpful to understand some basic guidelines for what is healthy and what is not. Having no clear knowledge of boundaries, people who are codependent do not know what is and is not healthy.

BASIC GUIDELINES FOR PSYCHOLOGICAL HEALTH
People who are relatively mature, and appropriately functional psychologically and emotionally, usually make healthy choices. People who are immature and dysfunctional make unhealthy choices. Here are some general examples that can help distinguish the difference between more appropriate, healthy choices and those that are inappropriate and less healthy.

HEALTHY CHOICES
People who take personal responsibility for their thoughts, emotions, and behavior, and are committed to continual learning and spiritual growth, are more likely to make healthy choices. They own their choices, and do not blame others for a bad outcome. They are largely in control of their thoughts, and do not engage in out of-control, disaster thinking, and thus are able to maintain relative psychological balance. They do not overreact, but instead pause to make a realistic assessment of the facts, and try to respond appropriately. They clearly establish and maintain personal boundaries, and are able to understand the value of honoring and respecting the boundaries of others, even when they do not always understand their reasons why.

UNHEALTHY CHOICES
People who do not take personal responsibility for their thoughts, emotions, and behaviors are not concerned with, or committed to, personal growth, and do not try to make healthy choices. They see themselves as powerless victims, and blame others for their life's misfortunes and consequences. They perpetuate personal psychological imbalance by indulging in out-of-control, disaster thinking. They quickly overreact, make distorted assessments of the facts, and usually react in inappropriately disproportionate ways. They do not set personal boundaries as a rule, and have difficulty honoring and respecting the boundaries of others

without arguing, judging, or demanding an explanation when they do not understand them. They have great difficulty maintaining a healthy psychological balance in life, and their lives are more often than not wrought with chaos and trauma.

A definition of mental health can be that whatever we endure, we are able to process out to its natural conclusion in a healthy, proportionate and accepting way. People who are considered to be psychologically and emotionally mature, balanced, and appropriately functional with healthy boundaries are self-governed with their "adult ego" in charge most of the time. They practice healthy processing and expression of their emotions and thoughts in a moderate and responsible manner that enables them to continually grow and change throughout their lives. This principal does not change if you are a highly or less sensitive person. One out of four people are born highly sensitive. They usually feel and perceive more than less sensitive people, and may require more time to process their experiences.

People who are psychologically and emotionally immature, unbalanced, and dysfunctional without limits, allow their "overly-adapted child ego" to be in charge. They often allow their thoughts, and consequent emotions, to run wild; what Sigmund Freud referred to as the unleashed "id" of uncoordinated instincts. They will repeatedly abuse their bodies and minds by flooding themselves with stress hormones, such as cortisol and adrenaline. These primary stress hormones are also called "death hormones" because they can become addictive, and this kind of repeated self-abuse eventually can cause serious health problems.

Without their adult ego in charge, these people allow themselves to be swept away by neurotic, irrational fears and imaginings, and they create negative mental movies with compulsive worrying that can distort their judgment and ability to assess their reality accurately. Consider that the derivation of "to worry" means "to devour one's self", and causes unhealthy, unnecessary anxiety. We all know someone that we call "a drama-queen (or king) on wheels." They are prisoners of themselves, and misery always loves company. So don't allow these unfortunate people to insinuate themselves into your life. Have compassion for them, or not, but set boundaries of distance and time against them. They are energetic black holes.

Note: Both suppressing and avoiding emotions (emotional constipation) and over-reacting and dramatizing them (emotional diarrhea) are unhealthy choices. It is healthier to express your thoughts and feelings in moderation in a responsible and timely manner, without suppressing them or allowing them to erupt in an uncontrolled, explosive outburst.

Virginia Satir wrote, *"I want to love you without clutching, appreciate you without judging, invite you without invading, criticize you without blaming, and help you without insulting. If I can have the same from you, then we can truly meet and enrich each other."*

When I think of all the years of codependency I suffered, and the unhealthy choices I made without even realizing I was sacrificing myself for the sake of disordered people, I truly regret not seeking professional help or guidance throughout this period of my life. I had to drive myself into the depths of despair from putting others first too often, before I was forced by chronic illness to take stock of my life, make the much needed and long-overdue changes, and take responsibility for my self-care by learning to value myself appropriately and set personal limits with those who were unhealthy to me. Looking back, I can see now that all these years of suffering were so unnecessary.

In my early years, if I had been accepted and loved by my family for who I was apart from my mother, my life would have been so very different. I knew what I wanted and didn't want, what I liked and disliked, what felt good and what felt bad. I just didn't know that I had the right to do what was best for me, and say no to the people who were destructive and harmful. I knew things weren't right with the relationships in my family, especially between my mother and me, and that these things would not likely ever change. The only piece I was missing that I didn't know was that I did not have to be there. However, I have come to believe that "All roads lead to where we stand" as Don McLean's sang in *"American Pie,"* and that I am in charge of where I stand now. I also know that where I go from here is within my power to choose. I do not regret the path that has led me to where I am now. I honestly believe this path has always been toward a higher good, and is unfolding for me as the path I have chosen to take, and feels right because I am finally being true to myself.

Codependency is a serious condition. It literally kills. People can die from its depleting and harmful effects. When a codependent perpetually sacrifices themselves by throwing their vital life-force energy into the bottomless pit of the endless needs and desires of others, they can eventually deplete themselves beyond recovery. You have no doubt been told by flight attendants before your plane takes off, that if the oxygen masks drop from the ceiling, you should put on your mask first before aiding your child sitting next to you. If you run around helping everyone else on the plane before putting on your own, you will most likely suffocate.

Also, from their inability to say no when it is appropriate, the codependent person may even allow themselves to be led into potentially harmful or dangerous situations that could ultimately cost them their life. Recovering from codependency can literally make the difference between life and death, and will certainly determine your quality of life. If you suspect that you are codependent, choose to begin your recovery process now by practicing boundaries. Begin immediately. Do not wait!

For the first time in my life, I can honestly say I can keep myself reasonably safe from being harmed by another human being, and that I can trust myself to use sound, healthy judgment in my assessments of what is going on around me. I have learned to trust my instincts that tell me what I cannot discern with the naked eye, the open ear, or the careful touch. I know that mistakes in assessments can be made by the most functional and balanced people, no matter how tuned in they usually are, and I allow for this without fear, dread, shame, or anxiety.

I forgive myself when I make a mistake as easily as I can forgive others who own theirs, and I take responsibility for doing what I can to self-correct without diminishing my self-worth. I try to be gentle with myself and with others, and I have learned how to ignore my mother's angry, scowling voice in my head that used to say, "Oh, Val!" each time I asserted who I was apart from her.

When I asked my father during our final conversations before he died, why he chose to lead a solitary life, he replied, "Because I am protecting myself from being hurt." This is very sad. This man, who so freely gave unsolicited advice about how to get along in relationships, and love everyone unconditionally, stayed on the sidelines all his life, and never learned how to be in the game with rules and limits. I replied, "Well, Dad, that's where we are different. I have learned how to choose healthier relationships with people who will not hurt me."

It is easy to believe in unconditional love when you avoid involvement with everyone. But when you are in the game and playing to win, you must first have the sense to choose a winning team, and then play by mutually agreed upon rules that are based on standards and principals geared toward winning. If you do not, you are sure to lose. To win in human relationships, the foundations must be based upon the standard of mutual respect and loving kindness, and honoring and using healthy appropriate limits. I address this in detail in my next chapter.

I see that what sets us apart from other animals, what makes us human (free will), is exactly what allows me to experience what I choose in as meaningful a way as I wish. It's healthy to stay away from unsafe people, and to see and accept things the way they truly are. I can relax in life now, and know I am leading myself in the right direction overall. I understand that the intrusive, angry disapproval from my disordered family regarding the path I have chosen, has been a sure sign that I am on the right track.

I know whatever is beyond my control, I have the ability to accept and endure with appropriate boundaries, and go on. I blunder now and then, but that's okay. I stay the course, remembering to live and let live, to assess others for how they might support or challenge my safety and health, to understand when possible and not judge, to allow others to be responsible for themselves, to be in the present as much as possible, and to live within the mystery of life as gracefully and responsibly as I can. What more can anyone do?

"IF"

If you can keep your head when all about you are losing
theirs, and blaming it on you,

If you can trust yourself when all men doubt you, but make
allowance for their doubting, too; If you can wait and not be
tired by waiting, or being lied about, don't deal in lies, Or
being hated, don't give way to hating, and yet don't look too
good nor talk too wise...

If you can dream and not make dreams your master,

If you can think, and not make thoughts your aim,

If you can meet with triumph and disaster, and treat those
two imposters just the same;

If you can bear to hear the truth you've spoken twisted by
knaves to make a trap for fools, or watch the things you gave
your life to, broken, and stoop and build 'em up with warn-
out-tools;

If you can make one heap of all your winnings, and risk it on
one turn of pitch-and-toss, and lose, and start again at your
beginnings, and never breathe a word about your loss...

If you can force your heart and nerve and sinew to serve
your turn long after they are gone, and so hold on when
there is nothing in you except the will which says to them:
"Hold on";

If you can talk with crowds and keep your virtue, or walk
with kings nor lose the common touch;

If your neither foes nor loving friends can hurt you,

If all men count with you, but none too much;

If you can fill the unforgiving minute with sixty seconds'
worth of distance run, yours is the Earth and everything
that's in it, and—which is more—you'll be a Man, my Son!

Rudyard Kipling

FIVE

BOUNDARIES
The Key To Recovering From Codependency

When individuals are brought up in a dysfunctional family system, they often enter into adulthood with little or no knowledge of the existence of boundaries (limits). They are also unaware of the importance of functional boundaries as an essential component in their relationships with other people. Lack of boundaries is central to destructive behavior, and can seriously prevent a person from maturing mentally into a functional, healthy adult, one that is capable of mature love and intimacy. People who have grown up without boundaries often lose their sense of self in the perpetual chaos and trauma, and are unable to recognize the presence or absence of abuse, because abuse has been "normalized" by the family's enablers.

Therefore, establishing healthy boundaries is imperative for self-protection and developing a healthy sense of self (identity). Self-awareness, self-control, memory, and reasoning are all higher mental functions. Mental maturity can be measured by the increase of these functions, just as mental degradation can be measured by their absence or loss. There is a saying in Buddhism, "To say no means you have to know what yes is." It is within the process of figuring out what you do not want, that you figure out what you do want. Mental maturity includes establishing healthy boundaries, and the self-awareness that comes as a result of having them.

Functional boundaries are also imperative to psychological, spiritual, and physical healing because they protect against the destructive forces of evil behavior (behavior that is destructive) that threaten health on all three levels. Very often, evil behavior is simply a bi-product of mental illness. Evil behavior may or may not be intentional or conscious, but the accountability is the same either way. It has to be. A person does not have to be purely evil (for instance, a devil worshiper who is an active member of a satanic cult that practices blood sacrifice, etc.) to be spiritually, emotionally, and psychologically harmful and dangerous.

104

Destructive behavior is always harmful because it results in the suppression, and even prevention, of overall spiritual growth and enlightenment (total-self knowledge in the here-and-now). Establishing a "code of honor" for yourself in the form of a system of limits will move you toward self-discovery and spiritual maturity. In this age of consciousness, the ideas that come to us from quantum physics, Zen Buddhism, and psychology, etc., are not meant to be entertainment, ego-enhancing, or warn as a "mask of consciousness" to wear out socially to impress people who are "consciously correct." These ideas are meant to be applied to our lives to propel us forward into our natural evolution as a species. These ideas are meant to guide us and change us. Boundaries are the most basic foundation for this process of personal discovery, change, enlightenment, and the spiritual evolution of mankind.

As soon as you become someone with healthy boundaries, you will attract a higher caliber of person, and repel the rest. People who know how to protect themselves in appropriate ways can do this easily and graciously. People who will respect your boundaries without hostility, resentment, or argument, and can simply say to you, "Okay, we'll miss seeing you this time, but we'll catch you another time." Adults have good boundaries, and they respect the limits of others, even when they do not understand the whys and wherefores. Healthy adults do not expect people to sacrifice themselves to the selfish demands of other's, and they appreciate and respect the rights and freedoms of others to live their lives as they see fit.

When you come across people who become angry or hostile when you say "no," set strong physical and/or emotional boundaries against them, and let them go their own way. You are not responsible to engage in a discussion or argument to make someone who is being intrusive understand your private business, or convince them of your reasons for setting a personal limit. Neither is it is healthy to argue with them, and say things like, "What part of NO don't you understand?"

Mature adults keep their own counsel, and are not accountable to anyone else for their personal decisions regarding their wellbeing and safety. If you wish to explain your reasons to someone you feel is safe, or are intimate with for the sake of sharing, do so. You are never required to explain a boundary someone else. The only requirement is to be brief, clear, and make sure that the fact of the boundary is understood, even if its reason is not. The most effective way to protect yourself against people who behave badly is to utilize a system of personal boundaries that combines internal and external limits.

BOUNDARIES

Boundaries are like the fence around your property that protects everything that is yours that you value. They prevent others from trespassing on your rights and freedoms to lead your own life, and keep yourself safe and healthy. When your boundary fence has gaping holes of ambiguity, an intrusive element can enter into your space and harm you, or rob you of a piece of yourself. In addition, your fence can have a locked gate that leads in and out of your life and personal space. You not only have the right and the power to decide where and how far out to put your fence at any given time, you can decide when to unlock the gate and open it to some extent, or not.

These decisions are yours to make, and no one else's, no matter how willfully ignorant they are about boundaries. There will always be outside pressure from intrusive personalities who have not yet learned to have internal boundaries of their own (self-control), and therefore do not value and respect the boundaries of others. This is when good judgment and common sense help you maintain the boundaries you feel are appropriate to set at any given time. Only you can know what is best for you.

Remember one thing: when you have your boundary fenses in place, they not only keep unwanted elements out, they simultaneously keep you in. Sometimes this is what is necessary for self-protection. However, living your whole life behind a fence with a locked gate can be very lonely. What I am talking about here is risk. There are times to close the gate and lock it, and there are times to unlock it and let people and events into your life. There are no guarantees that you will not get hurt in some way when you do this. Even when you eliminate the intrusive people from your life, there comes a time when you must risk letting new people in, experience them, and learn.

Not every person or situation requires being faced with a locked gate. Over time, you will learn to discern when and with whom a locked gate is or is not necessary. But when it is, you must endure the difficulties of standing by your decision, and not cave in when disordered, harmful people picket your fences with vicious accusatory signs, jeers, scorns, and guilt trips they are bound to inundate you with. Otherwise, you might as well put out the "welcome mat" for all who happen by, and suffer the diminishment that comes with allowing your self to be trampled on, suppressed, and potentially destroyed by others.

You are the keeper of your mind, your body, and your soul. You are responsible for your life, and the choices you make. This fact is an inescapable part of having been given the gift of life. This is a beautiful world, and the world we create for ourselves within the world we all share can be as wonderful as you choose to make it. Making these choices, however uncertain they may seem at times, are always worth the effort!

DEFINITION AND PURPOSE OF BOUNDARIES
Boundaries are a personal system of internal and external limits that enable people to gain some control over the effect they have on others, and the effect others have on them. Their specific purpose is to provide a framework for you to have a clear sense of your own reality, and a clear sense of yourself. There are four areas of boundaries that define and contain your reality, and who you are apart from others. Who you are apart from others is your identity. You can have no clear identity without boundaries.

BOUNDARIES DEAL WITH FOUR AREAS
1) The limits you set for your physical body (your appearance).
2) Your thoughts (how you interpret what you experience, and the meaning you assign to it).
3) Your feelings (the emotions that result from the thoughts you choose, and/or messages from your body intelligence).
4) Your behavior (what you choose to do or say, or not do or say about any given situation).

Your reality literally consists of how you look, how you feel, how you think, and what you do and say, or not do and say. This self-defined reality is different for each person. Some people have a clear and healthy system of boundaries in place, and are comfortable with having them. While others, such as people who are suffering from codependency, for example, do not have a consistent and functional system of boundaries at all, and therefore do not actually know who they are.

Moreover, these people have their internal boundary in reverse, which tells them they are responsible for the feelings and choices of others, and that others are responsible for theirs. This reversal of misplaced responsibility creates the role of the "victim" when a person is being their most immature and dysfunctional. As I have said before, they unwittingly have everything backward.

On the other hand, when people have both their internal and external boundaries functioning together while sharing their reality with someone else, or while someone else is sharing their reality with them, a wonderful thing can happen. When both boundaries are functioning strongly at the same time, the spiritual boundary is automatically present and is very powerful. It is the feeling of being one with the other person while at the same time being separate, and is the spiritual awareness of knowing where responsibility lies for each one. This is what God intends for us all. The understanding that we are all connected through the same life-force energy, yet at the same time separated by our physical body and by our internal and external boundaries in our responsibility for self-care.

INTERNAL BOUNDARIES
Internal boundaries have to do with owning your responsibility to what you choose to think, and what you feel as a result of what you think, and the actions you choose to take or not take, even when you are responding to someone else. Although we need to be sensitive to the effect we have on others if we want to be in relationships, the only time we are responsible for the feelings of another is when we are intentionally disrespectful, abusive, or harmful. Then we must take responsibility, show remorse, and make amends. It is that simple.

EXTERNAL BOUNDARIES
External boundaries have to do with protecting the body and keeping it healthy and safe from harm. This applies both to non-

sexual and sexual situations, and deals with decisions such as when and how close you get to another person physically, and when and who gets to touch you. These boundaries are meant to control distance and touch.

When someone has their internal boundary reversed, and they are playing the proverbial "victim," their life is a perpetual series of crises and dramas. It is impossible to have a healthy, adult relationship with them. No one likes to be around a perpetual victim who cannot take responsibility for their behavior, and blames others for their unhappiness. However, even though we are not responsible for the way someone responds to us, based on the meaning they choose to assign to what we do and say, we are still responsible for noting the impact we have on others, and how we handle that impact.

We cannot always change the way others assign meaning to what we say or do, or how they choose to feel about us. Let others think of you what ever they need to think. There is an old saying, "What other people think of you is none of your business!" All we can do to avoid being an offender is to not knowingly do harm.

Whenever people deliberately commit a major offense, they are accountable for it. They are then obliged to make amends, which means taking personal responsibility for their behavior, showing remorse, and promising to work hard at never doing it again. If they are not willing to do this, then they are not capable of a healthy adult relationship of an intimate nature. It then becomes necessary to evaluate and assess the psychological health and safety of those you are attempting to have a relationship with, and the nature of the relationship you can have with them, if any.

Note: A legitimate victim is someone who has been harmed by the destructive actions/behaviors of a major offender.

EVALUATING INTERNAL BOUNDARIES
1) The healthy, intact internal boundary is always functioning when you are taking responsibility for yourself and your reality, and it allows others to be responsible for theirs. At the same time, you are able to remain sensitive to the effect you have on others, and can freely and moderately communicate the effect

that others have on you. Remember that adults keep their own counsel, and your power can be demonstrated in not reacting to others (picking your battles), or by taking action for self-care by setting needed boundaries (living in action for yourself).

2) The non-existent internal boundary is when the boundary of responsibility is reversed, where you blame others for your reality, and you blame yourself for theirs. This is the proverbial blame game that is played by every victim, and gets to be a real drag.

3) The intermittent internal boundary functions inconsistently, depending on the internal and external environment and circumstances (how you feel, where you are, and whom you are with). Ideally, this boundary should be functioning as consistently as possible.

4) Finally, there is the internal wall when you could not possibly care less about another person's reality, nor do you wish to share yours. You intentionally wall out the other person, and wall your self in. You do not open up to anyone, and you are not the least bit interested in anyone else in return.

EVALUATING EXTERNAL BOUNDARIES

1) The healthy, intact external boundary constantly evaluates distance and touch in your interactions with others. You protect yourself by controlling how far away you are from someone, and whether or not you allow them to touch you. You are still vulnerable to attack or harm, but have some basic protection with containment of your own reality and sense of self.

2) The non-existent external boundary is when you do not evaluate distance or touch in your interaction with others, and have no awareness that something is lacking. You are extremely vulnerable to attack and harm, and are providing yourself no protection with no containment of your reality and no sense of self.

3) The intermittent external boundary utilizes healthy boundaries part of the time, and other times does not use them at all, depending on your circumstances, where you are, and whom you are with. Also, if you are sick or fatigued, you may not have the energy to be able to utilize them fully. Here you only have partial containment and protection of your reality and sense of self.

110

4) The extreme alternating external boundary is continually alternating between having no boundaries at all to having impenetrable walls, shifting back and forth between one extreme and the other.

5) Finally, the perpetual wall. Walls provide complete protection, allowing no intimacy at all, and should always be used when you are interacting with a chronic or major offender. Walls consist of extremes in behavior that completely separates you from another person without offending or harming them. These can be demonstrated as anger, humor, talking, silence, politeness, distance, etc., allowing no intimate contact, and keeping you safe. With these walls you are completely protected, contained and isolated. However, they take an enormous amount of energy to maintain. The least draining wall is the wall of distance and time (physical distance).

When your internal or external boundaries are intermittent, it means you have holes in your fences. Pay attention to what happens to your boundaries when you are around certain people, or in certain situations, that seem to cause them to function intermittently. Don't be a chameleon. Practice activating your boundaries any time they are not functioning as consistently as they should. Again, learning to utilize consistent boundaries is like learning to play a musical instrument. All it takes is practice, practice, practice, and soon it will come naturally. The holes in your fences will eventually be repaired, and you will be protected most of the time. However, do not ever tolerate abuse!

No one's boundaries are fully functional all of the time. Learning to be responsible for your own reality and leaving other people's reality to them is the key to being a healthy, mature adult, and is an important goal to set for yourself. Nobody can be human, endure stress and illness, and the ups and downs of life, and keep a perfect boundary system going all the time. Just practice doing your best, and you will become more aware in time. Remember, practicing boundaries at times in a situation that requires them will make your boundary setting skills stronger than if you never practice them at all.

HEALTHY BOUNDARIES

The Bible is the most popular and widely read book ever written, and with the right interpretation, can be useful for providing healthy role models for appropriate boundary setting. Matthew 18: 15-18 says, "Moreover, if thy brother shall trespass against thee, go and tell him his fault between thee and him alone; if he shall hear thee, thou hast gained thy brother. But if he will not hear thee, then take with thee one or two more, that in the mouth of two or three witnesses, every word may be established. And if he shall neglect to hear them, tell it unto the church: but if he neglects to hear the church, let him be unto thee as a heathen man and publican. Verily I say unto you, whatsoever ye shall bind on earth shall be bound in heaven: and whatsoever ye shall lose on earth shall be loosed in heaven." This means some people will get to be in your life, while others will not. It is just the way a healthy, adult world works, so set boundaries and see who gets to stay.

HEALTHY MODELS FOR BOUNDARY SETTING

1) All adults are responsible for both setting and honoring boundaries. In setting boundaries, you do not owe an explanation, nor do you require permission to set them.

2) Boundaries are for self-preservation, and they do not have to be explained. The person who you are setting the boundary with does not have to understand your reasons, or agree with your boundary. They do not even have to like it. The only things they need to do are hear it, clearly understand what the boundary is, and most importantly, honor it. Honoring boundaries, whether they are your own or the boundaries of others, is something adults are *supposed* to do, and should not be seen as a "favor" given with guilt messages or a quid pro quo attached.

3) Boundaries are to be celebrated in ourselves and in others. Healthy adults who take good care of themselves love the boundaries of others. They respect and honor them without complaint and make an honest and willing effort to remember them.

4) If you are faced with a chronic boundary violator, such as a narcissist or a borderline, you can remind them a couple of times, and if they continue to violate your boundaries, or make no effort to remember them, then it is appropriate to distance yourself from them for a while (sometimes permanently) by

creating a physical boundary of distance and time between you. Chronic boundary violators only care about themselves. They do not care about the wellbeing of others, and are not capable of healthy intimate relationships or mature love. Why would a self-respecting person want to share their most valuable assets, their time, energy, and personal space, with a chronic offender?

Apply a healthy yardstick to your relationships. Give them the litmus test of boundaries, and carefully observe how your boundaries are honored. If your boundaries are ignored, resented, or demeaned with complaints about how inconvenient or disagreeable they are, then the quality of your relationship with that person does not measure up. What you will find out is that there was never truly a healthy relationship with that person to begin with, and what seemed to be a relationship connection was only an illusion. Gracefully let these people go.

Find out with whom you can have a healthy, adult relationship, and whom you cannot. When you become a boundary lover, you will attract other boundary lovers. There are plenty of adults out there who can honor and celebrate your boundaries without judging you, and can set boundaries for themselves graciously and respectfully, and make a sincere effort to respect yours.

Naturally, children do not have the capacity to always remember boundaries. Patience and consistent consequences are therefore required to help them learn the importance of honoring boundaries so they can become adults who are capable of loving, intimate relationships. Remember that boundaries exist to teach "self-control'" and not "other-control."

An immature person would rather have you accommodate or enable their inappropriate behaviors, needs, and selfish demands, than have you take the healthier position of setting up boundaries against them. They need to grow up. The book, "Boundaries," by Cloud and Townsend states, "I would rather be around people who are capable of taking personal responsibility, who honestly fail me, and can own their behavior, apologize and make amends (promise to try in earnest never to do it again), and repent (make a true change in direction), than people who dishonestly deny ever doing anything wrong, and have no intention of taking personal responsibility for their behavior, or doing better in the future." I wholeheartedly agree! This sums up why I cannot be around my dangerously disordered biological family. None of them have ever admitted to, or taken personality for, their destructive behaviors, nor will they.

HOW TO SET BOUNDARIES
The word "no" is the most effective and most solid of boundaries. In fact, the word "no" is actually a complete sentence! There are no ifs, ands, or buts about it. It is very clear and non-negotiable. Sometimes, based on the information at hand, a "no" boundary is required. When it is, you must do your part, and stand by your boundary. This is not to say when you receive new information, you may decide to change your mind, and adjust your boundary to some degree. You most certainly may. The point here is that you are in control of your boundary, and can change it according to your on-going assessment.

Upholding your boundary is the beginning of the work of boundary setting. This means resisting the demands and guilt-trips laid on you by others, resisting giving up your moral principals out of fear of rejection, condemnation, or loneliness, and resisting the temptation to abandon your position out of the fatigue all these battles inflict. This also means not giving in to the self-doubt caused by the voice of that "critical inner-parent" who says you are wrong, or have no right to think, feel, or believe what you do.

The truth is you must base all of your decisions in life, including your reasons for setting a boundary, on what you truly think, feel, and believe at the time. Otherwise, you will be abandoning yourself time and time again in the most fundamental way possible. You will be abandoning your responsibility for self-preservation, and this can be seriously self-destructive.

People who are passive compliant are not able to say "no." They literally believe they either belong to others, or do not have the right to say "no." As a result they are chronically dishonest, both with themselves and with others, and routinely say yes when they really mean no. There is an old joke about the passive-compliant: Question: "What happens when a passive-compliant meets an egocentric-controller?" Answer: "They get married." The tragic reality is that the passive-compliant usually does not realize they are in an abusive or destructive relationship until it is too late, if ever.

Furthermore, people who cannot say "no" are not just willfully ignorant and immature. They also enable inappropriate, evil behavior through fear, and often combine passive compliance with denial, and refuse to recognize destructive behavior, or confront it. We all have the responsibility to grow up into mature adults, and set boundaries to preserve a healthy life. We must learn to value the importance of distancing ourselves from or letting go of people who cannot, or will not, love and respect our "no."

People who attempt to badger and manipulate you out of your "no" boundary, are acting as if something is being done "to them" when in reality something is not being done "for them." For a small child, running up against a "no" boundary is very painful, but no one is actually hurting them. They are simply being prevented from doing something they believe they are entitled to do. Adult children respond in this same way.

Mature adults with good boundaries use the word "no" as easily and as automatically as they use the word "yes" without guilt, animosity, or second thoughts. They are as gracious and accepting of the boundaries of others as they are in the way they set boundaries for themselves. Without them, relationships cannot work, and no one can be at ease, happy, or healthy.

Setting boundaries can be as easy as politely saying "Thank you, but I'm not up to it just now. Maybe some other time" or "I'd rather not, thank you" or "It's best for me that I pass on this one" or "I'm afraid I'll have to say no" or "I'm sorry, I just can't do that for you" or "I'd rather not talk about this right now."

If you are up against a major offender who will not accept your gracious "no" and insists on being intrusive, attacking, judgmental, or argues against your boundary, you may have to beef it up a bit by saying "Just so you know, my private affairs are off limits" or "If you won't get off the subject, I'll have to leave" or if you are on the phone with them, you can say, "I'll give you ten seconds to change the subject, or I'll have to hang up and talk to you another time."

Immature people will likely call you crazy or worse, but do it anyway. Boundaries can actually be enjoyable, and can even make you closer through your mutual respect for their importance. I find that using the phrase, "It's best for me…" preceding a boundary is very effective, because who can argue with what is best for you without being seen as extremely selfish?

A good strong system of healthy internal and external boundaries is the only way we can keep ourselves safe from harm, and become mature, happy, functioning, adults capable of loving, intimate relationships. Boundaries protect us from people who are rude, intrusive, manipulative, deceitful, controlling, and judgmental. They protect us from those who use lies, guilt, coercion, and emotional blackmail to control and use others to meet their selfish needs and covert agendas. Learn to recognize these destructive, exploitive behaviors and say "no" to them. Stay away from people who are accustomed to these destructive behaviors, and allow them to go their own way. They have every right to be who they are, and you have every right to protect yourself from them.

Give your adult relationships the litmus test of boundaries so you can weed out immature, destructive people from your life. They may even reject you, and save you the work of defending your boundary. Become a liver of the way of boundaries, and you will attract healthier, like-minded people who can contribute to your life in a positive way, instead of taking away a piece of you, and leaving you less than you could be. Get with it! Get boundaries! And become aware of what to expect.

WHAT TO EXPECT
(Setting them means defending them)
The most immature, dysfunctional reaction to a boundary you are setting is going to be, "What do you mean? Are you crazy? Now you've really gone over the edge!" So count on it! You are going to be scorned, jeered, laughed at, ignored, judged, labeled, and in the worst cases, the unhealthiest family members will attack you and call you crazy. You will hear all forms of guilt trips and personal insults, and may even be viciously rejected altogether.

You will become the hot topic of discussion as your dysfunctional family members get together and share their willful ignorance, while you are being resented and even condemned.

There will even be some family members who will approach you under the pretense of "genuine concern" about your mental and spiritual wellbeing. They may even believe they are being sincere, all the while behaving inappropriately condescending. If you have any religious family members, the Bible may be quoted in a warped and self-serving fashion in an attempt to manipulate you into relinquishing your new and healthier position. Every form of manipulation will be tried, so expect your dysfunctional family members, and even some of your friends, to pull out all the stops, and become your self-appointed travel agents for guilt trips. But hold tight! Don't pack your bags! Defend and maintain your needed boundaries!

The reason for this reaction is simple. Lack of boundaries is a hallmark of the average dysfunctional family system, and the idea of limits being imposed that force people to control themselves in your presence, when they are used to being freewheeling and behaving as they please, is going to cause a lot of anger. Immature people do not want to grow up as a rule, and will only do so kicking and screaming, if at all.

Their becoming personally responsible for their choices, actions, and behaviors no matter what, is an idea that requires an entire reorganization of their internal belief system, and the values they built their lives on. Setting healthy boundaries requires honest self-examination, and a lot of work that can be very uncomfortable and sometimes painful.

When you apply healthy standards to unhealthy people, it is going to hurt, like fitting them with new shoes that need breaking in. They are not going to want to cooperate, and are going to feel and act like victims. The guilt trips they lay on you will be proof of this. In addition to judging you and calling you names, the worst of them will likely condemn your new boundaries and healthier values, and call it all "bullshit"... or some like remark.

This is where the rule "you do not need to explain your boundary" comes in handy. There is no arguing with this type of reaction, nor should there be. You simply cannot make sense out of the non-sense of others. They are going to think what they need to think for their own reasons, so let them. Allow them the discomfort of their negative thoughts about you and the situation, and maintain your boundaries and healthier values anyway. Their discomfort is their problem! They are simply experiencing the natural consequences of their inappropriate behaviors.

There is another deeper reason for the inevitable resistance and unpleasantness you are sure to encounter. When family members educate themselves and attempt to apply what they learn about self-care by setting limits, it threatens the unconscious psychological core of a family system that has perpetuated and cooperated in dysfunctional behaviors that have so far gone unchecked. When one family member changes, and stops playing the family games by family rules, it causes an imbalance in the dynamics of the way things operate, and shakes up the entire structure.

When your family is unsuccessful in manipulating you out of your new position, and cannot coerce, shame, or guilt you back into the old one, they will become angry and defensive. You are betraying the family code, disrupting the order of things, and exposing what could be called an "unconscious conspiracy of denial" about how unhealthy and disordered the family really is. No one in the family is going to want to look at this disorder and the evil it enables, and no one is going to like you for forcing them to look at themselves by changing the way you relate to them.

The dysfunctional family is like a rusty, rigid, mobile. I call this the "immobile mobile." When one piece of the mobile oils up, breaks loose, and changes position, the rest of the mobile becomes strained and creaky, and is eventually forced into changing positions relative to each other, in an attempt to maintain some kind of new and awkward balance.

They creak and they squeak, and they jerk about in unwieldy ways. This causes a ripple effect of discomfort, anger, and even rage, because this change was imposed upon them, and is not a choice they are ever likely to make. Dysfunction does not like to change. It prefers the familiarity of sameness and predictability. Everyone is accustomed to adapting to what they are used to adapting to, they identify with their roles, and they are wedded to the status quo.

Furthermore, when someone can predict how you will act or react, they feel they have some power over you. When you begin to set boundaries and limits to protect yourself, and stop participating in what you recognize as unhealthy behavior, you are no longer predictable to them, and therefore no longer easy for them to manipulate or control in a shared role. They may even say they do not know you anymore, when the truth is they never did.

By honestly defining yourself by your boundaries when before you had none, they feel you have "changed" and that you have a lot of nerve! How dare you change! Well, guess what. All of these reactions are a positive sign that you are on the right track. Consider the source, and shout "Bravo!" Pop open the Champagne, and celebrate these reactions as a mark of your own success! This is not debasing the disordered individuals in your dysfunctional family. It is acknowledging the fact that you have made an important step in your own recovery, and are rightfully celebrating your progress.

When you maintained your healthier position long enough, the family dynamics will change, and the system will have a glitch. If you are not rejected, you will surely be a source of irritation and discomfort, and probably will no longer be very well received. Sooner or later, the family is going to have to stop challenging you by attacking you, and will no longer see your behavior as a temporary aberration.

The ones who truly love you may come around to a point, and tolerate your boundaries with subdued grumblings and suppressed judgments. The more selfish ones are likely to judge you openly, are not going to be at all interested in respecting your autonomy, and will maintain, and even dig in deeper into their willfully ignorant judgments. They will consider you an irredeemable traitor and will back away from you, or push you out. They will not want to – be able to – be with you anymore. They will no longer get to share your time and space. Consider it a blessing. Again, let them think what they need to, and go their own way. Remember, what others think of you is none of your business.

These are all possible scenarios. Depending on how enmeshed or central a player you have been in your dysfunctional family system, your pulling out of the game quietly and solidly might have the effect of changing the way the family interrelates. Exposing the lie that the family system is based on (that there is nothing wrong with the way things are) may only change things to a point. However, once lies are placed into the floodlights of truth through the use of boundaries, where are they going to hide now? When the truth is out there, even if no one wants to look at it, it's out there! It is no longer an X-file.

It is important to understand that all this "re-activeness" toward your sudden honesty and boundaries setting is going to be natural, and more importantly, unconscious. You will be threatening the way in which your dysfunctional family views their lives, their relationships, and even their entire reality. This can be terrifying to them, and in truth, can constitute a very real threat of unconscious psychological annihilation.

In the final analysis, it is perceived this way because a radical shift in their current view of themselves feels like the death of their identified "self." This death naturally precedes the birth of a new and healthier self, but your family will not consciously perceive this as being spiritually desirable, and will only perceive this as an enormous threat.

This accounts for their attack response. When an animal, any animal, feels cornered, it will naturally and automatically attack as a primal survival response. One thing is for certain in this scenario: when it comes to their psychological survival, they are not going to care about you, or the fact that you are trying to do what is best for yourself. They're only going to care about themselves.

Try to have compassion and patience, and allow them the discomfort of your boundaries, but never allow anyone to be abusive. Remember, it is their responsibility to grow up and learn self-control, and not your responsibility to fix them. So hold your position, maintain your boundaries, and see what happens. You may need to create some distance from some of your family for a while, a few years, or maybe even permanently. Wait and see, and let the chips fall where they may! "Nothing splendid has ever been achieved except by those who dared believe that something inside them was superior to circumstance" – Bruce Barton (1886 – 1967). Rise above the circumstances of your family dysfunction, and be true to yourself.

You cannot expect other people to behave appropriately and honor your boundaries without being willing to do the same. When you make an agreement with someone about a limit you need, you must try to stay within that limit yourself, and maintain it. "To accomplish great things we must not only act, but dream. Not only plan, but also believe." – Anatole France (1844 – 1924). We must act as though we believe that the dream of a better, healthier self can emerge from what we are now, and that there is a way to achieve this goal. Dream of a better life, educate yourself about what is healthy and what is not, take action by applying what you learn, and things can only get better.

PREPARE FOR THE STORM
(Avoiding lightning bolts, earthquakes, firestorms, and tornados)
When you begin setting boundaries against family dysfunction, you will need to prepare for a perfect storm of collective descent, and stock your storm-shelter with some appropriate boundary statements that defend these new limits, to keep you safe. There are a great many forms of dysfunction to become aware of, but they can all be limited either by setting verbal or written boundaries, or when these fail, by removing yourself from the game.

When you've grown up in a severely dysfunctional family, taking charge of your health and standing up to them with boundaries will seem terrifying at first. You may feel like a gazelle in a lion's den, and it can be awfully difficult to protect yourself from getting bit or eaten alive. Remember, zoos keep the gazelles and lions separated for good reason.

121

The first boundaries you set will serve as a way to expose who is healthy enough to respect them, and who is not. This is the only way to find out whom you can be in contact with, and whom you need to distance yourself from. This is the most important step on the path to healing, because eliminating unnecessary stress is crucial to healing, physically or mentally, and you cannot become healthier without doing this first.

The sooner you stop enabling and/or participating in dysfunctional behavior, the better. Such behavior may consist of circular conversations, triangulation, intrusiveness, dumping, blaming, attacking, judging, emotional blackmail and manipulation, and most destructive: lies and deceit. Learn to recognize these behaviors, and set internal and external boundaries against them.

It is essential that you prepare yourself for the possibility of the perfect storm that is likely to come your way. The best way to stock your storm shelter with boundary statements is by anticipating some of some various forms of resistance that occur within dysfunctional families. One is the circular conversation. This is like being sucked up into the vortex of a tornado, and being spun around until you say, "Okay, Okay, I give in!" But do not give in. Do not even get close enough to be sucked up in the first place. As soon as you see a tornado forming in the clouds, head for cover, and set limits. Remember, the most important battles in our lives are often fought alone.

CIRCULAR CONVERSATIONS
Circular conversations are full of "mind" fields and booby traps, ready to explode or trap you at every turn. These hazards are automatically set into place instinctively and habitually by the people who live by them. This peril can appear at the very first boundary you set. Say you want to stop commiserating and/or gossiping about a family member's bad behavior, and have decided to stop.

The circular conversation can look like this:
Boundary setter: "Well, I've decided not to talk about this person anymore."
Reaction: "What do you mean, we've always talked about them before."

Boundary setter: "I know, but I have decided to stop."
Reaction: "Why? What has changed all of a sudden?"
Boundary setter: "Nothing, really, I've just been thinking, and have changed my mind about a few things, that's all".
Reaction: "Thinking, huh? That's interesting. What prompted this?"
Boundary setter: "I'm working on becoming healthier, and I am making some changes."
Reaction: "Healthier? Are you saying the things we used to talk about aren't healthy now? Who died and made you judge and jury?"
Boundary setter: "No, no, I don't mean to judge anybody. I'm just thinking about what's appropriate and what's best for me."
Reaction: "So, then what's okay for me isn't good enough for you now? I can't believe what I'm hearing. Who do you think you are? It sounds to me like you've really gone over the edge!"

This is the type of reaction to expect from the most immature and dysfunctional members of your family who will naturally be the most threatened by your new position. A way to avoid getting caught in these kinds of "mind" fields and booby traps (questions that are meant to get more information/ammo to argue, judge, and attack you with) might be to simply say, "Truth is, I'd rather not discuss it" and stand by this boundary, and do not reveal any more information.

The more hostile their reaction, the deeper their unconscious denial about the family illness is. Respect their right to be who they are. It is not your job to try to educate them. It is not even appropriate. Your only job is to protect yourself and your right to keep yourself safe from destructive, dysfunctional people.

If you choose to take part in a circular conversation, it can escalate into a very dangerous argument that can last for hours and even days. I experienced this phenomenon when I tried to save a relationship that I needed to let go of, to no avail. If you find yourself sucked into one of these arguments, pull out as soon as you recognize it. That would look something like this: "OK, we're going around in circles here, and I'm not going to do this anymore. I'll talk to you some other time." Then walk away, or hang up the phone if you are on the phone. If they call back out of anger and you answer, your final boundary can then be, "I'm hanging up now, goodbye," and do not answer the phone again, and allow them to leave a message.

Only people who are completely out of control will leave a scathing message on a recording. If they do, then you know you are dealing with a major offender, and you need to get some distance between yourself and this person. If you are face to face, and not on the phone, it can then be, "I'm sorry, but I have no choice but to leave. Please stop talking to me." Then get up and leave, and do not respond to them at all. If they follow you and heckle you, just keep your feet moving, and get out of there.

Once my mother wanted me to lie to her guests at one of her parties about a scholarship I won to a two-week vocal training program in Italy that had been cancelled due to a flood. She was going around telling everyone about it as though it were still on, to make herself look good, and tag me as an extension of herself. She expected me to lie and give details if anyone asked. I was so humiliated I left the party, and told her if she ever asked me to lie to good people again, I'd tell the truth instead. She was so outraged, when I got home there was a scathing message on my answering machine that said, "You're nothing but an ungrateful bitch, and I don't want to lay eyes on you for a long, long time!"

My boyfriend, now husband, was there when I played the message, and said in horror, "Who on earth was THAT?" I said with great embarrassment, "That was my mother." He said, "My God, who has a mother like that? That's horrible!" It was his introduction to my true, narcissistic mother without her charming mask of sanity. The next day she called back and left a message sounding like a little girl who accidentally stepped in a mud-puddle saying, "Hi Val, it's momma. I didn't mean what I said before. I love you." Oh dear me, I had so much to learn about how to set a boundary of distance and time with major offenders who chronically exacted their psychological abuse on me. But I learned.

TRIANGULATION
Another dysfunctional game is triangulation. This means two people are talking about a third person that is not there. First of all, it is inappropriate to say anything critical about someone else that you are not prepared to say to their face. It is not a good

habit to do this anyway, because what you say usually gets back to the other person, and is not always represented accurately.

To bow out of a conversation that is beginning to triangulate, you can simply say, "I'm sorry, but I'd rather not talk about that person behind their back. Let's change the subject." Then bring up another topic, and steer the conversation in another direction. It can be as simple as and gracious as that. There is no need to be hostile or confrontational. Just set the limit and move on. No big deal.

INTRUSIVENESS
Intrusiveness is a major hallmark of disordered, entitled behavior and a red flag for a total lack of boundaries. Someone is being intrusive when they are prying into your private business, your personal life, your reasons for doing things, giving unsolicited advice, or simply showing up when they feel like it and expecting you to make time for them. If this is happening, quickly stop it.

When you set a boundary against intrusive people, they are likely to feel like a victim because they believe you are taking away something they are entitled to. When you say, "Yah know, I don't appreciate your prying in my personal business when it is none of your concern," they are likely to say, "Well, it does concern me, and I'm making it my business!" These people major offenders, and you need to set a strong boundary against them right away.

To set a boundary against a major offender, you need to be short, clear, offer no explanation, and ready to exit. Do not stick around for the games to begin. If you have to explain something like an appropriate boundary in the first place, you are wasting your time. Pulling out of a dysfunction family system means you are choosing to no longer waste your valuable time and vital life-force energy playing destructive games, guarding yourself against the insanity of others, or enabling them. Being insulting, offensive, or sarcastic when you set a boundary is also not appropriate.

DUMPING
Dumping is another big problem with lack of boundaries. If someone is spending all their time with you sharing their problems and talking about themselves, without demonstrating some

restraint, moderation, or personal responsibility, or taking into consideration your time and energy, then you need to set some limits. It is one thing to be there for someone who needs some occasional support, but not when it's at your expense. A boundary against dumping can look like, "It's best for me that you not lean on me." So be kind and respectful, but do not hesitate to set a boundary against dumping, and do not allow anyone to lean on you all the time.

BLAMING AND JUDGING

There will be times when you are setting a boundary, and to your amazement you will be blamed and judged. Blaming is a tactic that diverts responsibility away from the offender, and judging is a tactic that focuses the attention on you. It is a senseless game that goes nowhere and accomplishes nothing. When you are the one initiating a change in a dysfunctional relationship, the brunt of the backlash is going to fall on you, and you'll be called unfair, or even crazy, for causing discomfort.

Furthermore, explaining a boundary only invites more blame and judgment. Once the blaming-finger begins to point and wag, the blame can ripple as far back to as many generations as you can dig up. It is a fact that family illnesses are unconsciously passed down through behavioral conditioning and DNA.

MANIPULATION, LIES, AND DECEIT
(Evil: a destructive force)
The last scenario is the toxic, destructive, and abusive behavior of manipulation, lies, and deceit. This is the insidious form of dysfunction that can be extremely violent psychologically, and causes serious deterioration within any relationship that it appears in. This form of behavior can be invisible, and frequently goes on behind the scenes because it is covert and calculated. It can be shrewdly covered up by a charade of good intentions, and is usually perpetrated with no other witnesses aside from the person being abused. Often the person that is being manipulated and deceived does not realize it consciously, but there can be a feeling that something is not right.

When someone is chronically abused in this way, they can lose their ability to recognize this kind of treatment as abusive, and

126

become conditioned to accepting manipulation, and habitually excuse it. Unconsciously, this is very toxic, and consciously very disabling. The effects of frequent manipulation can paralyze a person, and render them unable to protect themselves against evil in other forms. The dishonesty and lack of moral integrity inherent in manipulation, and in all those who enable it, erodes any chance of intimacy and love because this behavior is so disturbing.

Ultimately, this behavior destroys love, and that which destroys is evil. When people use manipulation, lies, and deceit to coerce you into doing something you would not do if you knew the truth, they probably sound a little like an Amway salesman who tries to recruit under-salespeople. They will not give you a straight answer when you come right out and ask them for one about what they represent. When you try to find out more, each structured answer seems a little more slanted than the one before, until pretty soon the entire structure begins to look like the leaning tower of Pisa. When you have to tilt your head sideways to look at something, it is probably not upright.

I am not trying to say Amway people are liars either. The business world calls them capitalists. I am simply saying that in personal relationships, manipulative people are extremely dangerous to the soul, and need to be avoided. There is usually no boundary to protect yourself from evil that works, other than physical distance.

Note: The hypothetical examples of dysfunctional behavior I have been discussing are common, and I have personally experienced them all. I use them because I feel they are patterns that disordered people so often fall into. I do not use examples of physical abuse because its marks are obvious, and should never be tolerated under any circumstances. I have experienced both kinds of abuse, and know first hand that both psychological and physical abuse can be equally devastating. These wounds are those of a shattered heart, a broken mind, and a shredded soul.

If you are being mistreated in any way, you must learn to protect yourself from further harm by using boundaries. A good therapist will help you and get you the protection you need. Do it! Do it now!

Journey To The Garden

I grew up in a vast wasteland of despair that bordered on a
great abyss; I felt alone and afraid. I had only one hand to
hold on to. It was the hand of my brother.
One day he was killed, and I began to wander.
Lost and empty, and during a dark and turbulent storm,
I tumbled, abandoned, into the great abyss.
After many years in darkness, a light began to dimly flicker.
I looked down and saw my own path,
and I knew the light was coming from within me.
I looked back and saw the face of evil,
and decided to go my own way.
With all I had, I slowly climbed the jagged edge,
and never looked back again.
I did not lose heart, but began to lose hope.
As I reached the top, I could feel my brother's love,
and when I reached out my hand, it was met by another.
This hand began leading me on what would become
a long journey through an arid and treacherous wasteland,
toward a beautiful garden. Such a place as I had never seen.
Along the way my light began to sparkle and glow, and as I
grew nearer, I saw farther and more clearly than ever before.
My heart began to fill with hope, and my soul began to sing.
I knew this wondrous garden was where I truly belonged,
and I believe it was my brother who led me there.
And now, as I enter the garden, I want to sing with joy and
gratitude, and touch the hearts of all who hear my song.
I want to climb to the treetops, and watch the eagles soar.
I want to hear the earth-music in the wind, and be
a part of the miracle of creating heaven on earth.
It is a lot to ask, but I pray each day this dream will become
the truth, and what was true before will become a dream.
I pray to become strong enough to be the person I am
meant to be, fulfilling a long-awaited destiny.

Valerie Lumley

SIX

YOUR OVERLY ADAPTED INNER CHILD
The force that runs your life

Within the human mind there exists three basic modalities of the human ego: the "adult," the "parent," and the "child." These three modes exist together, while at the same time they alternate in their predominance, depending on circumstances and what is appropriate at the time. Even though a person can choose to activate any of these three modes at any time, in a mature person, the "adult" ego is nearly always in charge. Ideally, the chosen mode, and the appropriate time to activate it, is natural and instinctive. I believe this choice is inherent in the ubiquitous nature of the human being in that we can choose to transform ourselves from one minute to the next through spontaneous choice.

When we are at work, our adult ego is not only in charge, it is predominant. When we are interacting in a relationship with our kids, we are first and always in adult mode, but can simultaneously choose to activate our child ego in times of play and festivities, or our parent ego when it is time to guide and instruct. How freely we are able to activate, move within, and function between one mode to the next depends on how healthy our parents were, and how well we were nurtured and guided during the development of the ego as a whole throughout our formative years.

In a book by Muriel James & Dorothy Jongeward called, *"Born to Win,"* which I highly recommend, they discuss the human ego in depth as it relates to Transactional Analysis (TA) and Gestalt experiments, developed by Fritz Perls (1893 -1970). To paraphrase a small portion of these discussions, in combination with my own knowledge and observations, I would like to establish the need for a balanced and functional ego to aid in the process of becoming healthier. I believe that fortifying and/or reconstructing a functional ego system is vital to our potential for inner peace. I also believe this is a lifelong, ever evolving process, and is both monitored and nurtured by conscious choice.

When developing children suffer the transgressions of a severely dysfunctional family, one or more of these ego modalities can become deformed, or overly adapted due to an unnatural environment of abuse and neglect, in an effort to survive emotionally and psychologically. When these children grow into adults, and cannot readily make decisions for themselves, cannot take personal responsibility for their behavior and choices, or suffer from neuroses or psychoses, this means they are overly adapted (or maladapted) in one or more of the three basic ego-modalities. When the ego system is out of balance, one or more negative adaptations may be controlling your life. The right therapist and guided education together can help you learn to create a healthy, balanced and functionality within the three ego-modes.

THREE MODES OF THE HUMAN EGO
(The adult, the parent, and the child)
1) THE ADULT EGO (The grand supervisor)
The adult ego is the grand supervisor that works at gathering and processing data. Unless the brain is severely damaged or disordered, everyone is capable of using these abilities to gather technical and operational information to store it for future reference, to evaluate external and internal stimuli, and to reason.

The adult ego enables a person to be highly selective in choosing their responses in order to function and survive independently. The appropriate use of the adult ego can be assessed in ego structure analysis to observe the difference between maturity and immaturity.

Eric Berne said, "The adult ego is an independent set of feelings, attitudes, and behavioral patterns adapted to current reality, and are not affected by parental prejudices or archaic attitudes left over from childhood. The adult ego makes survival possible." Keeping the adult in control is making a conscious choice to direct your psychic energy in such a way so you can easily shift from one ego-mode to another when appropriate, based on the circumstances in your current reality.

Choosing to put the adult ego in charge of your life gives it executive control over the others. People are emancipated and able to make autonomous decisions only when they are freed from negative and irrelevant influences of the parent and child egos. Without the adult ego acting as executive controller over the parent and child, outside stimuli are more likely felt and responded to by the parent and/or child, instead of the adult.

Instead of reacting with a kneejerk response from the parent or child, the adult stops to think about what is being seen, heard, and felt, assumes responsibility for subsequent thoughts, behavior, and actions, and then determines which possible response from which ego-mode is appropriate. A person's executive adult ego can opt to tune into the impulses of their parent and child egos, and decide what is okay and what is not, and can either agree with or reject either impulse, depending on what the adult decides the situation calls for.

The adult ego deals with reality objectively. Activating and strengthening the adult ego is like activating and strengthening a muscle. The more you use it and exercise it, the stronger it gets. Almost everyone has the potential to do this, even if they don't know it. The adult ego is influenced by environment, education, and experience, and is not related to age per se, yet there are many older adults who do not even realize it exists. Just because a person looks like a grown up adult, does not mean that their adult ego is in charge.

When people activate their adult ego, they are able to collect and organize information, and make the kinds of conscious decisions that can help to minimize regrettable behavior, and increase their potential for success. When their parent and child egos are causing inner conflicts that interfere with the decision making process, the adult ego can intervene to find solutions and compromises. The adult can outright reject the parent when it is clearly being overly critical, punishing, cruel, or brutally withholding affection. It can comfort and educate the child ego, when it is viewing life through the lens of a former childhood trauma, to prevent the child ego from contaminating present reality through old prejudicial belief systems, fears, delusions, and childhood adaptations.

Giving the adult executive power over the parent and child ego allow the expression of the other ego modes so that they can contribute to the whole of the personality. This can help guide you through life much more intelligently and creatively with fewer painful outcomes. With the adult supervising and allowing the positive qualities of the child to emerge and express itself, while subduing the harmful effects of a critical parent, the creative and functional self can experience a liberating sense of fulfillment.

When the parent and child egos are allowed to run amok and control your every response and decision, your own children will become disordered, and life can be a painful, unfulfilling, and lonely journey, even when people are around you. Einstein said in his remarks on good and evil, "The true value of a human being is determined primarily by the measure and the sense in which he has attained liberation from the self." The liberator is the executive adult ego.

2) THE PARENT EGO
(The script inside your head)
The parent ego is the internal script that was written by your parents (the spoken dialogue on the circulating tapes that play inside your head). This script contains the examples set in their parenting methods, and the behavioral and relationship role models that were portrayed by your parents during your formative years and beyond. Be it warm or cold, mild or harsh, safe or terrifying, the atmosphere your parents created in your home determined the development of either a constructive, encouraging script, or a destructive, discouraging one. The most responsible thing any parent can do is apply a healthy yardstick to their own internal script, and decide if it merits passing on to their children. If not, erase it, and start from scratch with a clean slate.

Widely accepted studies show that, like other primates, humans learn how to be parents from their parents, and not from innate instinct. It is up to us to choose how we want to teach our children to be parents, determining how they will consequently, eventually treat us. Evaluating your parent ego is the best place to start, whether you are parenting your children or re-parenting yourself. The interesting thing about your own parental script is that because your script was written by your parents, and because people automatically tend to raise their children the way they were raised, the parental script inside your head is most likely that of your grandparents. This is why you may have noticed that the behavior of one of your parents may resemble their parents.

TA, as it was used in Gestalt therapy is not new. It is the study of the origin of what people do and say to themselves in their relations with the world. In TA, we see that the internal messages from our parent ego are heard most frequently by our child ego. Sometimes our adult ego hears what our parent is saying to our child, but most of the time the dialogue is occurring between our parent and child exclusively. It is up to you to activate your adult during these exchanges to evaluate whether the messages from your parent are predisposed to being nurturing or prejudicial.

It is also important to become aware of the types of daily inner conflicts you may be suffering from. It may be the tyranny of a domineering parent ego over an oppressed, inhibited child ego, who then cannot express its joy and creativity. The adult ego must intervene, correct the errors, and give truth to the lies from the negative parent. This is the process of the adult ego re-writing the script on the internal tapes, and is one of the most important tasks your adult can undergo for you. Practice makes perfect. You must work at correcting this script daily, hour to hour, and eventually a new, healthier, nurturing parent ego of choice will develop. This process is called re-parenting the negative parent.

REPARENTING THE NEGATIVE PARENT EGO

Rewriting the script of your parent ego may be the single most liberating thing your adult ego can do for you. Because parents that come from dysfunctional families usually make sorely inadequate parents themselves, there is usually not much they can offer the developing parent ego of their children that is useful. Most of it is self-defeating, and should be discarded altogether. Working to turn off these negative tapes through counseling is one option, but a more effective way to neutralize the debilitating effects of a negative inner parent is to restructure it.

The way to do this is to first recognize the negative characteristics that have been incorporated into your parent ego. These may have come from parents who meant well, but behaved in destructive ways such as; being extremely punitive, protective, nurturing, needy, sweet (false), fearful (neurotic), contradictory, used inconsistent or no boundaries, were obsessed with or uninvolved with their children, or self-involved and neglectful.

Secondly, read and educate yourself about what a healthy, nurturing parent is like with the guidance of a good counselor, and also look for and observe healthy role models wherever you can find them. There are plenty of healthy and relatively well-balanced parental figures out there to model yourself after. Serious personality disorders, such as those in my family, are the exception, not the rule.

Thirdly, engage in a considerable amount of nurturing inner dialogue between your adult and child egos, and determine what particular unmet needs your inner child still has. The adult ego uses this information to act as a substitute parent ego, and eventually this new parenting over the child restructures the old negative parent ego.

The result is that the negative characteristics of the old parent ego become balanced by a more positive new one, and a healthier, more appropriate parent will emerge. Even though our nervous system originally incorporated into our personality many of the unwanted, negative aspects of our defective caregivers during our childhood, we have the ability to upgrade our script through the power of choice. We can begin to see our own parents more clearly, and understand the inner conflicts they most likely experienced between their own parent and child egos. We can then perhaps forgive them their transgressions and inadequacies from a standpoint of them being merely a product of their own upbringing: whether or not it is healthy to have contact with them in our current reality.

3) THE CHILD EGO
(The most fascinating and complex)
The child ego is the most fascinating of all because it is the only ego modality that actually has four aspects. The first three are given to us in TA. These three are called the natural child, the little professor, and the adapted child. Theoretically, it is here in the child ego that the way we experienced impulses from outside stimuli as a child are permanently etched into our brain and nervous system. While it is in the parent ego that we incorporated

134

the personality traits of our emotionally significant authority figures in our childhood, it is in the child ego that we store the inner world of our experiences, how we feel about them, and our adaptations to them, be they healthy or maladaptive.

When people respond to outside stimuli in the same way a child would, such as being curious, manipulative, inquisitive, playful, affectionate, selfish, mean, and deceitful, they are responding from their child ego. Some people, such as those with a personality disorder like the narcissist or the borderline, respond almost exclusively from their child ego. Healthier, more mature people move in and out of their child ego naturally in appropriate ways, depending on the situation and surrounding circumstances.

Inherited genetic characteristics and environmental factors that influence the development of each child produce children who are each unique, even when they are siblings from the same parents. Additionally, when a mother or father identifies with one child more than another, they often project themselves onto that child in an effort to mold the child into the mother or father's own image. These various influences directly deform the natural development of the child's individual identity, and create multiple factors that influence and distinguish the personality of one sibling from another. The result is that even when children grow up in the same household, no two children experience the same childhood, or the same parents. These various influences are also instrumental in the formation of the four aspects of the child ego.

Note: When one sibling insists that their childhood experiences were identical to those of their siblings, they are being narcissistic.

FOUR ASPECTS OF THE CHILD EGO
1) THE NATURAL CHILD
The first aspect of the child ego is the natural child, the youngest and most infantile. The natural child is expressed as the impulsive and unrestrained infant inside each of us that responds to outside stimuli as an infant would; with cold, angry outbursts when its needs are not met, or with affection and love when they are. When an adult responds with uncontrolled angrer when they are being crossed or cannot get what they want, they are being their most infantile and immature.

The natural child is as uncensored, sensuous, curious, affectionate, and impulsive as a baby when they are being their most charming. On the other hand, it is as self-centered, willful, aggressive, rebellious, obnoxious, self-indulgent, and fearful when it is being not so charming. The survival of a child often depends on the use of these traits, or they would perish. Later on in adulthood, the natural child can be manifested in many roles, such as the tyrannical employer, the intrusive relative who feels entitled to special treatment, and the most dreaded parent of all: the parent who chronically responds to every crises or stress from their natural child, and routinely batters their children spiritually, psychologically, emotionally and even physically with their infantile selfishness, immaturity, and uncontrolled aggression.

2) THE LITTLE PROFESSOR
The second aspect of the child ego is called the little professor and is expressed in the form of our natural unschooled wisdom. The little professor consists of our innate intuition that instinctively reads and responds to nonverbal messages and hunches. It is intuitive, creative, and manipulative, and all babies use these abilities to figure out how to get what they want; knowing when to cry, when to be quiet, and when to smile. Like the natural child, the little professor is also a necessary part of every infant and child's ability to survive, and is able to intuit what is going on around them with no training in human behavior at all.

Through their little professor, a child receives the nonverbal messages of approval and disapproval from their primary caregivers, and figures out the best way to respond to them in any given situation. The little professor also has the ability to create something new and original without guilt or fear, and during adulthood, it can express that creativity in purposeful ways when used in tandem with the adult ego. Also in adulthood, the little professor is still active in discerning how to interpret what is going on around them, and along with the adult, can make wise choices and solve problems. When the data gathering and analytical aptitude of the adult ego, teams up with the imagination, intuition, and creativity of the little professor, a moment of genius can occur.

3) THE ADAPTED CHILD

The third aspect of the child ego is called the adapted child. The adapted child modifies the impulses and inclinations of the natural child, and creates what are expressed as behavioral adaptations. Every sort of adaptive behavioral impulses from the natural child that was created by the adapted child is a direct response to training, experiences, traumas, and most significantly, the demands of the strongest authority figure throughout a child's formative years. A great many of these behavioral adaptations are positive to the natural development of a child as they grow, and are healthy to carry into adulthood. Examples are: learning to sense the difference between right and wrong, which is not knowledge we are born with, or when their actions are hurting or harming someone.

These are positive adaptations that make it possible for a child to fit into the changing world around them, and function in a strong, safe, and productive way throughout their life, while at the same time being considerate to others. However, there are also many negative behavioral adaptations that are not appropriate that only serve to diminish the potential of a person's life, and can possibly destroy it if they are carried into adulthood and used as primary coping mechanisms. These negative behavioral adaptations are what I call the overly adapted child.

4) THE OVERLY ADAPTED (MALADAPTED) CHILD
(The force that runs your life)

The fourth aspect of the child ego is what I call the overly adapted (maladapted) child. Influenced primarily by parental authority, some children experience negative over-conditioning and training that is oppressive, destructive, and crippling. When a parent is extremely abusive, the adaptations formed in the child to cope with the demands of surviving these conditions become so excessive they cause severe dysfunction in their personality as a grown adult.

These children often exhibit a profoundly unnatural inability to connect with or express their true feelings, respond appropriately to abuse, make friends easily, be curious about the world, clearly process the events of their outside reality, or allow themselves to give or receive affection in healthy ways.

Instead of learning to be their authentic selves with their individual identity intact, they disconnect from their self, and are unable to relate to others in social ways that can fill their own needs. They develop irrational psychological patterns, such as automatically complying without question, justifying and excusing the evil in abuse, withdrawing when there is no need, holding onto unhealthy positions even when they are presented with healthy alternatives, and procrastinating when they need to be responsible.

These children lack any motivation to battle for a saner position that is based on their own ideas and identity, because these had to be sacrificed to adapt to the demands of life with a psychologically abusive parent. They become adults who literally do not have their own ideas, or any sense of their own identity. They unknowingly exhibit three common patterns throughout their lives.

THREE PATTERNS OF THE OVERLY ADAPTED CHILD
1) COMPLIANCE
(The proverbial doormat)
The first pattern of the overly adapted child ego is compliance. Parents who are overbearing and domineering rob their children of developing in natural ways toward establishing their own sense of self (their individual identity). These parents give their children unconscious negative messages that read, "Do as I say, and not as I do" or "You're not good enough the way you are" or "If you do not comply, I will reject you," and make unreasonable and unrealistic demands of perfection on the child. These parents are overtly hypocritical, and hold their children to standards that they do not hold to themselves. For these children, this abuse can be extremely frustrating, confusing, and impossible to sort out or make sense of.

The stress of trying to cope with the insanity of these kinds of messages and demands become so intense for these children that the easiest and least painful thing for them to do is comply, stay out of the way, paste on a smile and pretend to be happy, and literally utter not one peep of defiance. Fighting for a more rational and sane position in an attempt to hold on to their sense of self may not to be an option to them.

Tragically, compliance becomes a habitual, unconscious survival mechanism that is often carried into adult life. Then, unless they experience a major eye-opening event in their adult life, and retain what they learn as a result of this event, they can live their entire lives not ever knowing who they really are. These are the tragic, overly adapted adults who enter into cults and/or radicalized religious groups, whose fanatic, cult-bubble mindset has become maladaptive and pervasive in their interpretation of their outside reality, and in many cases, for their entire lives.

2) WITHDRAWAL
(Escape into denial and fantasy)
A second pattern of the overly adapted child ego is emotional withdrawal. These children feel so overwhelmed and unable to cope with their toxic and dysfunctional external reality, they learn to withdraw into themselves, solitary activity, and hobbies as another form of self-protection. In extreme cases of emotional withdrawal, a child can retreat into an inner world of fantasy and denial (La-la land) to protect themselves from the extreme pain and conflict that exists outside them. It is easier to distort reality and pretend that their created world is a happier, safer place than it is, than engaging and confronting its injustices, abuses, ambiguities, and deficiencies. These children are often seen as being developmentally disabled, or obtuse because they are noticeably slow in perceiving, acknowledging, processing, and responding to outside stimuli.

As adults, these children often suffer from serious memory lapses of certain periods in their childhood, ranging from a few months to a few years, and in extreme cases they can even suppress a decade or more of their childhood memories. Innocent children do not have the mental facility to cope with an environment that is excessively cruel and stressful, and consequently they must adapt any way they can to survive and not go completely insane.

There are many possible environmental factors and forms of abuse that can cause a child to retreat into a fantasy world of denial of their reality, such as extreme poverty that produces hunger and freezing conditions, neglect, physical or psychological abuse, abandonment, and chronic crises and conflicts in the home. However, it is also unrealistic parental demands and expectations that cause the child to distort their reality and overly adapt in this way. To grow into healthy adults, children must be allowed to be children and express themselves within reasonable, consistent boundaries, and feel the safety that comes with it. When they make a natural misstep, they should not have to live in fear of rejection, extreme retributions, or disproportionate punishment beyond what is reasonable. Warranted consequences are not a justification for abuse!

3) PROCRASTINATION
(The passive-aggressive "no")
A third pattern of the overly adapted child is the behavior of procrastination. Procrastination is a solution to the intense inner conflict that occurs between the natural child who wants to rebel and say "no!" and the overly adapted child who is used to being compliant, and does not dare say "no." So, the intuitive little professor steps in and strikes a bargain between the two. The little professor decides to use procrastination as a passive-aggressive way to partly placate the authorities, while at the same time filling an inner wish to rebel and say "no."

Procrastination eventually can become a predominant way of reacting to and acting out the drama of life by stalling, not responding, and putting things off. This behavior can become a habitual part of the adult personality (maladaptive) that is being controlled and operated by their overly adapted child.

The overly adapted child is most likely the troubled part of a person's inner psychological life, whether it is conscious or unconscious. When a person with low self-esteem believes themselves to be "less than" in some way, this belief fuels the fires of their over adaptation. This can become a real personality handicap that can potentially take over and run that person's entire life.

Recovering from an over adaptation of one kind or another, usually requires the help of a good therapist in order to rediscover the positive impulses of the natural child, and recapture the ability to respond to life with honesty, spontaneity, laughter, and healthy love. Everyone has a child ego, and when we act, feel, and make decisions in the now the same way we did as children, we are experiencing our child ego being in charge in one form or another.

The freedom of our natural child enables us to be playful, curious, expressive, and joyful, or selfish, rebellious, and able to say "no" to stand up for ourselves. The natural wisdom and intuition of the little professor is activated when we experience moments of joyful creative genius, or manipulate someone to get what we want. It is the adapted child wherein we experience our social training and awareness, and possible feelings of low self-esteem. When we are experiencing the "less than" feelings of the three patterns of over adaptation - compliance, withdrawal, or procrastination - we are experiencing our overly adapted child.

When someone comes on like a parent, or when we are sick and dependent, our child ego is activated. Our adult then filters these impulses, and decides which to act on or ignore, depending on what is appropriate at the time. When the adult ego is in charge, our other ego modalities and aspects can express themselves freely with guidance and oversight, resulting in wiser choices, more effective responses and creative solutions, and appropriate feelings of self-esteem.

I believe with the help of a good therapist, the disabling effects of the overly adapted child can be healed. I also believe the problems of the overly adapted child in adulthood are based primarily on an unconscious, inappropriate choice: the choice to identify with something that you are not. When your identity is founded on a beliefs from negative "this or that" messages, such as, "I am stupid" or "I am not good enough," you are being driven by a false identification of self. In truth, you are the *conscious observer* (mind-consciousness) of your internal and external reality, responsible for choosing the internal experiences of your ego as a whole.

When you fully recognize yourself as consciousness, the unhealthy ego is removed, and you are freed from the master that has enslaved you thus far. You are free to be yourself as you truly are. Egoic attachments to an inappropriate, false identification of self become exactly the force that runs your life. Making choices from the standpoint of the conscious observer puts you in charge of how you assign meaning to all you experience in your outside reality, and can help detach you from old, ingrained response patterns. This prevents enslavement by the crippling mal-adaptations and false identifications of self that can control your life and keep you an illegitimate prisoner of an unhealthy ego.

Add to this equation the knowledge that our higher power is the collective consciousness that exists within every living thing as a guiding force. Then it follows that you, as a part of this collective consciousness, and you, as the individual conscious observer, can become "consciousness observing consciousness." This resolution can be nothing short of total freedom of the true self from the master of false ego identifications. This freedom will give you the power and will to make the choices you must make to put yourself on a healing path toward becoming a healthier version of your true self.

Within the struggle between the false self and the true self, the true self can prevail through the power of conscious choice. In the now, choose to identify yourself as consciousness, and become the conscious observer of your life and of your external and internal world. Observe what you are thinking while you are thinking it, and make choices from a place of freedom, and not slavery to false identifications of self – the overly adapted child – and wait and see what happens.

THREE COPING MECHANISMS OF THE OVERLY ADAPTED CHILD
(Roles associated with personality)
There are three main coping mechanisms (roles) of the overly adapted child that are common among dysfunctional family systems. These are the "over achiever" (often the oldest), the "rebel" (often the middle child), and the "good child" (often the youngest). These roles can shift between children in the family as the years go by according to significant changes within the family dynamics, such as a death of an immediate family member, a divorce between the biological parents, a child going off to college, or the rejection of one or more children by a biological parent (usually the rebel). However, the primary and most practiced role taken on by a child while growing up is often the role that they carry with them throughout their adulthood as maladaptive.

1) THE OVER ACHIEVER
(The "type A" personality)

The over achiever is often the oldest child who attempts to control reality and protect their sanity and sense of self from a harmful external environment by immersing themselves in the pursuit of achievements. Somewhere along the way, their intuitive little professor decides that focusing on a project, a job, a study, or a task, will insulate them emotionally from the painful whirlwind of dysfunction and crisis that is perpetually going on around them in a dysfunctional family.

These children keep very busy, often with many different things going on at the same time, keeping their focus on doing well with all of them. They always seem to be going, going, going, and never seem to get there. You have probably heard of the "type A" personality who rarely stops to enjoy a state of rest to recover their energy naturally, or process their experiences. The role of the over achiever can become engrained so deeply into a child's nervous system, it will more likely than not be carried into adult life, and continue to be played out for as long as they can.

For the over achiever, every accomplishment seems to be directly followed by yet another undertaking. They can even thrive on the stress of spreading themselves too thin, and can sometimes become addicted to it. Sadly, the over-achiever rarely takes time out to take proper care of themselves, relax and enjoy the fruits of their labor, or smell the roses along the way. Re-evaluating their priorities or how they want to expend their time and energy, may only come after the over-achiever is forced to stop and take stock of their life by a sudden catastrophic event, or by the onset of a severe or chronic illness. Sometimes this opportunity may come too late, such as in the case of a fatal heart attack or stroke, or an aggressive terminal illness.

Even when they do not survive, it may be possible for them to become enlightened to a degree, and although the illness may ultimately take their life too soon, they can still die with a significant amount of healing on board, maybe not physically, but psychologically, emotionally, and spiritually. To me, the saddest thing of all would be to die without ever having a sense of enlightenment about who you are, or a comprehensive understanding of the life experiences that shaped you. This would mean that some people have lived their entire life in an unhealthy, self-oblivious, maladaptive state, and were never really able to truly be themselves, or experience the natural results of healthy living efforts.

2) THE REBEL
(The difficult child, and the ultimate family scapegoat)
The *rebel* is often the middle child who attempts to confront a harmful external environment through fighting back in an effort to protect their sanity and sense of self. Here, their intuitive little professor, along with their natural child, decides that the only way to preserve the identity of the developing individual self is to rebelle, fight back, and stand up against the evil oppressive forces of their dysfunctional external environment. The rebel is a wearisome role to play, and is the hardest of all three positions to take. If contact with these harmful forces is maintained, the fight can be ongoing for the duration of this contact.

The energy that is expended in this on-going fight for self is enormous, and extremely depleting. For the young rebels, their youthful vitality can provide them with enough energy to keep up the fight for a very long time, and allow them to hang on to their identity and relative physical health for many years.

Eventually though, as the energy of youth wanes, this struggle becomes so depleting that it can contribute to manifesting physical symptoms in some way. In some instances, the suppressed anger and rage toward the continuous oppressive forces of dysfunction and abuse can become enormous. In an effort to prevent exploding outwardly toward others, sometimes the rebel will choose a conversion reaction, turning the frustrated rage inward. This inward implosion can manifest in psychological breakdown and immobilization, and/or physical illness.

The child who is physically and/or psychologically ill becomes the identified patient in the family, and is the inadvertent whistle-blower to the overall state of the family's health. Where there is a sick child, there are usually sicker parents. This child is often the one with the most conscious and accurate perception of their external reality and the family disorder that is working so hard to conquer them. Even though we are not born with a natural sense of right and wrong, children from dysfunctional families can often see that other families and their children are different from them, and can sense their own home life as being not quite right.

Rebels perceive that something is very wrong with their family and with the way they are being treated, even though they do not know how to define it in terms they can understand. So for the rebel, fighting back in the light of this perception is often the only option for psychological survival, albeit being potentially emotionally and physically draining.

Ironically, with the help of healthier outside influences and surrogate alternative role models and support, many children from severely dysfunctional families can emerge from their childhood successfully developed into relatively well-balanced, productive, and functional adults. In these instances, the stronger and more enduring the rebels, the greater their chances of surviving childhood with both their sanity and identity relatively intact, and the more likely they are to become the healthiest and most well-adjusted of all three roles later in life.

However, children of dysfunctional families do not always experience the benefit of helpful outside influences. If they do, if they hang out with healthier neighbors and friends, this alone can be the saving grace that can offer them the promise of recovery, and the ability to enjoy a full and productive life. The rebel that does not have this kind of support, nor the strength not to choose a conversion reaction, can develop a pattern of uncontrolled angry outbursts.

This pattern can be accelerated and intensified if the family dysfunction is serious enough to include a parent who is a chronic substance, physical, or psychological abuser. The behavior pattern of the raging rebel is usually carried into adult life, where it ultimately results in a significant contribution to society's most tragic social woes, from domestic violence to public and community violence. Our jails are full of them. James Dean brought this role to light in his most famous movie role in *"Rebel Without A Cause."*

3) THE GOOD CHILD
(The escape artist)

The good child is often the youngest child in the family who attempts to escape a harmful external environment by withdrawing into a world of fantasy and denial in an effort to protect their sanity and sense of self. This withdrawal from reality serves to shield them from emotional and psychological harm and annihilation. At the same time, they partially or completely disconnect from their sense of self, and exhibit complacency in the face of the insane demands of their severely dysfunctional external environment.

The compromise is that by quietly staying out of the way, and appearing happy with a pasted on smile, their sanity and emotional wellbeing is partially protected, but their sense of self suffers, and can even erode altogether. This pattern of withdrawal and compliance can become so deeply engrained in this good child's nervous system and psyche during their childhood, they are prone to continue playing this role into adulthood as maladaptive, and throughout their adult lives to varying degrees.

As adults, these individuals often do not know who they are or what is best for them, and consequently end up in relationships that require their maladaptative skills. They continue to unwittingly play the role of the compliant spouse to an overbearing, neglectful, and abusive partner, while at the same time living in a fantasy that tells them everything is hunky-dory, and that they are living their dream. Ironically, there is more truth to this than they realize. In reality, they are living in a dream world based on a lie.

They are often drawn into cults, or subservient group practices where compliance and fantasy are exploited as the norm, and living life as a doormat feels like fulfillment. The good child in some ways may be the easiest role to play, and the safest position to take in the severely dysfunctional family system. However, those playing this role sadly pay the price of a lost sense of self, living a life that is based on a lie, and in most cases is a song of individual potential unfulfilled.

By now you may have some idea about yourself, and whether or not your child ego suffers from some kind of moderate to severely disabling negative adaptation. Maybe you can even see yourself and your siblings in some of the lines on these pages. It would be natural to recognize at least some of these concepts, because most people are from families that are dysfunctional to some degree, and have various degrees of issues to correct.

If you have one or more parent that is a substance abuser or is psychologically imbalanced or disordered in some way, such as an overly-emotional, fearful and protective mother, or an overly-critical, authoritarian father, chances are you had to become maladapted in some way to survive the abuses inherent in this emotionally and psychologically violent environment. It's possible you may have carried one or two negative adaptations into your own adult life.

Whether you pass on your negative adaptations to your own children depends on how conscious you are of them, and how much you have allowed them to control your life. The power you have given these adaptations depends on how fully you have developed your adult ego. Your adult ego can offset destructive impulses from your overly adapted child through re-parenting your child ego. And again, how well you have developed your adult ego depends on how much help and support you received from outside influences, alternative role models, and/or therapy and guided education.

If you suspect you have an overly adapted child ego that is running your life, it is time to get some help in teaching your adult ego to re-parent your overly adapted child. It is time to recognize that as a grown adult, you can choose to eliminate the circumstances in your life that seem to mimic the same childhood traumas and threats that caused you to become overly adapted, that activate your maladaptive tendencies in the present. You can get rid of the triggers.

Whether it is detaching yourself from a long and painful enmeshment with a severely dysfunctional family, leaving an abusive partner or friend, or quitting a job with an unreasonable and tyrannical employer, the way to begin finding your inner balance is to take responsibility for making the necessary changes in your life. There is no sane reason to recreate a similar environment in your adult life in order to match your unhealthy childhood adaptations that are now outdated. It is far saner to choose a healthier environment for yourself, and shed those old adaptations that keep you from becoming a healthy, self-governing adult with your adult ego in charge. That was then and this is now, and in the now you can choose to be healthier.

In my family, my older brother was the classic over-achiever, I was the rebel who became the identified patient, and the youngest sibling was the withdrawn and compliant good child. When my brother died in a tragic auto accident at age 19, I took on the role of the over-achiever in addition to the rebel, in a promise to him at his grave that I would live life fully enough for both of us.

It was actress Joanne Woodward in the movie *"The Three Faces of Eve,"* whose character's two deviant personalities suddenly gave way to a third, healthier individual. After becoming aware of the brutal chaos I suffered in my seriously dysfunctional family. I finally realized that I was not created to live my life serving false masters as a twisted bundle of unconscious, unhealthy adaptations, and neither is anyone else. I believe we were all created to have an intact, healthy, functioning ego system that can be activated naturally, can alternate easily between the adult, parent, and child egos according to the ever-changing circumstances of daily life, and with our adult ego in charge, at least most of the time!

So choose to work, play, love, feel your joy, and feel sad or mad too, all when it is time to do so, without dragging along the ball-and-chain of inappropriate adaptations wherever you go. Kahlil Gibran wrote, "To understand the heart and mind of a person, look not at what he/she has already achieved, but at what he/she aspires to do."

Dame Jane Goodall said, "Unlike our primate ancestors, we have the intellect to monitor our behavior. We all have that indomitable spirit, but we don't always recognize it, we don't always feed it, we don't always grow it, we don't always let it out into the world to do good, to inspire, to take action."

Take action. Choose to become free.

I SAY GOODBYE

I say goodbye to an innocent buried
I say goodbye to a childhood missed
I say goodbye to the unseen blossom
To the twisted vine by the dew not kissed
I say goodbye to a poisoned youth
I say goodbye as it finally ends
I turn my back and am not defeated
I boldly go where the road now bends
I say goodbye to the beguiled young beauty
I say goodbye as she lived unknown
I say goodbye to old dreams escaping
To the pearl whose host was blindly sewn
I say goodbye to the misplaced promise
I say goodbye to the years that died
To the terror, and mercy, and pain repeated
To the untrained pilot who charmed and lied
I say goodbye to the spirit shredder
To the grizzly's claw as its grasp uncurls
I see its retreat and its dissipation
And the lifeless pose of its face unfurled
I say goodbye to the unknown God
To the un kept faith, and the un felt trust
To the blind man's staff, to the warlord's treasure
I leap from the mountain, as I know I must.

Valerie Lumley

SEVEN

REJECTION
The double-edged sword

There are two sides to rejection. It can be used in a positive way as a constructive tool for initiating necessary change in a belief system or circumstances or situations that are unacceptable and beyond your control. It can also be used in a negative way as a destructive weapon to punish or control others. It is an action that, when taken, can ultimately result in profound inner peace, or extreme inner conflict. It can either make things turn out right, or make things go very wrong.

Rejection is like a double-edged sword that cuts both ways. With surgical precision it can carefully cut away unwanted chaff, and after winnowing away the hulls, a purer, healthier grain is revealed. Conversely, when carelessly executed for the wrong reasons, rejection can cut away an essential element, and cause something to wither and die. There are times when rejection is an appropriate action to take to make things safer, healthier, or saner. It is the act of choosing what to allow or not allow into your life. Other times it can be the worst possible choice of action, and can cause lasting negative ramifications.

All things considered, the act of rejection remains a necessary phenomenon. We need the courage to reject what is not healthy or working, whether it is an idea or school of thought that does not make sense, a standard that does not seem realistic, a judgment that does not seem fair, or a person that is doing you harm. The inability to constructively reject what is necessary is an act of self-neglect, and prevents self-care in a most basic way. Not rejecting can destroy you. The question then becomes "When does rejecting become unhealthy and destructive?"

Anyone who has been rejected by someone they love – a spouse, a friend, or an employer, for example – knows that being rejected is painful. Having to reject someone, especially someone you care about, can also be very painful, even when it is for the best. The lessons inherent in rejection are profound, and provide everyone involved an important opportunity for self-examination and growth. Defining your priorities and doing what is best for you is being proactive. Also, the people being rejected are forced to face a new and unsought view of themselves. Rejection is sometimes a necessary part of the pain in life, and all meaningful relationships include the experience of pain. This cannot be avoided.

The fact remains that rejection in relationships with other people is sometimes necessary. It may be the only way to break a destructive pattern, and restore a healthy balance in your life, and is thus constructive. However, when the threat or act of rejection is used as a weapon in a cruel or thoughtless way to punish or gain control over someone, it is obviously destructive. An example of this can be as subtle as a parent disapproving an inherent trait in its child, such as sensitivity.

Adults who are stuck in a pattern of using compulsive rejection as their primary coping mechanism have brought this pattern forward from their childhood. For them, this pattern of rejection is an infantile and outdated survival strategy, developed to protect against and offset trauma. This pattern can imprison people later as adults, cause them to become an abusive parent or partner, and prevent them from experiencing any true and lasting intimacy with another person.

Compulsive rejection is developed in children who perceive their primary caregiver as abusive or unavailable. Often, they become parents who batter their own children with this kind of psychological and emotional assault, and cause them to experience chronic self-doubt and fight-or-flight stress. Children will often deal with this by distancing themselves from this parent on the premise "I will reject you before you have a chance to reject me." This behavior is among those that contribute to an inherited cycle of dysfunction that is typically passed down.

In the story *Alice in Wonderland*, the Queen of Hearts stormed around her castle shouting, "Off with their head!" each time someone displeased her. Sometimes, infantile adults cruise through life using the threat of rejection as a knee-jerk reaction to nearly any situation of difficulty, and are oblivious to the destruction they leave behind them in their wake. Ultimately and tragically, they often end up being the one rejected, bringing upon themselves the very thing they fear most and are unconsciously trying to avoid. They end up cutting off their own heads to spite their hearts.

Healthy, self-respecting adults prefer to have intimate relationships with people who also have some maturity, self-respect, and self-control, and not people who are chronically immature. I heard a great line in an old Lauren Bacall movie when her bad-girl character in "Young Man With A Horn" said to her male pursuer, Kirk Douglas, who she was trying to stave off, "Only people who respect themselves can give love freely, and I don't happen to respect myself." Respect yourself enough to stay away from immature and destructive people who cannot love freely in healthy ways, and reject who and what is bad for you. Examine your motives, and when necessary, you be the one who does the rejecting for the right reasons.

FORMS OF DESTRUCTIVE REJECTION
1) DESTRUCTIVE REJECTION
When rejection is used in the wrong way, such as abandoning a healthy lifestyle, disobeying rules created for domestic harmony, or violating laws created to keep society safe and functioning, it becomes extremely destructive. While these are all unwise choices, they are also overt and very plain to see. However, hidden, covert forms of destructive rejection in dysfunctional families are not as obvious. They are the psychological rejection of neglect, lack of nurturing and guidance, and abandonment. These forms of psychological violence are insidious, and very difficult to recognize because the effects cannot be easily seen from the outside.

Neglect from a self-absorbed and/or emotionally disordered parent – absence of expressed love, guidance, and nurturing – can be felt by a child as a form of deep personal rejection. This can be perceived as not being worthy or deserving of natural parental love and nurturing. Constant covert criticism, disapproval or sarcasm, are also experienced as profound forms of personal rejection. Children of the narcissist and/or borderline all too frequently inherit rejection as a birthright.

All forms of destructive rejection prevent children from learning healthy self-care. It teaches low self-esteem, and a sense of deep personal worthlessness. These children can spend their childhood in profound, unacknowledged emotional pain that can cause such deeply ingrained feelings of worthlessness that, if gone uncorrected, can last a lifetime. The self-doubt that these adults experience not only makes them vulnerable to being exploited by disordered personalities, it can lead them to suicidal thoughts.

EFFECTS OF DESTRUCTIVE REJECTION
(The shattered heart, the shredded soul, the annihilation of self-esteem)
When a parent chronically uses subtle, covert, or violent rejection, or the threat of rejection on their children as a primary means of discipline, punishment, or control, they are tattooing a message on their child's soul that they are worthless. Consciously or unconsciously, narcissistic parents use chronic rejection with the intention of destroying their children's individual identity to mold them into the parent's own image. They systematically seek to create clones of themselves by discouraging their children's natural born selves, and only approving of characteristics that mimic or resemble the parent's. The narcissist is only capable of seeing their offspring as extensions of themselves, thus they never really see them at all, rendering their invisible to them.

This phenomenon alerts children on a deep, unconscious level that the only way to receive approval and positive attention from their neglectful and self-obsessed parent, is by imitating their behavior, which eventually can take the place of the child's natural inclinations. This is the process through which children of the narcissist so often relinquish who they are, and grow up into self-oblivious adults who cannot develop their full potential. They tragically become cases in arrested development, too crippled to mature into healthy adults, and wind up becoming a distorted version of themselves.

In a dysfunctional family that is full of rejection and other forms of psychological violence, there is often a child that is called *the* identified patient. This child is typically used as the family's sacrificial lamb and scapegoat, and winds up being held responsible for many of the family woes, and for the untidy public image of the dysfunctional family. The identified patient is often the rebel who acts out against the chronic dysfunction, and the one who evokes most of the family's disdain and hostility. When the identified patient ends up seeking outside help for the trouble they cause, they inadvertently shine a light on the family pathology, and often wind up being rejected and scorned for doing so.

Ideally, family therapy is a choice that with work and cooperation can often turn around many of the destructive patterns in a dysfunctional family system. But this choice is not always made. More often, family members do not want to experience the pain and humiliation of honest personal introspection, or take personal responsibility for their own actions and behavior, or acknowledge that there is something wrong with the way things are. Parents often fear that therapy is about being blamed for their inequities and inadequacies when they feel they did the best they could.

This is the most common put-off to family therapy. However, accounting for unhealthy personality traits, understanding where they originated, and how they were formed is the only way to heal and forgive wounds through this newfound understanding. It is not about blame. It is about understanding and growth, learning to take personal responsibility, and realizing that we are all in the same boat when it comes to being a parent.

When no one in the family recognizes a need to get help, or refuses it when it is indicated, the result is almost always that the rebel child is sacrificed (abandoned) and scapegoated (blamed) for the family dysfunction. This way, everyone else can avoid the discomfort of self-examination, and maintain the status quo in the family in order to protect their personal image, comfort zones,and world view. Why look at the family as a whole when you can blame the difficult child, the one whom around most of the problems whirl? It's so much easier throw them under the bus.

After my parents got divorced, I grew up feeling abandoned, frightened, struggling for psychological and emotional survival, fighting for my own identity, and dependent upon my older brother for protection and expressed love. When I received the news that my brother was accidentally killed in an auto accident at his college, I was 18 and he was 19. I felt the hungry dogs of life consuming me a bite at a time, and I was not receiving the help, counseling, and support I needed.

I remember after the funeral, everyone in my extended family went on their way, and I was left alone with my overwhelming grief. I had lost the one person in my family who made me feel safe and loved. My mother, who was in shock and heavily medicated for the next year, and my stepfather were unable to tolerate the additional discomfort of the way I was acting out my desperation and despair. Consequently, the people who were supposed to love me and keep me safe decided to kick me out of the house, and threw me to the dogs six months after my brother was killed.

While my mother was in bed under sedation, my stepfather said to me, "You are a zero and we don't want you around here anymore! You have three days to move out." I realized then this was his chance to destroy me for his own unsavory reasons, and that I was now being expected to survive on my own without any help or support at all. With my brother gone, I had no one. My biological father who was dealing with his own grief, was remote and far away, and never even checked on me to see how I was doing after the funeral. As far as I knew, he was as unavailable then as he'd always been. It didn't even occur to me to call him for help.

I understand that losing a child is the worst thing that can happen to any parent, and that families do not always come together during this kind of loss. I also understand it is natural for parents and children to clash and bump heads during their children's adolescence, and even natural for the parents to have thoughts of rejecting their children. This is a common phenomenon during the time when adolescents are attempting to establish their independence, and are getting ready to leave the nest.

During this time, they naturally want to create their own identity in the world, and learn how to do things for themselves. However, parents should never use total rejection as a coping strategy during this time, especially if their child is going through a major life-altering trauma that is beyond their control and ability to handle.

This is cruelty beyond measure. The compounding wounds inflicted by this kind of insane abuse can cause a child such intense psychological pain that the results can cripple them for life. The wounds of a shattered heart, a shredded soul, and the annihilation of self-esteem are all wounds inflicted by destructive parental rejection. These wounds can contribute to the eventual manifestation of serious physical, psychological, and emotional illnesses. Deep wound such as these can be healed over time with work and the right kind of help. The following are a few tips to help reverse the effects of destructive rejection.

REVERSING THE EFFECTS OF DESTRUCTIVE REJECTION
(Some handy tips)
1) CHOOSE AN APROPPRIATE LEVEL OF SELF ESTEEM
The first way to reverse the harmful effects of destructive rejection is to concentrate on choosing an appropriate level of self-esteem. A lingering, outdated childhood belief that you are worthless or do not matter, is no more than a silly, inappropriate delusion. The truth is, even if you grew up in an environment where your welfare was not your parent's first concern, everyone matters, everyone has worth, everyone has a sacred identity of their own with their own path to follow. Even if you have committed offenses against another person, as long as you own up to your actions by taking personal responsibility for your behavior, make your sincere apology and a commitment to do better, you can update your level of self-esteem.

There is no sane reason to go on believing you are worthless or "less than" others in some way. Drop this self-defeating persona, correct this illegitimate delusion, and set out on a higher road. Choose to take charge of your level of self-esteem, and choose to heal it. Rachel Carson said, "Those who contemplate the beauty of the earth find reserves of strength that will endure as long as life lasts." Contemplate the beauty of the Earth, and draw strength from the fact that you are a part of this beauty. In spite of your past, you can absolutely summon the strength to undertake changing your view of yourself. Any thoughts telling you that you do not matter are evil lies, so stop believing them!

In *Desiderata* by Max Ehrmann, he tells us, "With all its sham, drudgery, and broken dreams, it is still a beautiful world." He also added so eloquently, "You are a child of the universe, no less than the trees and the stars; you have a right to be here." In order to repair my damaged self-esteem, I had to put these truths to the lies. Remember, the only chance a lie has to exist is that someone will believe it. I had to learn that, even though I was treated as though I did not matter while I was growing up, it was not true. Although I felt invisible and disregarded, and was told in many different ways that my thoughts, feelings, and needs did not count, it was up to me to eventually decide that they did, and that I mattered.

When I look back on my life now, "with all its sham, drudgery and broken dreams," I choose to believe the truth that I have value, my life is indeed worth living, and anything else is a mistake, a delusion, a lie. There is a worthy principle from the Christian Science school of thought that states, "The only power error has is to destroy itself. Silence the lie with the truth." Today in the present, I choose the truth, and not the old lie of an echoing childhood delusion. I understand that what happened yesterday no longer has power over today, and how I choose to feel about myself today will set the tone for tomorrow. So why not choose the truth, and let it sparkle and ring in your very soul!

2) COMMIT TO SELF CARE
The second way to reverse the harmful effects of destructive rejection is to make a solid commitment to self-care. Maybe it is time for you to honor yourself by being the one doing the rejecting, and eliminating who and what is not good and wholesome in your life. Honoring yourself means to pay attention to how you feel about something or someone, and valuing yourself enough to act in your own best interest. This may also mean you need to learn to enjoy being alone, and appreciate the value of solitude, which I will talk more about next. To abandon and dishonor yourself by ignoring your feelings is a sure way to devalue yourself by default. To be committed to self-care means to stop pretending that what you feel does not matter.

Also, just because something makes you feel bad, does not mean you should reject it. The ancient prophet Kahlil Gibran said, "Pain is the breaking of the shell of understanding," and sometimes we hurt and get hurt by the people we love. This should be taken into account and allowed for. However, if your relationship to something or someone is chronically bad for you, meaning: unhealthy, unwholesome, harmful or destructive, or someone is being chronically disrespectful, intrusive, judgmental, abusive, and so on, then maybe it is time for you to do the rejecting.

Honoring yourself also means honoring your inner guide, or body intelligence, that alerts you when something is harming or violating you in some way, and then taking the appropriate action to stop it. The opposite is an unhealthy martyrdom and the mental illness of denial.

The resolution that you will not abandon yourself by ignoring your feelings, that you will not allow others to abuse or disrespect you, that you will not do something you do not want to do, or put yourself in harm's way, is what committing to responsible self-care is all about. This means there may be times when you have to reject some people or things, even if it causes pain. You cannot take care of yourself and take care of the way someone else feels about it at the same time, nor is it healthy or appropriate. You may take note of the way others feel, but you are only responsible for yourself. This is why the way you reject should be as respectful, as brief, and kind as possible. There is always a reason someone is being rejected, so allow them to be responsible for their consequences, even when they are incapable of understanding them.

First and foremost, you must be able to trust yourself to be the one who keeps you healthy and safe if you want to feel true self-worth, and reverse the effects of destructive rejection. You'll never feel self-worth if you chronically abandon yourself, and continue exposing yourself to abusive behavior, or unsafe situations.

It is also important to understand two things. One, a presumptive source of love that is chronically harming you is not love. It is something else. And two, love can always come from within (your inner guide, inner knowing, higher power, and the universal life force). You can treat yourself with love, respect, and compassion by choosing what and who gets to be in your life, based on an honest assessment of who and what is safe and healthy, or not. You can love yourself by taking loving action on your behalf, and choosing to eliminate the evil, destructive forces from your life that are within your power through constructive rejection.

3) VALUE AND ENJOY SOLITUDE

The third way to reverse the harmful effects of destructive rejection is by learning to value and enjoy solitude. Ardis Whitman wrote of "The Secret Joys of Solitude" and I would like to paraphrase a couple of her lovely thoughts while contributing my own experience on the subject. I have learned that solitude is an inevitable and unavoidable part of life. Sooner or later, we will all experience it for one reason or another, whether it comes through the death of a spouse, the end of a marriage, departure of children, loss of a ley friendship, or simply choosing to be alone.

Whether solitude comes into our lives on its own, or we choose it, when you are trying to become healthier it is sometimes necessary for the sake of recovery to choose being alone, whether you need it on a 24/7 basis, or only for blocks of time throughout each day. Solitude may be the only way to get the peace and serenity necessary to heal yourself, process a new understanding of your life and the people in it, and figure out what your true feelings and needed boundaries are.

Sadly, fear of being alone keeps people stuck in bad relationships or situations more than any other single reason. People who are not afraid of being alone can demand healthy relationships that work. They can pick and choose whom they want in their life, instead of clinging out of fear and neediness to whoever will have them, or staying in a destructive relationship out of psychological codependency, or an inappropriate sense of responsibility or obligation. Fear of solitude should never be a reason for maintaining a destructive lifestyle, or staying in a destructive relationship that is no longer working. But there is hope for those who fear being alone.

For those who fear solitude and the waves of loneliness that come with it, it is possible to learn to view solitude in an entirely new way. Despite a longing for the joy of sharing experiences with someone else, you can actually learn to appreciate the value and satisfaction of experiencing things alone, and discover that there are hidden benefits in solitude. There is a lot of peace in being able to enjoy the here and now in your own company, in dignity and grace, and the fulfillment of feeling free and autonomous. Theologian Henri Nouwen calls this transition, "The conversion of loneliness into solitude." This is not narcissism. It is developing the ability to sense, appreciate, and enjoy your own presence in the world in relationship to the here and now, and all that it has to offer. You don't need someone else's company to experience this.

Solitude offers many meaningful benefits. It enhances and strengthens memory by providing a sense of continuity to our lives that we can only acquire when space and time are available to us. When combined with memory, it teaches us to develop a stronger sense of our own individual identity, and a clearer understanding that we are multi-faceted beings. We get in touch with our inner conflicts, and begin to ask questions about what is going on inside us. Out of this process comes a new and deeper understanding, a clearer view of life, and is a handy opportunity to go on a journey of self-discovery.

We can then step back and view our lives from a distance, and get a better and more unobstructed view. All the pieces to the puzzle called life, come together and form a colorful picture, and we can see what we have lost and what we have gained.

It is important to know as much about yourself as you possibly can without becoming pre-occupied with yourself. In solitude you can become privately introspective, maybe even for the first time. It forces us to ask the mature and important questions about life, and provides the time to experience what is in our hearts, and come to understand it. If you get yourself into a quiet space and sincerely ask yourself a question, you are very likely to get an answer; especially if the answer is a simple one.

The experience of solitude gives us the opportunity to overcome our fears by having to continually cope with new situations by ourselves. Very quickly, it teaches us about what kind of human being we are by revealing our strengths and weaknesses, and helps us forge a new and truer identity. This can be viewed as a kind of re-shaping of the soul, and is a noble task to undertake. The spiritual growth that comes with solitude has been written about by many a poet, and is what the Quakers call "That of God in every man." German poet Rainer Maria Rilke said, "In solitude, there is nothing that does not see you."

Carl Jung said about solitude, "Loneliness is not necessarily inimical to companionship, for no one is more sensitive to companionship than the lonely man." He indicates that we are freer when our hearts are empty, and therefore more open to others than when our hearts are focused on loving just one person. There is an old Bushman tribal saying that is used when one Bushman meets another in the wilderness. They cry, "Good day! I have been dead, but now that you have come, I live again." Solitude puts focus on the actual worth of every single living being.

Solitude is a necessary part of the human maturation process. It illuminates your life experiences, and allows the opportunity for suppressed or unacknowledged unfinished-business to surface, and come into the foreground to be dealt with and resolved. This can be an interesting and enjoyable experience as clarity is developed, or it can be a painful experience that can change you forever. You will come out of it either more peaceful, compassionate, loving, and understanding, or not. It often depends upon the way you chose to handle life before solitude came.

If you resist the temptation to be a victim and feel sorry for yourself, and choose instead to see solitude as an undetermined amount of time for growth, without dwelling on "the way things used to be," you are more likely to transmute your loneliness into a tool for making yourself a person more appreciative of new things.

Use the benefits of solitude to deepen your ability to be a more "well-rounded" human being. Use it to learn to treat yourself well, and increase your ability to live life more fully in the present. Playwright Christopher Fry, said, "No man is free who will not dare to pursue the questions of his own loneliness. It is through them that he lives." I would like to add that it is through answering the questions of our loneliness that we also heal the wounds of our lives.

If you must leave a relationship that is bad for you in order to heal yourself and your life, befriending solitude may be a necessary choice for you to make. When you really look at your life in the physical sense, you come into the world alone, live alone inside yourself, and die alone, even when others are around. No one else can experience your reality in the same way that you do. However, it is where you live spiritually that you are never alone.

I believe we are all spiritually connected through the same life-force that created and animated us to be separated from one another physically, and that this life-force makes all living things "members of one another" on the physical plane. With this understanding, choosing to experience solitude with courage, humility, and grace is something everyone has the capacity to do.

The right therapist can help you make the transition into and through a period of solitude, and this may be an effective way to help yourself arrive at a place of inner peace if you cannot seem to get there on your own. You might first try going for long private walks in nature every day if possible, where you could clear your negative thoughts in the peace around you.

If you have experienced destructive forces in your life, you are going to need as much inner peace as possible to heal yourself of their effects, and sometimes you may have to remove yourself from a bad relationship, situation, or job to get it. If you have no means to live independently, and are financially dependent on someone who is destructive, then set boundaries that allow you to experience as much distance from them as you can.

There is always a way to get the experience of solitude into your life if you need it. Conversely, there is always a way for life to get solitude into your experience through unexpected loss, for example. There is really no way to avoid it, so embrace it, choose it if you need to, and allow it to do its work on you. You will likely become stronger, larger, wiser, healthier, more confident, more autonomous, and more peaceful as a result.

NOTE: Nowhere am I advocating becoming a recluse. That is something entirely different than accepting a period of solitude for healthy reasons, or as a turn of fate. Choosing to become a solitary recluse is choosing to opt out of spiritual growth and evolution. It is not a healthy choice. It is a tragedy. At the time I was writing this book, people were being forced into seclusion – alone, with a partner or family member – by government edict to handle the coronavirus. For some people, this might be a gift.

4) LET GO OF YOUR PAST

The fourth way to reverse the harmful effects of destructive rejection is to let go of your past, but only after you have learned to understand it, the people involved, and the role you played in it. After two years of therapy and guided study, I was able to understand that, as the rebel child, I had been fighting against the dysfunctional ways of my family for most of my life.

As an adult, the only piece of the puzzle I'd been missing was the realization that I no longer had to be there, braving the endless struggles that sapped my energy and kept me from fully living my own life and reaching my individual potential. I learned that my biggest fear in life was losing control of my sanity, and becoming mentally disordered like my family, and I realized that the true value of my family was in their serving as the ultimate unhealthy example of how not to be. I grew to understand that they were actually my most valuable, yet uninvited, of all my teachers. I also appreciate that had my family not been so brutally dysfunction, I wouldn't have needed to learn those lessons.

Of course, I now understand that my parents always did the best they could with what they had at the time, that they did not know any better, and that they were suffering from the personality disorders that were formed by their own childhoods. They became prisoners of themselves from an era gone by, when mental health guidance was not available the way it is today. They had been struggling on their own misguided path in life for a very long time, and I have compassion for them in this regard. I also have the responsibility not to allow their tragedy to become mine.

In most cases, learning to understand someone makes it easier to forgive them. I now feel a detached, impersonal love, compassion, and forgiveness for my parents that came from the enlightenment of education. Because I learned to understand myself, my past and the people in it, I can let go of my fear of becoming lost in adapting to someone else's disorder, and can relax and be myself.

Another fear from the past I needed to let go of was the fear of being rejected or abandoned by someone I loved. It was not until I learned to understand the meaning of the stories in my past that I could see them like scenes out a window of a passenger train, and could view these memories as scenery gone by. There is a delightful little poem I ran across in recent years that is unsigned called "Life." It goes like this:

"Life is like a journey taken on a train, with a pair of travelers at each window pane. I may sit beside you all the journey through, or I may sit elsewhere, never knowing you. But if fate should mark me to sit by your side, let's be pleasant travelers. It's so short a ride."

I have learned that as you travel through life, it is best to keep with healthy, pleasant people, and remain focused on the scenery in the present, because it is all we ever really have. However, forgetting the morals of the stories in your past, or pretending they never happened, is not healthy. Furthermore, you need an honest and accurate memory of past experiences to aid you in making healthy decisions in the present.

If you are not bearing in mind what you have learned from your life experiences, then you are probably viewing and living life today very much in the same way you did as a child. This means you are not likely growing or evolving naturally, that you may be stuck in an old position, handling reality the same way you always have, and are therefore apt to repeat past mistakes and misperceptions. But it can be fixed. With resolved intention, commitment, and hard work, you can almost always get yourself unstuck. Everything worthwhile in life usually requires some hard work from time to time. Life is not a smooth, easy ride, nor is it always fair. No one gets a free pass through life to avoid hard work and pain.

You must remember that you are not your life stories. You are the consciousness of your soul that naturally wants to expand through every lesson you learn. Your life is made up of the choices you make from the wisdom you subsequently gain from these lessons. Retaining the lessons is wisdom (accumulated learning) that creates better choices, and better choices create a better life, better health, and the gift of more wisdom. My paternal grandmother said to me once, "You are today exactly where you put yourself yesterday." And if someone did not own their behavior or live up to this standard, she'd slap her knee, and say, "They're no damn good!"

In spite of the inner storm of approach/avoidance conflicts I experienced with my family most of my life, more than anything else, I wanted to be a good person, capable of experiencing healthy love and intimacy. I wanted to be strong, courageous, loving, joyful, compassionate, creative, resolved in healthy values, and clear about who I was apart from others. Over the years, I was becoming exhausted from keeping my protective wall of humor intact whenever I was in their presence. These were dangerously disordered people, and I had to protect myself from all of them, and constantly be on my guard at the expense of my life-force energy.

However, my desire to become healthier was thwarted by the frustration, anger, and internal conflicts from a conditioned betrayal-bond that my narcissistic-borderline mother had created, and I was plagued with anxiety. I can see now that the result of my anxiety was depression.

My therapist said my mother's personality disorders had not, nor would they ever, become part of my personality because inherently it was my greatest fear, and I had fought against my family ways so valiantly all my life. I had a degree of codependency disorder going on, was constantly sabotaged by self-doubt, and my behavior with men was nearly always controlled by my fear of abandonment and rejection. In short, I was a mess.

However, after I spent two years in therapy in mid-life with guided education, I was able to distinguish my own identity apart from my family, reject who and what was unhealthy and destructive for me, and gradually began to understand and heal myself psychologically and emotionally. With help from the right therapist, I was able to correct the errors in my belief system, make the necessary changes in my life, and acquire the understanding and strength to set the long-overdue boundaries against the abuse that was continuing to happen.

165

Until I detached emotionally from my dangerously dysfunctional family, and set boundaries of distance and time against them, I was unable to evolve spiritually, because the past was continually being recreated in the present through my interactions with them. I was changing, but they were not. Today, in assessing relationships, I base my conclusions on the present behavior of others, using the past as a source of information. It is handy to remember that in most cases, the present can be judged by the past, because most people don't do the work they need to do to free their soul, and their behavior and world view rarely changes over time.

Now that I am more in charge of my life and my wellbeing, I feel reasonably healthy and safe, and I trust myself to keep me that way. I naturally work at being the kind of person I want to be each day. I understand that even people who had the advantages of a relatively healthy upbringing and happy childhood have the rigors of life to cope with, as we all do, and they too have to work at life daily. Everyone has to work at being a good person, to do no harm, and to keep an eye on themselves and others. It is simply a part of being human. Life just seems a whole lot easier when you are no longer dragging around the ball-and-chain of unenlightened past wounds and unresolved issues, or allowing the relationships that handicapped you to persist in your life.

Learning to reverse the effects of destructive rejection, one of the most mortal of psychological wounds, can be most liberating. There are still times when I hear my mother's voice after she read the poem I wrote called "Journey to The Garden" that outlined my life. She said to me with smug indignation, "Huh, I didn't know your life was so bad!" I observed that her lack of empathy and knowledge of me were in keeping with her narcissistic inability to see me as apart from herself, and this was not conscious.

So, I have chosen to allow memories such as these to be irrelevant and insignificant in the now, as I allow them to drift through my mind like hazy zephyrs without resistance, as I peacefully move on to other thoughts. I feel neutral about memories of the past now, and feel quietly detached from the echoes and ghosts that once lingered. When they do appear to me, they no longer stir me. They are simply passing bio-chemical impulses traveling through the neural net of memory clusters in my brain, and like tiny sparks, they dissipate as quickly as they fire, as I do not offer them a place to catch on, take hold, and smolder. The hurricane inside my head has become a gentle cleansing breeze.

Genuinely freeing yourself from the past must be done if you want to experience the kind of inner peace that comes from understanding, and "living in loving detachment." When there are relationships in the present that continue to re-create the distructive behaviors and patterns of the past, letting go of the past may also mean letting go of these relationships, if only for a time. You will need to be able to experience as much detachment from the past as you can, if you want enough energy to heal yourself in the present.

Kahlil Gibran said, "Yesterday is but today's memory, and tomorrow is but today's dream." Choose to live in the now, and do not cover it over with a blanket woven together with memories and dreams that are not even real today. Remember that the power to heal yourself lies in the choices you make here and now, being detached from the past and the people in it, healed of old wounds, freed by newfound understanding, and at peace in acceptance of what is.

This place of inner peace is something we all strive for, and it is not wrong to do what you must to achieve it without intentionally hurting others. But keep in mind some people may feel hurt when you set a fair and honest boundary with them when their behavior is destructive to you. This is their choice. Remember the rule of thumb that if you have to explain, you're wasting your time. Regaining your health may depend upon it. I know a wise man who once said to me, "I don't have time to worry about what other people think of me. What really matters is what I think of myself."

Do not concern yourself with the arrogant, willfully ignorant judgment of others. Other people's view of you is naturally going to be filtered through the limits of their own experience and knowledge, their current state of mental health, and will also be biased by the choices they have made that they are now justifying and living with. Other people cannot possibly be qualified to judge the choices you must make in taking good care of yourself, nor do they have a right to. Simply ignore them.

You know what to do and why you must do it, and if others do not possess the capacity to understand you, and feel compelled to judge you, be willing to allow them their thoughts, keep your distance, and stay the course. It is not your job, nor is it appropriate, to convince anyone of your reasons for the choices you must make in your own life. It is their job to grow up, learn to stay out of other people's business, and mind their own.

To give an example of putting a boundary between you and someone who is being inappropriately disrespectful of your healing choices, I will offer a couple of handy tips on how to identify a problem, get in touch with and own your feelings about it, and handle the decision to create a boundary of distance and time between you and that person or situation for as long as you need.

Remember that the behaviors of chronically immature, disordered and dysfunctional people are extreme and destructive. While these behaviors seem atrocious, obnoxious, and repugnant to the self-respecting, mature adult who would not consider them acceptable, they seem normal for the infantile, out-of-control people who display them, and to those who enable them. To them, these marbleized, dysfunctional behaviors are an acceptable dynamic to their own family's status quo. You cannot reason or communicate safely with people who behave like this, or the people who are enabling these destructive behaviors. It is best not to try, since it is almost always self-defeating.

When you are striving to heal yourself, you will not get support from everyone from a dysfunctional family; however, you must always demand respect, even when others do not possess the capacity to understand you. Basic human respect is not dependent upon understanding, and if others are disrespecting you because they do not understand your healing choices, then they are being immature and selfish, and are not behaving like a healthy adult. Summarily, dysfunctional families are made up of people who do not know how to behave like healthy adults in the first place.

This is not your problem. As long as you are making an effort to behave appropriately, and making the necessary choices to get to a healthier place in your life, you need not concern yourself with this type of person. Do not waste your time or energy on people who cannot completely respect that you are in the process of becoming healthier and are simply acting in your own best interest, who are threatened deeply by your undertaking. Arguing with people about your personal choices is inappropriate anyway, and is simply not worth it. Wish them well, and go your own way. Remember to walk away from the dysfunction and to yourself!

USE BOUNDARIES
(Some handy tips)
Boundaries can solve problems, protect you, and heal old wounds. But unlike Paul Simon who sang, "There are 50 ways to leave your lover" – there is no limit to the number of boundaries you can come up with. Just remember the three keeps of boundaries: Keep it short, Keep your feet moving, and Keep quiet about why.

Although disordered people deserve considerations, they are not your responsibility, nor do you have to keep exposing yourself to them. If someone is behaving badly toward you, set a boundary. Say things like, "You may not speak to me unless you are kind and respectful", "I do not appreciate your tone", or "You may not treat me this way." If they still insist on behaving badly, detach and set a boundary of distance and time between you.

Note: Read the chapter on boundaries for more information

Finally, it is simply a fact of life that in some relationships there is no middle ground to be found. Recognizing this when it occurs is wisdom, and going your own way is as inevitable as it is necessary if you want to live a serene, healthy, fulfilled life, reaching your full potential, with a heart filled with understanding, empathy, compassion, forgiveness, appreciation, and love.

THE VELVETEEN RABBIT

The Skin Horse was bald in patches and showed the seams underneath, and most of the hairs in his tail had been pulled out to string bead necklaces. He was wise, for he had seen a long succession of mechanical toys arrive to boast and swagger, and by-and-by break their mainsprings and pass away, and he knew that they were only toys, and would never turn into anything else. For nursery magic is very strange and wonderful, and only those playthings that are old and wise and experienced like the Skin Horse understand all about it.

"What is REAL?" asked the Rabbit one day, when they were lying side by side near the nursery fender, before Nana came to tidy the room. "Does it mean having things that buzz inside you and a stick-out handle?"

"Real isn't how you are made," said the Skin Horse. "It's a thing that happens to you. When a child loves you for a long, long time, not just to play with, but REALLY loves you, then you become Real."

"Does it hurt?" asked the Rabbit.

"Sometimes," said the Skin Horse, for he was always truthful. "When you are Real you don't mind being hurt."

"Does it happen all at once, like being wound up," he asked, "or bit by bit?"

"It doesn't happen all at once," said the Skin Horse. "You become. It takes a long time. That's why it doesn't often happen to people who break easily, or have sharp edges, or who have to be carefully kept. Generally, by the time you are Real, most of your hair has been loved off, and your eyes drop out, and you get loose in the joints and very shabby. But these things don't matter at all, because once you are Real you can't be ugly, except to people who don't understand."

"I suppose you are Real?" said the Rabbit. And then he wished he had not said it, for he thought the Skin Horse might be sensitive. But the Skin Horse only smiled.

"The Boy's uncle made me Real," he said. "That was a great many years ago; but once you are Real you can't become unreal again. It lasts for always."

The rabbit sighed. He thought it would be a long time before this magic called Real happened to him.

Margery Williams

EIGHT

DENIAL
Living in hiding within the fortress

You have probably heard the one about Cleopatra, the intrusive Egyptian queen, who traveled up and down the Nile river "barging" in on everyone, being a general pain in the "asp" and blissfully unaware that others were not as pleased about her arrival as she was. She soon earned herself the name "Queen of DeNile." Simply put, denial/fantasy, or cognitive dissonance, is when one's inner perceptions do not match one's outside reality.

By some standards, the unconscious pattern of building a psychological wall of denial around a problem or situation, and escaping into a world of fantasy and lies that say everything is hunky-dory, can be seen as personally irresponsible, cowardly, and even insane. However, denial is a two-sided coin. There are times when it can be used to save one's sanity, when other times it can be used so pervasively that denial itself becomes the insanity. Then it is no longer protection. It becomes the thing you need to protect yourself from.

Think of the proverbial ostrich who chooses to respond to threats by burying its head in the sand, and is consequently unable to see the reality of what is going on around it by virtue of its self-imposed blindness. He actually believes that if he doesn't see it, it doesn't exist. This is a very sad and costly way to live one's life. Everything that is important for health and spiritual growth in life can pass by virtually unseen. In denial, you simply cannot see what you refuse to see, and thus, you do not know what you will not know.

In denial, there is a false sense of safety, when everything is perceived superficially and taken at face value, and has no underlying meaning. The tragic deficit of living life in a blissful state of unwitting blindness creates a quiet form of covert insanity that carries with it the enormous price of unfulfilled personal potential and development. The truth is: ignorance is not bliss. It is simply ignorance.

DENIAL AS PROTECTION (A temporary survival mechanism)
In his remarks on the plight of science, Einstein said, "In times of crisis, people are generally blind to everything outside their immediate necessities."

There are two basic types of denial. The first type I will talk about is denial as protection. This form of denial can be a very natural, necessary, yet temporary coping mechanism for surviving a sudden and severe trauma. The response of psychological denial in the case of experiencing the sudden death of a loved one, or any other type of serious emotional trauma, can shield the mind and the soul from being mortally wounded beyond repair by a savage spiritual blow, or help survive a major crisis.

Temporary denial following such a trauma can also buy people enough time to gather their strength so they can begin the struggle of getting their bearings in a new and suddenly imposed reality. It allows people time for them to come to grips with their feelings in a more gradual way, and find the support they need. It can also help buffer their pain through the taxing journey of working through their grief and arriving at acceptance.

The grief process is commonly known for its five key stages. These can begin with psychological shock and denial, then move into anger and rage, depression, bargaining, and finally acceptance. The order of these stages may change and vary in length of time and intensity. In addition, not everyone experiences each one of these stages. Sometimes one or more of these stages is skipped, or a person gets stuck in one or more stage and will need help to get unstuck, to keep moving through the process. Eventually this kind of denial response is discarded by most people who come out the other side of the grieving process and begins to heal. As a stage of grief, denial is seen as a natural and healthy part of the process.

DENIAL AS AN ILLNESS (A form of insanity)
The second type is the illness of denial. Denial can become an illness when a person becomes stuck in denial, or uses it as their primary coping mechanism to life's stressors and challenges. Denial can actually become a habitual, maladaptive part of a person's personality. In his remarks on religion and science, Einstein said, "Everything that the human race has done and thought, is

concerned with the satisfaction of felt needs, and the assuagement of pain." What more effective means to satisfy the need to assuage emotional pain than the use of denial. The problem with holding on to a posture of denial is it requires a tremendous amount of unconscious energy to maintain, energy that could otherwise be used toward facing facts, solving problems, learning, growing in an upward direction, and evolving spiritually.

Over time, a pattern of denial can develop into a complex system of evasive maneuvers, and can become an impenetrable wall. This wall can build upon itself, and eventually become a fortress that is strong enough to protect and contain an entire internal world of fantasy that is nurtured by lies and misperceptions, where all that is unhealthy and destructive is externally enabled.

When people wall themselves off from reality by living in hiding inside a fortress of denial, they may avoid a lot of pain in the moment, and protect themselves from seeing what they really don't want to look at, but they also avoid and prevent self-knowledge and spiritual growth. While remaining self-oblivious, they also prevent themselves from being capable of understanding the reality and feelings of others, except in ways that support their personal comfort zone and worldview.

Furthermore, people who live in denial can be perceived as being slow, obtuse, impervious, impenetrable, unavailable, lacking in empathy, nonresponsive, and not entirely psychologically present. The lights are on, but they're not answering the doorbell. The remoteness and falseness of an adult living in denial can be exasperating for someone who is attempting to have a healthy, intimate, relationship with them, because they seem, and are being, entirely artificial.

Their unnatural, flat non-responsiveness to their external reality prevents them from reaching any kind of meaningful understanding of themselves, others, their situation, or their circumstances. It makes it impossible to connect with them for the purpose of reaching a mutual understanding, or simply receiving real personal acknowledgment. There is almost nothing more frustrating or energetically draining than trying to reach someone who cannot, or will not, be reached.

Also, children who depend on this person for their nurturing, guidance, boundaries, and safety can become full of anger, frustration, and fear. They simply cannot tolerate the intense, overwhelming anxiety from the fact that their primary caregiver does not live in the same world they do, or even seem like a real person. How can any child feel safe in their world when the person they depend upon for protection lives in another, and cannot set safe, appropriate boundaries that enable the child to relax?

In the final analysis, it can be said that people who live in habitual denial of their reality are in effect insane to some degree, as they are not in-reality. Children can sense this. This form of insanity can manifest itself in ways that can be conspicuous and obvious, or too subtle and insidious to easily see. People living in denial most of the time know how to wear the mask of sanity to avoid being too conspicuous, and can act normal from time to time, and this is especially confusing for their children.

The onset of perpetual denial can result from something as visible as a major trauma early in life, or something less visible such as a series of minor, cumulative traumas from things like chronic neglect, unexpressed love, and lack of boundaries and guidance. The pain of these traumas can be so far beyond what developing children can cope with, that the coping mechanism of denial can subsume their perception of reality. This is not a conscious choice. It is a survival mechanism that becomes maladaptive if carried into adulthood.

Without the right help, denial can become like quicksand, and a child or adult can psychologically sink in so deeply, they can literally become stuck, and in some cases can disappear altogether. There is an old joke that goes something like this: A man says to his friend who has just experienced a major life-changing trauma, "How are you feeling?" the man asks. The friend replies, "I've never felt better. I'm in denial!" Denial may feel like a peaceful place to be temporarily, but in the long run, it rarely pans out to be peaceful. Over time, it can only serve to perpetuate dysfunction, block intimacy, and can frustrate and prevent fulfillment of personal growth and potential.

The bottom line is that people who deny reality are not really protecting themselves at all. They are merely denying who they are in relation to an outside reality that will always exist, whether they acknowledge it or not. Therefore, they are only protecting themselves from self-knowledge. Eventually, all the painful and external problems that were not faced come home to roost, as all accounts eventually come due, and in most cases with interest and heavy late fees. Better to face life as it is, and pay along the way, than later on all at once, and become completely tapped out.

UNDERSTAND THE ABUSE/NEED/DENIAL TRIANGLE
Within the dysfunctional family system, there exists an interesting triangle of cause, effect, and result that supports the dysfunction. I call this vicious cycle the abuse/need/denial triangle. When you look at denial, it's one thing to look on the surface and see the abuses and traumas that created it, and another to look beneath the surface and see the place where denial lives and breathes inside the dysfunctional family system.

Firstly, it is safe to say that all forms of abuse create various degrees of unmet needs. Secondly, when we consider that these unmet needs result in chronic emotional pain that can cause a posture of denial to assuage or hide this pain, then we can say unmet needs create denial. Thirdly, when we consider denial can only serve to enable (allow) more abuse to occur, then we can say denial creates abuse. This is the vicious cause, effect, and result triangle perpetuated and supported in dysfunctional behavior.

I believe that when you expunge denial from a dysfunctional family system, the abuse/need/denial cycle can be broken. When you recognize denial as a survival strategy, and that your unmet needs can now be met by other sources, the cycle can be broken. When you educate yourself, and learn to face things as they actually are, and set healthy boundaries to stop the abuse, the cycle can be broken.

Once you reject denial as a tactic, you can make the necessary changes that will break the abuse-need-denial triangle that you were caught up in, and the process of becoming healthier can begin. This must happen so that personal responsibility can exist to stop the denial from enabling other illnesses of the mind to develop.

Perpetual denial has no place in a healthy life because it is a major obstacle to psychological health. In developing denial as a primary coping mechanism, most people begin by experiencing a major trauma early in life. This trauma can be as violent as experiencing an earth-shaking event, as subtle as persistent chronic neglect, or the result of witnessing something traumatic. When the trauma is neglect, it is "accumulative trauma." Every parent has their lapses in responsibility, and cannot cover all bases with their children at all times. I am talking about a constant pattern of neglect and lack of boundaries that creates an intense and ongoing anxiety in children, and leaves them with serious wounds and intense unmet needs.

An environment of trauma and abuse also teaches children to become used to adapting to trauma and deprivation. In a constant state of anxiety, the "fight-or-flight death hormones" of adrenaline and cortisol, along with endorphins and norepinephrine, pour into the blood stream. When a state of anxiety or fear becomes chronic, it can become addictive. During adulthood, this addiction can manifest in many different ways (the addictive personality type) and is always destructive in that it perpetuates more trauma and deprivation.

During childhood, intense psychological and/or physical abuse victims can become so overwhelmed by anxiety and terror, they can become unable to respond at all (catatonic), or they can distort their reality and escape into a world of fantasy and lies. In the latter, denial may be the saner and lesser of the two evils, yet it is still an insane survival mechanisms as maladaptive.

In addition, when denial becomes maladaptive in adulthood as a coping mechanism in relationships, it is very destructive. Therapists Blizard and Bluhm describe the phenomenon of denial in this way: "These defenses are highly adaptive in childhood because they permit the child to survive in an abusive family. In adulthood, the defenses become maladaptive, because they prevent the survivor from accurately perceiving the presence or absence of abuse. By permitting the adult survivor to maintain a relationship with someone who resembles the original abuser, these defenses perpetuate the cycle of abuse."

Many people unconsciously marry their abuser, meaning they marry someone closely resembling an abusive parent's personality disorder that replicates the treatment they received, perpetuating the abusive/maladapted relationship they are accustomed to. I married my primary abuser in my first marriage, a man who was a psychological and emotional terrorist, like my mother. The maladaptive defenses of perpetual denial can become manifested in various ways. Here are some common telltale signs of denial.

COMMON TELTALE SIGNS
1) Pretending that a problem does not exist when it does. (Pure denial)
2) Being willing to admit a problem exists, but not admit to its true nature and severity. (Minimizing/diminishing)
3) Seeing a problem as caused by someone else. (Deflecting)
4) Use of endless excuses and justification to avert responsibility. (Enabling)
5) Dealing with a problem without an emotional acknowledgment of evidence. (Impervious)
6) Changing the subject to avoid facing a problem. (Avoidance)
7) Becoming irritable, indignant, or angry when confronted by a problem. (Intimidation avoidance)

Perpetual denial is an extremely destructive force. When used in an ongoing basis, it demoralizes relationships, and destroys what is beneficial to personal and spiritual growth in an effort to avoid pain. Without pain, we cannot gain the understanding we need to expand our conscious mind.

When we consider life's challenges, the way we choose to handle and respond to them is far more important than what occurs. I believe that it is through these choices our character is formed. Hardship brings out in the open the content of our character for all to see. We are all responsible for choosing healthy, appropriate responses to situations and challenges, and retaining what we learn from them. We cannot do either when we are in denial.

Therefore, choosing to recover from denial can be one of the most important steps a person can take. Recovery will enable you to see things differently, and this can transform your entire life. Choosing fantasy over reality is foolhardy and cowardly. Wake up and face your reality so you can learn from it, grow from it, and make your reality better. You will emerge healthier, more mature, more secure, and less fearful. There is more true peace in creating a healthy relationship with reality than there could ever be with living a fantasy that can come crashing down around you at any time.

RECOVERING FROM DENIAL
Learning to view your reality in a whole new way can be a monumental task. It will probably require the help and guidance of a good therapist, along with guided study, patience, and most of all, courage. It will also require an unrelenting commitment to fully recognize your present life as it truly is. This will include your life-style, living environment, eating habits, job satisfaction, financial status, relationships with others, behavior, and the state of your physical and mental health, and that of the key people in your life.

Choosing to recover from denial can be the greatest gift you can give your spirit. Learning to see things differently can be unavoidably painful, however the realizations that come to you one at a time, or sometimes all at once, can be buffered by remembering a few simple rules.

FOUR SIMPLE RULES FOR RECOVERY
1) Make assessments of health, safety, and appropriateness, instead of judging.
2) Have aspirations and goals, instead of expectations.
3) Have faith that the unplanned events in your life are a form of spiritual guidance toward a greater good that will eventually be revealed. Do not allow yourself to wallow in despair; climb out of it. Choose to wait and see what happens next.
4) Remember the "Serenity Prayer" that says, "God grant me the serenity to accept the things I cannot change, the courage to change the things I can, and the wisdom to know the difference. And God, grant me the courage not to give up on what I think is right, even when I think it is hopeless."

Einstein noted to George Bernard Shaw, "There are few enough people with the sufficient independence to see the weaknesses and follies of their contemporaries, and remain themselves untouched by them. And these isolated few usually soon lose their zeal for putting things to right when they have come face to face with human obduracy." Human obduracy – the stubborn and total refusal to change an opinion or stance – is a human tendency that prevents the intake and processing of new information, thus preventing the natural spiritual evolution that is intended for us. We have witnessed a dangerously unhealthy growth of human obduracy in the political polarization in democracies around the world.

It is through our human freedom of choice that we can either free ourselves from, or doom ourselves to, a life of enslavement to what is false and destructive. People like Einstein and Shaw are among the many great thinkers of our time in the ways of personal and spiritual freedom. However, ultimately it is our own indomitable determination that will take us to the "promised land."

It is up to each of us to "set out on the lonesome trail" and take "the road less traveled" to discover our here and now as it truly is. From this point, we take the first steps toward learning to see things differently, and making new and healthier choices for a better tomorrow. Life will always present challenges, or blindside you with something you never saw coming, but as Lena Horne said, "It's not the load, but how you carry it, that matters."

LEARN TO SEE THINGS DIFFERENTLY
(Einstein versus Hubble)
There is a wonderful story I like to tell about when Einstein who, in the middle of his career, met with NASA astronomer Edwin Hubble who was the inventor of the Hubble Space Telescope. Einstein called this meeting "the conversation of my life." In this conversation, Einstein and Hubble naturally debated the nature of the universe.

By then, Einstein had already formulated many of his famous theorems, among them his *theory of relativity* ($E=mc^2$) that became the most famous equation in the world. He had already been hailed as one of the world's foremost leading thinkers, an accolade that professor Einstein found very distasteful.

In this conversation, Einstein asserted his belief that even though he saw the universe as infinite, he also believed it to be stagnant, or not moving. Dr. Hubble vehemently disagreed, asserting that distant galaxies were continually moving apart; this view was hatched in the 1920's based on his own observations. His conclusion was that the universe was not stagnant at all, but was continuously expanding at a determinable rate. Dr. Hubble's theory would later be called "Hubble's Law" which gave way to the famous "Big Bang Theory." After a lengthy argument and discussion, Dr. Hubble was able to present his view of an expanding universe convincingly enough to persuade Einstein to consider it.

Hubble's view was so radically different from Einstein's that adopting it would change Einstein forever. But Einstein was a man of courage, and courage was his middle name. He not only chose to adopt this radical new view of an expanding universe, he proclaimed he had formerly been enslaved by his old view to a point of frustration, because it held back his thinking on ideas he had been trying to develop for years. Suddenly, Einstein's thoughts were no longer constricted by his old view of the universe. He realized that many of the theories he had begun developing earlier in his life that seemed to have a solid basis, he had abandoned in frustration because they did not fit into his old belief in a stagnant universe.

Now freed to view things differently, from then on his thoughts soared into his future works, which he considered the greatest works of his life. With his new view of the universe, he said his ideals of truth, goodness, and beauty "have lighted me on my way, and time after time have given me new courage to face life cheerfully." By choosing to view things differently, Einstein fulfilled his greatest potential. He became one of the strongest and most beloved scientific, social and spiritual thinkers of all time, and a renowned humorist. While few of us are not all destined to become as great as Einstein, however, we are all meant to become our greatest selves, to reach our full potential, to learn to face life with courage, to have faith in ourselves, and again like Einstein, to enjoy cheerfulness.

Recovering from denial by seeing things differently can be as basic as opening up to, acquiring, and assimilating new information. My maternal grandmother, Grandma Tootsie, once said, "Sometimes it takes an extreme to counteract an extreme before you can find a balance." To err is human, however, in our human relationships and in the rest of the world, any extreme is out of control. I have witnessed and experienced many types of extremes first hand, and I know how harmful they can be.

I feel when you are learning to view the people and events in your life in a new way, it is important to resist the temptation to demonize or debase someone or something you find is harming you. This kind of judgmentalism can create a destructive pattern of anger and self-righteousness that can serve no good purpose, and it will chip away at your self-esteem and character. It is far better to concentrate on learning how to recognize and understand what is, and assess it for health and safety. This will mean making overdue, major changes, and a good therapist can help you identify and understand what these are.

Apply a healthy yardstick to yourself and the people around you, and see who measures up. Face your reality as it truly is, recognize the presence or absence of what is wholesome, and take a stand for what is healthy and safe. Muster the courage to believe the evidence of your eyes, and apply what you learn to your life. Have faith in what you know experientially, especially after you have learned to understand it. Trust yourself, and become the keeper of your health, safety, and reality. Open your mind to new possibilities, but don't let your brain fall out! As much as you can, keep in mind what you have learned.

You will become your own best assessor of what and whom you can allow into your life to protect your energetic livelihood. Protect yourself from negative influences that want to draw you back into your old familiar pattern of retreating into fantasy and denial. Even if you teeter on the fence between fantasy and reality now and then, as long as you hang on to what you honestly know, you will end up on the right side of the fence every time. This is simply a normal part of the transformation process of learning to see things differently. Remember Einstein when he said, "The only true source of knowledge is experience."

AVOID ENERGY DRAINERS

When looking at the people around you as the truly are, seek to recognize and distinguish the givers from the takers. There are people who drain your energy, people who do not, and people who actually contribute to your energetic wellbeing. People who drain your energy – deliberately or not – are exceedingly blind and selfish, as are those who enable them, and do not measure up to assessments of health, safety, and appropriateness. There is no sane reason to tolerate an energy drainer. Even if your family or others are ridiculing you for setting boundaries, set them anyway.

Being around my family's mental illnesses while I was healing myself of a chronic illness, always made my symptoms much, much worse, at a time when I was literally fighting for my life. It always took at least two weeks after seeing them to "detox" from their toxic, disordered energy. It does not matter if the energy drainer is a family member, a spouse, a friend, an employer, or just an acquaintance. In the healthy adult world, everyone is subject to the same assessments of health and safety and appropriateness.

I heard a story about a woman who survived a stroke, who recalled that while in her coma state, she sensed and perceived the people coming and going in her hospital room as energetic forms that drained her energy, gave energy to her, or were completely neutral. As an empath, this happens to me consciously every day. It is so true that sometimes people in their human struggle – especially the needy – can inadvertently drain the energy of those around them during times of difficulty, even when they are doing their best to cope. There are also people who simply feed off of the energy of others.

This is a normal part of the human experience, and if you want to be around other people, some of this must be tolerated, but only to a point. What I am talking about are chronic energy drainers – died-in-the-wool, willingly immature people who may have struggled to reach maturity, but for one reason or another, remained un-evolved. They still circle about in the same ways now as they did 20 or 30 years ago, and never seem to get anywhere. It is dumfounding and amazing at the same time!

There are many types of energy drainers, and they come in all forms. They can be covert, and wear a manipulative mask of sanity, charm, and sweetness and light, or blatantly obnoxious. If someone in your life is repeatedly draining your energy, recognize it, and don't have anything more to do with them.

You have probable heard the story about the frog that gave a scorpion a ride across a stream. The frog was instinctively hesitant at first, but the scorpion conned him by assuring the frog that it would not sting him. Half way across the stream, the scorpion stung the frog. As paralysis set in, and the frog began to sink, he asked the scorpion, "Why did you sting me? Now we will both drown!" The scorpion replied, "Because it's my nature. I couldn't help myself!" On the other hand, most people are not at all like the scorpion. Some can and will help themselves. Those who won't simply don't want to do the work.

Why people are the way they are in their behavior toward you has nothing to do with you most of the time. They most likely behave the same way toward everyone who will put up with them. So there is no need to feel the least bit responsible for how they treat you. Remember, assessing relationships with healthy standards is not judging. It is simply practicing responsible self-care to protect yourself from the scorpions. Learn to identify the people who characteristically poison or drain the energy of others, and choose to leave the scorpions on the shore. Respect their right to be who they are, have compassion for them, understanding that they are also limiting and depleting themselves in their unending struggle through life as unknowing prisoners of themselves.

IDENTIFY THE NATURE OF ENERGY DRAINERS
(Three short stories)
These are my three stories about "chronic energy drainers." They all suck the air right out of the room, and drain the life-force energy from whomever they come in contact with. These stories are titled: The Leech, The Vampire, and The Black Hole.

THE LEECH

When you are out in the world wading through the waters of life, you will come into contact with many things. One day you may stop to look at yourself and find that unbeknownst to you, a leech has attached itself to your body, likely more than one. Realizing this, you abruptly head for dry land to remove them. Because the leech exuded a toxin that numbed you, there was no way to tell one has latched onto you until you examine yourself. Also, because you cannot feel them after they've attached, they can skillfully sink their heads under the surface of your skin to establish a stronghold before you even become aware.

When you remove them, you have to be very careful. If you try to yank them out in a forceful way, their body will snap off and leave their head buried under your skin. The toxins from its poisonous head will cause an infection that can permeate your entire system, and make you very sick. The best way to get rid of a leech is to put something like salt on it to make it so uncomfortable it will back out on its own, and you can then remove it without harming yourself. It will never back out for your sake to ease your level of discomfort because it naturally wants to suck on its host forever.

Any leech that has latched onto you will simply be true to its own nature, and is merely trying to survive in the only way it knows how. To sustain itself, it must suck your blood, your life-force, in order to stay alive and maintain the only existence it has ever known. When you successfully remove a leech, and throw it back into the passing waters, it will simply return from whence it came, and float downstream until it finds another source of sustenance to latch on to. It's really nothing personal.

After you remove it, you will begin to regain the strength you had unknowingly lost. You will begin noticing how much better you feel. You will also begin choosing to stay in clearer waters, keeping your eyes open and watching out for leeches. If one comes along and unknowingly latches on, you will quickly notice, and gently remove it before it gets in under your skin. The moral of this story is, watch out for leeches and do not allow someone else's unhealthy thoughts or behaviors to disturb your serenity, drain your energy, or poison your mind or body.

THE VAMPIRE

Let's say you have the power to say "no" to a vampire. One night while you are enjoying a nice campfire in the outdoors with friends, a vampire walks up to you and says, "Hello, I'm hungry, and I want to suck your blood." A natural, healthy response would of course be, "No way, Jose! Be gone, and never return!" And you would feel no guilt at all. When Count Jose pleads, "But I can't exist without your blood! Won't you just allow me a little bite?" Your answer would be, "Sorry bud. That's your problem!"

Only a person with severe and inappropriately low self-esteem would feel sorry enough for the vampire to offer them their neck, and say, "Well, maybe just a little one." That's because they would feel too guilty to say no. Here is a news flash for you. It is inappropriate to feel guilty when saying no to a vampire! When someone is harming you by draining your life-force energy, it is utter nonsense to feel guilty for stopping them.

If you know your vampire stories, you'll remember that when a vampire preys on its victims, it is always under the cover of darkness when its true nature can be hidden, where their victims can be taken unaware, and are defenseless. The vampire will charm you into a trance, and pose as a friend, a loved one, or a charming do-gooder. Because of its mask of charm, you may not recognize it as something that wants to suck your blood, until it's too late.

Furthermore, after the vampire has taken its first bite, the victim becomes less resistant to its trance and is repeatedly bitten, and eventually dies. And what's worse, it turns into a vampire as well after being slowly drained of its natural liveliness by the evil vampire. Once this happens, the victim, now a vampire, loses their original identity altogether, has been is fully assimilated into a world of darkness, and has become completely maladapted. So much so, that when they look into a mirror, they can no longer see their own true image reflecting back at them. Their true self has suddenly vanished into thin air, has become something they no longer have control over, something devoid of compassion and free will, floating through life attacking victim after victim as a slave to their maladaptive state of being.

The moral of this story is clear. Stop floating through life with no identity. Wake up from your stupor, and turn on the floodlights of knowledge that will expose the vampires. As light destroys the vampire's power, so shall it discourage an energy drainer when you set an enlightened boundary against them. Learn to choose an appropriate level self-esteem, and gain the power to say no to a vampire without feeling guilty. The chances of coming out of a dysfunctional family with appropriate, healthy self-esteem may seem remote at times, but it is up to you to choose to prevail.

If you do not, and choose to go on being spellbound by the toxic trances of conditioned guilt and obligation, and continue offering your neck, you will run the risk of becoming as doomed as the maladapted vampire, either physically, mentally, or both. You will deprive yourself of truly seeing what you could have become as a fully energized and self-actualized individual. In all fairness, even the vampire was once a victim, and unnaturally turned into a monster. This may induce you to feel some compassion for them, and may even be a reason to forgive them. However, it is not a reason to join them in their dark, ignorant world by sacrificing yourself to their tragedy.

THE BLACK HOLE

Within our infinite universe of space, galaxies, and stars, exists a fascinating phenomenon called the black hole: the anti-star. Simply put, it is a large, black, vacant hole situated in space that appears black to astronomers. It has a gravitational pull powerful enough to suck into it anything that comes near enough to the foreboding edge of its infinite blackness, including light. Everything that gets too close to it becomes its victim, and is destroyed and consumed into oblivion, leaving not even the faintest trace of what once was a star, a planet, a nebula (un-coalesced matter and gas), space debris, and so on.

Once something has been devoured by a black hole, it is as if it never existed. The more a black hole consumes, the more it additionally consumes, and, of course, nothing is ever given back. It is the nature of the black hole to function in this way. In understanding its nature, the only way to protect yourself from being sucked into its overpowering vortex is to stay far enough away from its event horizon so not to be caught in its gravitational pull. The only way you can spot a black hole is by recognizing the absence of what would normally occupy the space where it exists, such as stars, or starlight, for instance.

People who are like a black hole can fool you at first, unless you know what to look for. But it won't take long for you to recognize a refusal to give of themselves. Like the black hole, taking is all that most selfish and disordered people know how to do. It is the only way they know how to try and fill the bottomless pit of their ego needs.

The moral of this story is that, because bottomless pits cannot be filled, these people will never feel as though they have something to give back. Thus, sadly and paradoxically, they miss the joy of giving, which is in itself fulfilling. This tragedy is the path they are on until they choose another. When you experience the dead zone around these takers, do a quick 180 and keep moving.

The moral of these three stories is: don't let anyone deplete you of your energy, either covertly or overtly, and don't be a chronic giver to a chronic taker. There are two good old sayings: "Do not cast your pearls before swine" and "Do not try to make a silk purse out of sow's ear." I love piggies – I do not eat them – because they are loving, intelligent, devoted animals, and can make as wonderful a pet as dogs. Comparing some humans to them is unfair… to the pigs! But you get my meaning. Make your own silk purse out of pure silk, and put your pearl inside it and keep it safe. String your pearls with a thread of impersonal compassion, clear assessments of health and safety, authentic forgiveness, and healthy boundaries.

These stories provide you practical awareness to help you put into perspective the pattern and nature of energy drainers, and the problems they pose so that you won't have anything to do with them. There is really no other option. Recognizing these people for who they are, and accepting the truth about their nature, is important of course. However, it is even more important to see yourself as you are, and address the truth about your own nature before you can change things in your self. Pull your head out of the sand, and stop sleep-walking through your life living inside foolish dreams, fantasies, and lies, pretending things and people are not what they actually are. Wake up from denial!

EPHESIANS 4:25-32

Wherefore, putting away lying, speak every man truth with his neighbor, for we are members of one another.
Be ye angry, and sin not; Let not the sun go down upon your wrath, neither give place to the devil.
Let him that stole, steal no more, but rather let him labor, working with his hands the things which are good, that he may have to give to him that needeth.
Let no corrupt communication proceed out of your mouth, but that which is good to the use of edifying, that it may minister grace unto the hearers.
And grieve not the Holy Spirit of God, whereby ye are sealed unto the day of redemption.
Let go all bitterness, and wrath, and anger, and clamor, and evil speaking, and put away from you all malice.
And be ye kind one to another, tenderhearted, forgiving one another, even as God for Christ's sake hath forgiven you.

The Holy Bible

NINE

ANGER
The gift of survival energy

During visits with my father, he told me repeatedly that anger was undignified, and that only the fool gets angry; the wise man understands. He'd also say things like, "Sex is strictly for procreation." He being a playboy made it seemed hypocritical to me. My mother, who was a raging psychological terrorist, often said, "Do what I say, not as I do." She'd also responded with anger when I was heart broken over breaking up with a boy, or when my cat got run over by a car, saying, "Oh, Val! Why do you always have to get so emotionally involved?" I knew early on my parents were not ever going to be healthy role models or any source of appropriate advice.

Needless to say, if you are from a dysfunctional family, some of the messages you were raised with may need to be thrown out! The most destructive message I received was that anger is undignified. The truth is, that anger is as natural an emotion as all the others, yet it creates tremendous amounts of confusion, guilt, and shame. I feel this is because it is so commonly misused and misunderstood. The truth about anger is actually fairly easy to understand. To clear some of this up, I would like to talk about what I call three key aspects of anger that are very important to understand: anger is a gift, it is felt for a reason, and it signals a problem (and a boundary) that needs to be addressed.

THREE KEY ASPECTS OF ANGER
ASPECT ONE (When we are attacked)
The first aspect is that anger is a gift. Not only is it a gift, it can be your best friend. We feel anger when there is a need to protect our mind, body, and soul from an intrusion, insult, or attack. Anger is neither bad nor good. It simply is. It is meant to give us important messages that help us survive, and keep us safe and healthy. Anger is as natural as fear, joy, sadness, jealousy, envy, and love. Because of the shame and guilt attached to anger I would like to offer some telling thoughts in its defense. Anger can either be constructive or destructive, and what distinguishes them is simply how it is used.

190

We may be told anger is undignified, that we should not get angry because it is unpleasant and destructive, or held to a too high bar of spiritual philosophy. I believe these concepts about anger have a potential to misguide us from its purpose, and cause us to become passive, complacent or inappropriately compliant. It is only when we suppress this energy, or express it in uncontrolled or abusive ways, that it becomes undignified or destructive. Anger is our survival energy and is sometimes the only emotion powerful enough to motivate us to face facts, isolate the truth, and take action to make the much needed and overdue changes.

ASPECT TWO (When we are supressed/oppressed)
The second aspect I see is that anger is always felt for a reason. We feel angry when our personal rights and freedoms are being trampled on, violated, or suppressed, when our boundaries are being manipulated or ignored, or our personal beliefs or decisions are being ridiculed, devalued, or judged.

We feel anger when our souls are being prevented from developing and evolving due to abuse or oppression of any kind. Entire nations have risen up against tyrannical dictatorships inspired by their natural anger about the inhumane oppression of their basic human rights and freedoms. There are always reasons for why we feel anger. It is simply up to us to identify these reasons, and take the appropriate action to protect ourselves.

ASPECT THREE
The third aspect is that anger is an indicator of a problem that needs a boundary around it. It may seem like a small problem at first, so small that it is hard to identify. But when you do identify it, you may find that this "small problem" is the root of an even larger problem, or an unhealthy pattern that could be solved or corrected with one simple boundary.

You alone are responsible for paying attention to and honoring the messages of your anger by responding appropriately. You are also responsible when your response is inadequate, or nothing at all. When this signal is ignored, the anger is repressed. When anger is repressed because it is believed to be wrong, which causes guilt and shame, or because it feels painful, uncomfortable, unpleasant or scary – the anger goes into a stockpile to accumulate along with all the previously repressed anger that came before it.

REPRESSING ANGER MAKES IT GROW

Repressing anger can prevent necessary action from being taken toward the situation the anger is calling your attention to. The result is the situation continues to exist, and more anger is created, repressed, and stored. This is why repressing anger makes it grow. We can only store up anger to the limit of our individual capacity, and when the stockyard is full, some people tend to explode to some degree. A cache of stored-up anger is often triggered to blown up by a "last straw" event, is felt disproportionately to the latest event that triggered it, and is therefore expressed in excess of what would normally be considered appropriate.

These explosions are a dead give-away to anger mismanagement. They indicate the exploder has not taken personal responsibility for honoring and expressing their natural anger with control and moderation, or for initiating self-care action through confrontation and boundary setting. The immaturity of this dysfunction may commonly be an oppressive childhood in which anger was not allowed to be expressed; from an on-going example of destructive anger being misused in out-of-control ways; or religious doctrines that frown on it.

WHEN ANGER IS DESTRUCTIVE

Children learn how to honor and express anger by the example set by their parents. If parents express anger in a healthy, controlled, and constructive way, the child naturally mimics this positive example. Conversely, when parents are immature and out-of-control in their expression of anger, the child will mimic this. However, when anger is repressed, causing some people to eventually explode, it causes others to implode.

When a person's repressed, frustrated rage is stored beyond their individual capacity to contain it, and the person is consciously inclined not to risk hurting others by exploding outwardly, they may choose to direct their anger inwardly, causing it to implode in their body. This is called an inversion response. Instead of an explosion of anger becoming toxic and destructive to the people around them, it becomes toxic and destructive to the body of the person containing it. This toxicity can permeate their entire body down to the cellular level, and overwhelm the body with what are referred to as the death hormones of adrenaline and cortisol.

These hormones are only meant to be experienced during a fight-or-flight response to danger. When the danger has passed, they are no longer being released, and the body washes them out of the system. When these hormones are regularly experienced in the body, they can become addictive, and their toxic effects on the body and the mind can be devastating. Chronic illness can eventually manifest on some level, be it mental, physical, or both. Also, these death hormones cause inflammation to occur in the body that condition can become chronic, manifesting in known inflammatory conditions such as arthritis and ulcerated gastritis.

I also believe that how deep an illness is manifested can depend on the intensity and regularity of repressed, negative emotions, the storage capacity of the individual to compartmentalize emotions, particularly anger, and the genetic weaknesses that are passed on through DNA. Genetic weaknesses are often triggered by stress, trauma, diet, or substance abuse. However, just because we may have inherited a predisposition toward a certain illness or trait does not mean we are doomed to experiencing this condition for life. Research has shown that if we learn to avoid the triggers of these genetic tendencies (miasmas), we can dodge these bullets. This is what boundaries and choices can do for us.

The two most destructive forces to the soul are repression and oppression. Repression is what we do to ourselves, oppression is done to us by others or societies. The energy that is compressed inwardly by these two negative forces intensely contradicts the outward flow of energy that is natural in the expression and evolution of the soul. Repression and oppression binds in chains both the mind and soul. Instead of being free to grow, expand, develop, and thrive on all three mind-body-spirit levels, repression and oppression causes a person to contract, whither, and deteriorate, with suffering on all three levels. The result is that we can tragically become stuck, stifled, unfulfilled, and very sick. Repressing emotions, including anger, is very costly.

You have everything to gain when anger is used in moderation in constructive ways to find solutions, and you take the appropriate action in a timely manner. Conversely, the only people an explosive person harms are the people around them. After they release their pent up anger they feel better, while everyone else feels poisoned by it. This is because their toxic energy flies out of them and into whoever is near. Nothing is gained, and everyone loses.

Even if the exploder feels better afterward, it is still a dangerous way for them to manage their anger. While they are building up an explosive charge, they are poisoning themselves, and the relief of "letting it all go" does not make up for the damage done to others, and to one's self while charging up for the next release. Not only does the receiver feel emotionally poisoned by the outburst, they are also poinsoned by their own fight-or-flight response of shock and fear. This is why exploding anger is so destructive to relationships, and so abusive to everyone it involves.

Note: Hate is not an emotion. Hate is the internal rehearsal and/or expression of negative perceptions and judgments directed toward another person about their behaviors and actions. It is making and taking the poison, and waiting for the other person to die first. It is not a wise choice. As Eldridge Cleaver averred in "Soul on Ice", "The price of hating someone is loving one's self less."

WHEN ANGER IS CONSTRUCTIVE
Anger can be used in a proper, positive way, and safe anger management and expression can be learned. With the guidance of a good therapist, and education about the nature and purpose of anger, you can learn to express your anger in healthy ways. Such behavioral modification is a good place to start. Honoring and respecting anger, and using it for good and constructive purposes, can actually be very rewarding. Instead of choosing a destructive method of expression, such as exploding or imploding, people can choose a more mature expression of anger that is healthy and helpful overall.

Anger sharpens your senses with its chemical responses, and provides you with increased energy to focus. Directing this energy toward changing things for the better can be a very powerful spiritual experience, even if it is not always pleasant or comfortable. Anger is supposed to be upsetting to motivate us to take action. If it were not unpleasant, what effort would likely be made to change anything? I doubt much effort would be made at all.

After all, human beings can be very lazy, and this innate human inertia, that some religions call "original sin," is believed by many to be at the root of all human evil. So, in our natural human unwillingness to endure pain needlessly, anger urges us to take action and set boundaries, resolve problems, and motivates us to overcome our human inertia that causes us to resist change, growth, and expansion.

When our efforts to resolve a problem are thwarted, or our attempts to communicate openly are not working, then a natural response is frustration and a degree of anger. Sometimes, when all else fails, we need to get angry to be heard. Focus your anger on identifying a problem, organizing your thoughts, thinking it through to its natural solution, framing this solution in clear terms, and expressing these terms a moderate tone in a truthful, respectful, self-honoring way. Though difficult, this can be very gratifying.

I don't mean gratifying in any egocentric sense, like what is commonly referred to as "ego-tripping," which in truth is weakness masquerading as strength in an attempt to feed the ego and control others. But gratifying in that there is no greater force next to love that is as powerful for evoking change than the unexaggerated truth, and the pure truth can be the hardest thing of all to find. Anger can motivate you to find it.

The fact is that honoring all your feelings is an expression of self-love in a healthy way, and is meant to produce an outcome that is constructive, instead of destructive. There is no ego trip in this. Only a desire for being committed to what is true and healthy can map such a path. Buddhists believe that every thought and action has a ripple affect that becomes a part of the universe and affects us all, and that we are all connected to each other through the same universal life-force energy (love) within us.

Honoring our true humanness that surfaces as our inner guide from the enormous trove of wisdom in our inner mind, is where we experience that gut feeling that grabs us, and hear that gentle, quite voice that speaks to us. Where we gain the inspiration that moves us to create and share our creations. Where we know the desire to love and to be loved. Where we experience the free will to choose "to be angry without sin." Where the feeling of all other emotions allows your mind, heart, and body to become aligned. When you are being congruent within yourself, these elements will not be at war with each other.

This means your energy will be aligned and resonating clearly, and without conflict or static. Within this resonance comes peace. When you find the peace that comes with honoring all your feelings in appropriate and healthy ways, only then will you begin to expand, see things in new ways, and begin realizing your full potential without being distractive by misperceptions about what is healthy. Use anger as a motivator to help you solve a problem, to evoke proper change, and to set protective boundaries. Use it as a constructive tool, without causing harm.

In a letter from St. Paul to the Ephesians, it states simply, "In your anger, do not sin, and do not let the sun go down while you are still angry, and do not leave room for the devil. Do not let any unwholesome talk come out of your mouth, but only what is helpful for building others up according to their needs, that it may benefit those who listen." So if you talk when you are angry, express yourself with moderation about what is in your heart and mind to successfully convey your message and protection of your serenity.

Be an example of how to express anger constructively. Observe how effectively you can solve problems, and help others learn to express their anger without being destructive. Remember, one of the best ways to becoming healthier is to honor all your feelings, love yourself in all your natural complexity, and listen to the messages of your anger.

PHOENIX RISING

Out of the pyre of life's injustice,
from events unearned and unforeseen,
emerges a caged and broken spirit,
now injected with the power of immortal love.

The spirit ascends like a shining phoenix
up and out of its rival darkness,
with a blast of comet-like force.
So furious a will that fuels its blazing wings,
as streaks of light glow wide beneath.

The phoenix rises and breaks free,
illuminating all that has gone before
in a single flash of comprehension,
never to sink or descend again.

The ignited intention of its recovered power
surges within the heart of its reclaimed spirit,
and courses through miles of electrified veins,
as the magnificent phoenix rises again as once before,
when, as its truest, most incandescent self,
is unfettered by events or time.

Brilliant with love and consciousness,
on fire with its natural blinding luminosity,
you, the phoenix, return.

Valerie Lumley

The Phoenix: An ancient mythological bird resembling an
eagle that lives for 500 years, and then burns itself to death
on a pyre, from whose ashes another phoenix arises.

197

TEN

AUTHENTIC FORGIVENESS
To cleanse and not absolve

To begin with, what I call authentic forgiveness is a process, and not an event. It is also a widely misunderstood pathway. There is so much confusion about forgiveness: how to do it, when to do it, if it can be done, if it really even needs to be done, what good does it do, and why. When people take personal responsibility for their own actions and behavior, apologizes sincerely, makes amends by promising to do better, and demonstrates an effort to change, forgiving them can be a relatively easy process, and take little time at all.

Conversely, when an insincere, or no apology comes from a person who has no intention of taking personal responsibility for their behavior, it can make forgiveness much harder. Whether or not the person you are trying to forgive feels personally responsible for what they have done, the act of forgiving them is ultimately meant to cleanse the heart of the person doing the forgiving. It is not meant to absolve the transgressor of their personal responsibility.

I want to sort all this out, and clear a pathway to forgiveness to show you that it is accessible, understandable, practical, and smart. If you are from a dysfunctional family, its inherent abuses have most likely left you with deep scars in you psychologically, emotionally, spiritually, and perhaps physically. Freeing yourself from the natural resultant anger through forgiveness, while at the same time setting up protective boundaries, is the best way to begin healing yourself from the wounds of the past.

You will also need to find peace with your past and the people in it through understanding, so you can use your energy in the present to heal your body, mind, and heart from the hurts of the past. Beginning the process of authentically forgiving your transgressors with the help of growing understanding becomes a physical, mental, and spiritual necessity. Actor, Mickey Rooney said, "Forgiveness is the only real power we have." We also have the power to direct our lives by our choices, and authentic forgiveness, like everything else, is a choice.

When you begin the process of forgiving, rushing to forgiveness is only a form of avoidance denial of emotions and not authentic, self-honoring forgiveness. The process of authentic forgiveness can be a relatively short path, or a long one, depending on what needs to be forgiven, the depth and severity of the wounds, and the length of time that the harm has been inflicted.

I feel the deeper wounds, especially those repeatedly inflicted over a long period of time, such as being in a relationship of some length with an abusive person, can take the longest to forgive. However long it takes to arrive at authentic forgiveness - be it a few minutes, hours, years, or a lifetime - the process is essentially the same. The process of authentic forgiveness is accomplished in the following ways. For me, it began with detachment on three levels.

DETACHMENT ON THREE LEVELS
(Physical, psychological, and spiritual)
1) PHYSICAL DETACHMENT
In the case of severe or chronic abuse, it is likely necessary to create a physical boundary of distance and time; stay apart for as long as it takes, even if forever. This boundary should precede all others to enable you to take a step back, assess the relationship, and learn to view it clearly from a safe distance. It should preclude all contact of any kind with the abuser, including in-person, phone calls, letters, emails, texts, and messages sent through others. Also, discuss this individual or individuals with those inside your immediate support system, such as your therapist, spouse, or a close friend who is safe and can be trusted.

It is also wise to utilize the support of a good therapist if you do not have one. Life-changing decisions need guidance and support, and the right kind of help can help prevent you from abandoning this process out of fear, guilt, false-obligation, outside ridicule and attacks, and/or separation anxiety. The distance and time boundary does not always need to be permanent, although in some cases it does, but it should never be adjusted or removed prematurely.

2) PSYCHOLOGICAL DETACHMENT

It is necessary to educate yourself thoroughly and become an expert on the nature of your wounds, the effects these wounds have had on you, and how they have manifested in your life, and the origin and cause of the abuse you have suffered. Again, you may need help and guidance here, and recommended appropriate reading that speaks to your specific experiences. Randomly reading from the self-help section of your local bookstore can become confusing, and very time consuming. The right information at the right time will give you the necessary understanding you need, and the added strength, clarity, and support this understanding can provide.

While you are learning to understand the nature of your wounds, you will simultaneously be learning to understand yourself. To "know thyself" is a very powerful way to be more clear and certain about your reality. A lot of peace and security comes from knowing yourself, and particularly in how you feel about what occurs, and why. This peace can open you up to the right choices, and allow you to put things into a more natural and healthier perspective.

Learning to recognize and understand the effects your wounds have had on your life, can make sense of how you feel about what occuring today. Learning new terminology will enable you to discuss event more clearly with others, and ponder them yourself. This can help you recognize and identify your feelings about the occurrences in the present, and separate them from your feelings about occurrences in the present that closely resemble the past.

If the present reminds you of the past in some way, you can now choose to respond more appropriately by seeing how this similarity can trigger past feelings, and supercharge your current emotional responses, causing them to become disproportionate. Separating the present from the past allows you to keep current events in their proper perspective so you can respond appropriately and proportionately.

Finally, understanding the cause and origin of your wounds includes learning to understand to an extent the true nature and personal dynamics of the people who have harmed you. This will be very helpful in separating yourself from them psychologically. It will help you see your abuser(s) objectively as damaged people, enable you to draw a line between where you end and they begin, and give you the strong sense of separateness needed to successfully detach.

3) SPIRITUAL DETACHMENT

It is extremely helpful to acknowledge the fact that arriving at authentic forgiveness is spiritually healing. The evolution of the spirit is meant to continue naturally throughout life. Blocking your personal evolution is unnatural and can cause illness, just as much as blocked, repressed, or unacknowledged emotions can. Recognizing the evolutionary nature of your soul and a higher power that created, it is a very important step that will enable you to ultimately free yourself from destructive belief systems and entrapments that can keep you stuck in dysfunction and/or bonded to your abuser.

Believing that one's spirit cannot release itself from another comes from incorrect conditioning by our parents that family is all we have, and we must stick by them, no matter what. We are all keepers of our own souls, with the power to release ourselves from the grip of pain inflicted on us by others (the betrayal bond), by directing our spirit onto the path of personal growth and healing.

Detachment brings with it a sense of peace and strength that supports the overall process on a very deep level. It also puts responsibility in the appropriate places by making the abuser responsible for their soul, and frees you to become responsible for yours. You cannot follow your own path toward health and enlightenment, and at the same time drag along the ball-and-chain of the degradation and self-depletion of an abusive relationship.

TAKE TIME

Take time for detachment to take hold and settle in, and grieve the loss, be it a temporary separation, or a permanent one. Absorb and process all that you are learning so that it becomes an integral part of your self and your choices. Learn to think and live life differently, get used to the strange newness and space that accompanies detachment, and select healthier and better people and occupations. Discover the wounded self now healing, now being redefined and creating a new, healthier identity. Experience your life within the limitless bounds of freedom that comes with detachment, and finally, experience the energy that was once chronically being depleted from tolerating the pain of abuse and dysfunction.

Chronic emotional pain can deplete your energy at an enormous cost to your health, and gradually collapse you into a state of resignation, complacency, and stagnation. It can rob you of your joy and ability to develop your unique gifts. It can so consume you that your life seems to be merely passing you by, instead of being fully lived and valued. This is the saga of the unfulfilled life and the un-evolved spirit. Do not allow this to happen to you. Take the time you need to walk away from the dysfunction, and to yourself.

HONOR THYSELF
Honoring yourself means to acknowledge, validate, and experience your feelings exactly as they are. Your feelings are not wrong. They just are. Experience them in all their simplicity or complexity, and allow them to surface uncensored. Don't try to interpret them to mean something you can feel better about.

What you feel may be painful, or feel like a frightening, unidentifiable blender of mixed emotions pouring out of your heart into your throat. In any way you can, feel your emotions, tolerate the discomfort they may cause, allow them all to well up, and wash them away with tears if necessary. Get rid of them. Process them out instead of holding them in.

Painful feelings have a life of their own. They may take a while to release, sort out, identify, and express. But know this, painful feelings cannot sustain themselves unless you hold them back, or choose not to acknowledge and express them. When you let painful feelings surface and make themselves known, they will naturally dissipate.

Conversely, when you hold them back, they grow in intensity, and can eventually permeate your entire body. Pent up emotional pain tends to warp, mutate, and combine with other feelings to eventually become unrecognizable, and can develop the power to chain your mind and oppress your soul. This result will tragically underwrite the unadulterated squandering of the natural self.

Ignoring and/or suppressing your feelings ultimately blocks grace, joy, and serendipity; the gifts that life offers that are not asked for. Dishonoring your feelings in this way can rob you of everything worthwhile in life. The pain of holding back your feelings and blocking their expression is said to be many times greater than the pain that comes from honoring them in a healthy way.

Experience their expression and all they have to teach. Releasing them to make room for a new, expanding self will enable you to come out on the other side of this process with more compassion for yourself and better understanding of others. You have everything to gain from cleaning house by honoring your feelings, and everything to lose by not.

"You are a child of the universe – no less than the trees and
the stars; you have the right to be here."
Desiderrata, Max Ehrmann

You have the right to be who you are, feel what you feel, think what you think, and live your own life as you see fit as a growing, flourishing, ever expanding human being, with a peaceful mind, a joyful heart, and fulfilled soul.

The only way out is to go into and through. Go into and through your feelings. It may feel terrifying or overwhelming at times, but you will come out safely on the other side, out of the darkness and into the light with the feeling of knowing what is deep within you, hiding nothing, seeing clearly, being honest with yourself and others, and living your life as the gift that it is. Nothing is more freeing than being true to yourself. You can walk more slowly with more assuredness, and feel secure in your own skin. It's wonderful. So, don't let anyone act like your feelings don't matter. It isn't true!

ASSESS YOUR REALITY
You must make a hard and realistic assessment of the big picture called your life. Detachment is a tool that allows you to stand back far enough to take a good look at your life in its entirety; maybe for the first time. Suppressed, unprocessed emotional pain can

create tunnel vision, and can put very narrow blinders over your view of life. When someone or something is harming you, your energy becomes significantly depleted by the task of surviving, and there is little or no energy left for assessing the very people and/or circumstances you are trying to survive.

Survival is our number one priority, and when we are stuck in survival mode, our assessment skills can become overshadowed, and sometimes we cannot see the forest for the trees. Under these conditions, making a realistic assessment of the harsh realities responsible for your suffering can be extremely difficult. You must look deep into the blinding light of the burning fire of truth. Be assured, it will not leave you sight impaired. Quite on the contrary. When you back away, your eyes will adjust, and you will have acquired the ability to see things with laser-sharp clarity. It will amaze you.

UNDERSTANDING MAKES FORGIVING EASIER

When you are being harmed and are locked in a battle for psychological, physical, and spiritual survival, you will want to consider at the capacity of the person causing the trauma to change. This is when learning to understand the nature of this abuser, and the origin of their behavior comes in handy. It is possible for some people to change with hard work, but only if they have a sincere desire and the ability to recognize what is out of order in themselves. This requires a capacity to extend themselves for the sake of others, to respect the importance of owning their behavior, and a willingness to take responsibility for changing it.

They must also possess the capacity to understand what is being presented to them for their cognition, and the willingness to apply what they learn to themselves and their life. Bear in mind that there is a distinct and significant difference between emotional illness and psychological disorder. Under the general category of mental illness, psychological disorders are identified as personality disorders, and are much harder to get on top of and deal with in comparison to emotional illnesses that can effectively be cured through talk therapy.

I am willing to forgive someone and give them another chance as long as they show true remorse for harming me, a willingness to take responsibility for their behavior, express an honest intention to do better, and prove to me that they are making the needed changes by behaving differently. However, the debilitating limitations of mental illness make all of this impossible, and it is not realistic to expect it.

If you are from a mentally ill, dysfunctional family, and struggling to assuage your anger for their abuse and deprivations, and are sincerely trying to forgive a major offender(s), a basic understanding of mental illnesses makes this easier. This is another important step in achieving authentic forgiveness. I have written a practical synopsis that is hopefully easy to understand and may help clarify your view of others, focusing on psychological disorders.

THE ORDER OF DISORDER
Psychological disorders have an order to their severity, and an individual potential for improvement with treatment, and a cure. I call this "the order of disorder." There are three basic types: psychotic disorders, personality disorders, and anxiety disorders. The following description lists first the most drastic disorders with a relatively poor potential for improvement or cure, down to the least drastic with a relatively good potential for improvement and cure.

1) PSYCHOTIC DISORDERS
The most serious psychological disorders are called psychotic disorders. Psychotic people are extremely difficult to treat, and usually require a lifetime of care, including antipsychotic drugs that produce little or no improvement. These people suffer from psychosis; an aspect that is marked by delusions, hallucinations, incoherence, and an overall distorted perception of reality, such as in the cases of schizophrenia or mania. Mental hospitals are full of these tragic suffering souls. The prognosis for improvement or cure in this group is very poor.

2) PERSONALITY DISORDERS

(Ego syntonic: thoughts, compulsions, and behaviors that are felt to be consistent with other aspects of a personality, belief system, and one's self-image)

The second most serious of the psychological disorders are called personality disorders, and contain ten prominent conditions. Personality disorders are generally referred to as ego syntonic when the disorder is marbleized throughout the entire personality and the sufferer believes that the drama, self-absorption, and other traits characterized by their condition are in fact reasonable responses to the way the world is treating them.

This makes them hard patients to treat and cure. Anti-psychotic drugs can alleviate some of the stress for some of the most drastic cases, and can motivate some patients to take on the harder work of therapy where they can learn to modify, and even control some of their behaviors. These ego syntonic disorders are grouped into three distinct subcategories, and I list them here from most drastic to least drastic. These are called the dramatic cluster, the anxious cluster, and the odd cluster.

A) The first and most drastic of these subcategories is the dramatic cluster. Of these, the best known are the borderline personality noted for their melodrama; the antisocial personality noted for being disruptive; the narcissistic personality noted for their self-absorption; and the histrionic personality noted for making too much of things. These are among the most toxic and destructive types of personality disorders, and commonly occur in combination with other disorders.

B) The second and less drastic is the anxious cluster. These disorders include the straightforwardly named dependent personality (the codependent); the socially withdrawn personality; the avoidant personality; and the rigid, rule-bound obsessive-compulsive personality (different from the anxiety disorder, see below).

C) The third and least drastic group is the odd cluster. These include the paranoid and schizoid personalities. The schizoid types have problems forming relationships and interpreting social cues. They are lone wolves (the classic recluse) that may also suffer from delusions, and skate along the edge of real schizophrenia.

An increase in family fragmentation and dysfunction in our society is producing more cases of personality disorder than ever before. As many as 9% of societie's general population is now reported to be suffering from some kind of personality disorder. As many as 20% of all mental health hospitalizations may be resultant of these conditions. Studies show that after two years of therapy, 40% of patients suffering from the less drastic personality disorders show improvement, leaving 60% with the more drastic disorders who continue suffering and believing the lie the disorder tells them: that there is nothing wrong with them. These nuts do not fall far from their tree, and are sometimes the hardest, and most impossible nuts to crack.

The best improvement that they can make is in eventually becoming more flexible and resilient. They are not likely to stick with therapy. Only a few will try it, and shortly afterward usually seek to discredit the profession altogether by concluding things like "all therapists are crazy." The prognosis for a cure in this group is poor.

3) ANXIETY DISORDERS
(Ego dystonic: thoughts, compulsions, and behaviors that are distressing because they are felt to be inconsistent with one's self-image)
The third and least serious of the psychological disorders are called anxiety disorders; they are phobias, compulsive worrying, eating disorders such as bulimia, obsessive-compulsive disorder (OCD), and depression, and are generally referred to as ego dystonic.

The difference from the syntonic sufferer is that the dystonic is usually able to acknowledge the problem and wants to do something about it, when the syntonic does not. These types of conditions are thought of as having a pathological rind, wrapped around an intact core. Peel away the layers of the dysfunctional conditioning through talk therapy, and/or melt them away with drugs, and the problem has a good chance of abating.

These are neurotic disorders, and can be successfully treated with hard work and dedication by the patient, and are not nearly as time consuming as the more serious cases. Neuroses such as these can be completely cured in as little time as six months to two years. It usually requires a correction in the person's belief system and replacing old outdated concepts of what is healthy and what is not with new ones, in order for the patient to be cured.

With the help of a right therapist, it will be up to you to determine which category the person or persons harming you may fall into. It will also be your responsibility to make a self-diagnosis, according to what you learn about your dysfunctional family and yourself. If you want a healthier life with healthier relationships, you may have to face some hard facts. Sometimes facing these facts means leaving some people behind.

You are in therapy for you, and are on your own path. Walking away from impossible relationships with authentic forgiveness is a choice you must make to be, as much as possible, a healthy, productive, loving, compassionate, joyful, fulfilled, human being. It is your responsibility to choose this by making the necessary choices to regain mental and physical balance, and the right therapist can help you.

MOTIVATION FOR AUTHENTIC FORGIVENESS
Forgiving is the kindest thing you can do for yourself, because grudges keep wounds festering. Forgiveness heals them. The amazing grace of authentic forgiveness is more than the result of the rudimentary transaction of a transgressor making amends – remorse, apology, promise to change – that can make forgiveness possible. But what about when amends are absent? Does a transgressor deserve to be forgiven, even if he or she shows no remorse, gives no subsequent apology, blames you for their behavior, takes no personal responsibility for theirs, and has no intention of making an effort to change?

The truth is that this does not morally concern you. What does is the act of authentic forgiveness: the deep, profound feeling in the heart that initiates transcendence above anger. That said, the act of forgiveness is not meant to absolve the transgressor of their personal responsibility. It is simply meant to cleanse the heart of the one doing the forgiving, and release them from the scourge of festering anger and grudges.

To forgive someone who you may not feel deserves it is truly the kindest thing you can do for yourself. Holding grudges causes the ongoing organic production and release of the toxic death hormones – cortisol and adrenalin – which are the result of the frustrated rage that accompanies long-term anger, whether it is active or suppressed. General hatred, disgust, distain, revulsion, the disappointment of unmet needs, and the frustration of unrealistic expectations, are all negative emotions that cause the periodic production and release of these hormones into the body that can permeate the body and eventually make you sick.

The bad behavior of any human being is never worth this kind of self-punishment. To forgive someone is to see forgiveness as a practical way to help you heal the wounds of the past and present. It is also a profound way to love, nurture, and respect yourself, and only you have the power to do this.

Be clear, the act of forgiveness never means going back for more abuse. It is very much the same as forgiving someone who has cheated you out of your life savings. You forgive them for your sake, but you will never be foolish enough to trust them with your money again. If someone is incapable of meeting your needs, and is instead harming you, then stop looking to them. Turn away, and look to someone else, someone who is capable. It is wisdom to do this.

I recently heard it said that wisdom and strength are not opposing forces. Wisdom comes from experience. Strength comes from self-love, which I believe acknowledges that our higher power (or God) is the ever-present guiding force within and not without. I'm not talking about the socio-civic businesses of organized religions. I'm talking about an ultimate spiritual truth. Connecting to this reality will give you the courage to stay the course, and not abandon yourself. Remember, when you no longer need love from someone who cannot meet this need, detaching and forgiving them is a lot easier when you realize this.

Tolstoy said in *War And Peace*, "The most difficult thing is to love life, even when you suffer, for to love life is to love God." So, to love life and all it teaches, even through you are suffering, is to love the self and the God, the higher power within us all. Authentic forgiveness will release you from the past and ground you in the present to help you face the whole of your life, come what may. It will free you to live your life with courage and grace, and as Einstein said, "with good cheer."

In the Holy Quran it is said, "He who seeketh to approach me one cubit, I will seek to approach him two fathoms, and he who walketh towards me, I will run towards him, and he who cometh before me with the earth full of sins, but joineth no partner to me, I will come before him with an equal front of forgiveness." Free yourself from the shackles of non-forgiveness, and forgive your transgressors for your own sake.

FORGIVENESS IS NOT RECONCILIATION

It is a common misconception that forgiveness is the same as reconciliation. There seems to be a lot of confusion about the difference between the two. The truth is that these two acts are entirely different in nature, and are mutually exclusive. Forgiveness deals solely with the past. Reconciliation deals solely with the future; a second chance, and the desire to change. Reconciliation is only possible when someone is willing to take personal responsibility for his or her behavior, express remorse, and honestly promise to do better.

When destructive behavior is brought to light, and people make an honest effort to own and correct it, this will be demonstrated by actions, not words. However, if someone is being unpleasant, sarcastic, or angry; playing turn-about games by calling attention to your past behavior; is unwilling to admit their present behavior is inappropriate, and change or do better; or blames you for their behavior… then reconciliation is impossible. No matter how badly you would like to reconcile with this person, if this is their position and response there is nothing you can do. This is narcissism, and it is their problem, not yours, nor is it appropriate to sacrifice your wellbeing to the pathologies of others.

When someone is unwilling to own their destructive behavior, to forgive and forget and go back for more is insanity. Wise men forgive, but only the fool forgets. Therefore, forgiving an unrepentant person is for your benefit not for theirs, and in no way does it make you obligated to continue your relationship with them. You are not even obligated to inform them that you have forgiven them. Forgiving them simply means that you have enough self-love and self-respect to not allow what happened in your past cause you to become frozen there, and it allows you to move forward into your future.

Forgiving the repentant or unrepentant transgressor means you allow yourself to acknowledge that the abuser was emotionally crippled as a child by an abusive environment and circumstances beyond their control that were not their fault. At the same time, you realize it is their responsibility to correct their destructive behavior, and not your responsibility to adapt to it.

Have compassion for them, and by all means forgive them for your own sake, but stay detached and keep your distance. Have the kind of impersonal compassion you would for all the suffering souls on the planet, but as long as they intend to continue with the same destructive behaviors toward you and/or others, you must put yourself first, and love your self too much to continue subjecting yourself to them. It means that even though you have forgiven, there are still going to be people and places you may always need to stay away from. You will know this in time. It is simply a part of life.

To forgive and forget and go back for more does not represent authentic, healthy forgiveness. It is self-destructive and purposeless martyrdom, denial of reality, denial of accountability, and denial of personal responsibility for self-care. Jumping to forgiveness without first acknowledging and working through your feelings of rage, betrayal, abandonment, fear, or grief is deep avoidance-denial of natural feelings. Making excuses for the evil in destructive behavior is minimization-denial.

Furthermore, understanding someone's bad a behavior does not excuse it. It merely equips you to make accurate assessments for health and safety. Disregarding a wrong behavior by making excuses for it, adapting to it, or ignoring it altogether, only enables and guarantees its perpetuation. Healthy adults say no to harmful behavior, and demonstrate the moral and spiritual integrity to refuse enabling it. Use your feelings as a guide.

In conclusion, by all means forgive, and reconcile when it is possible and equitable to do so. But when you are faced with an unrepentant major offender, choosing to squander your most precious personal resources – your time and life-force energy – by trying to reach someone who does not possess the capacity to understand what is healthy and what is not, is worse than foolish. It is pure, self-destructive martyrdom. We were not here to martyr ourselves to the incapacities of others.

Now, when I think of authentically forgiving my severely dysfunctional parents and family, I need to remember a simple fact. All they have done to harm me was done through their wounded, maladaptive child ego. All the insanity, neglect, abandonment, rejection, drama, disrespect, abuse, ridicule, misjudgments, et cetera, came out of the chronic unconsciousness of their psychological disorders, and had very little to do with me.

No one is consciously insane, and all the dysfunction that still permeates my family is due to unconscious emotional and psychological disorders. So I have had to ask myself, how can I remain angry at a mental illness? How can I expect someone to change, or become enlightened (do the hard work to gain a near complete understanding of themselves in their here-and-now reality), who does not possess the capacity or willingness to do so? How can I ask people to understand me who are incapable of understanding themselves? It would be insane on my part to expect anyone to listen to me who can't even hear me.

I have experienced this insanity firsthand, and suffered the pain, frustration, and disappointment from trying to reach people who do not share my adherence to reality and what is healthy and what is not. Due to my own past unwitting ignorance, and naive, unrealistic expectations, I have endured the pain I have caused myself from my participation in close relationships with many disordered people throughout my life.

Gaining freedom from dysfunction and disorder represents for me one of my life's greatest challenges and achievements. It also represents the greatest gifts I could offer myself: peace of mind, and the opportunity to live a healthier life. I am committed to continually educating myself so I can understand, forgive, and heal my family's legacy in me, and not pass it on to the next generation the way the rest of my family has. For my own sake, I have forgiven everyone who has ever done me harm. Meanwhile, the dysfunction stops here!

IT MAY BE HELPFUL TO REMEMBER
A person's psychological health is always reflected in those closest to them. If the people around you are struggling with mental illnesses, then maybe it's time to realistically and honestly assess yourself, and learn to understand your role within the inter-personal patterns of dysfunction in these relationships. There's an old saying, "water seeks its own level" – or we attract people on our own level of mental health. Also, parents recreate their own illnesses in their children. To see yourself, look at your children and the people around you. They are your mirror.

Your becoming healthier, by oiling up your position in the rusty family mobile, can often help move those close to you to become healthier by example. On the other hand, your putting yourself on the path to health may threaten some of your sickest family members so deeply, they may feel their only option is to attack or reject you, depending on how seriously disordered their egos are. No matter how badly people react to your choosing a healthier path, keep on marching straight ahead. Seek, and ye shall find your *freedom light!*

And so, as we go about creating each new and welcomed day, we can choose to treat ourselves with loving kindness, and consciously manage our thoughts and actions wisely. So remember that reasons do not equal excuses, forgiveness does not equal reconciliation or absolve responsibility, and a biological connection does not always equal family. We can continue to grow in an upward direction by educating ourselves, and evolving our spirit by expanding our capacity to absorb and apply what we learn. We can choose to have faith in what we know from our experience, teach by example, and monitor others and ourselves for health and safety. At any time, we can choose to nurture our unique gifts and develop them to their nearest and fullest potential with joy and gratitude.

If I had one sorry regret, it would be that I had the misfortune of being born into a severely dysfunctional family, and did not go out and find the help and support I needed to get away from them early enough in my life to have the chance to reach my full potential as a talented classical singer. Considering what I've done with my life in spite of them, I feel I could have cultivated a fulfilling singing career, had I gotten away in time. However, the near insurmountable obstacles inherent in growing up in this kind of unhealthy environment were something I had no control over. I only had control over how I chose to respond to them, and I eventually got myself on the right path. It doesn't make sense now to harbor this regret, but I will always feel the grief of missing out on what I could have been, and never had a chance to become.

Even so, I am content now in the knowledge that I am no longer a twisted, maladaptive version of who I was born to be, and live my days with true peace of mind. I am simply and authentically me, and that is the gift I have courageously fought to give myself. So even if it feels inappropriate at first, I strongly urge you to take charge of your life and embrace the unknown. Do what is healthiest for you, and be not concerned with what others think or feel about it! Love yourself!

I wish all of this for you, and leave you with my own personal motto: Never give up! Life, after all, belongs to the tenacious.

Sincerely,
Valerie Lumley

FREEDOM LIGHT

Within the sorrow of what almost was,
The visions in my soul are like zephyrs
That float through my being like ghosts.
Ghosts from a time that was ripe with splendid joy,
And tragic, epic, and forever.
A time that endowed me with mystery.
A time that discovered me, and all I could
ever be was revealed in one transient eternity.
And it was brought forth, shared, and given with
a force molten with the stern intent of
instilling the essence of strength of being.
An inner strength that, to me, became unknown,
unseen, and unfelt, while living a thrown upon life,
only to be revealed in one timely instant,
to emerge like an awakened dragon
from its restorative cave, leaving the darkness,
spreading open its sleepy wings without,
and exposing its giant and hidden heart within.
A heart that fought so bravely, was always
so steadfast, so heavy, and carried
among and through the un-chosen course,
and around the bends of unfriendly miles
that wound sharply into hazes, and disappeared.
A heart yet carried forth to dare the journey,
and hold itself against a truer, more intended fate.
A fate to find its freedom light
to illuminate each and every struggle,
and see that the strength, the courage,
and the love intended, were only moments away,
and always present within,
to be sought out through this determined agony,
and claimed forever as rightful.
To be melded together with every gift so freely given,
as this giant and brave heart begins to pass
through each new and welcomed day.

Valerie Lumley

DESIDERATA

Go placidly amid the noise & haste,
and remember what peace that may be in silence.
As far as possible without surrender,
be on good terms with all persons.
Speak your truth quietly and clearly; and listen to others,
even the dull and ignorant; they too have their story.
Avoid loud and aggressive persons;
they are vexations to the spirit.
If you compare yourself with others,
you may become vain and bitter; for always
there will be greater and lesser persons than yourself.
Enjoy your achievements as well as your plans.
Keep interested in your own career, however humble;
it is a real possession in the changing fortunes of time.
Exercise caution in your business affairs;
for the world is full of trickery.
But let this not blind you to what virtue there is;
many persons strive for high ideals;
and everywhere life is full of heroism.
Be yourself. Especially, do not feign affection.
Neither be cynical about love; for in the face of all aridity
and disenchantment it is perennial as the grass.
Take kindly the counsel of the years,
gracefully surrendering the things of youth.
Nurture strength of spirit to shield you in sudden misfortune,
but do not distress yourself with imaginings.
Many fears are born of fatigue and loneliness.
Beyond a wholesome discipline, be gentle with yourself.
You are a child of the universe,
no less than the trees and the stars; you have a right to be here.
And whether or not it is clear to you,
no doubt the universe is unfolding as it should.
Therefore be a peace with God, whatever you conceive Him to
be, and whatever your labors and aspirations,
in the noisy confusion of life, keep peace with your soul.
With all its sham, drudgery and broken dreams,
it is still a beautiful world. Be cheerful. Strive to be happy.

Max Ehrmann 1927

ABOUT THE AUTHOR

Valerie Lumley has lived on the Monterey Peninsula all her adult life. She and her husband of 30 years, Ron, now live happily with their two rescue dogs, Nina and Ricky, Valerie's African grey parrot, Mozart, her African Red-bellied parrot, Poquito, and her Cockatiel, Jake. She loves spending time with Ron, walking their dogs on the beach, caring for her birds, singing, and writing.

When Valerie was 25, she began a successful entrepreneurial venture as the creator in the field of independent medical insurance billing, after working as an office manager and medical assistant for an eye surgeon for five years. For the next 25 years, she grew her business, traveled the world extensively, studied classical singing and foreign language – learning to sing in five languages for opera – and educated herself in human biology and psychology.

She spent eight of these years training her voice, developing repertoire, gaining performance experience as a principal soloist for the Cabrillo College Opera Project, Burlingame Opera Company, and Monterey Opera Association (MOA). She also sang supportive and lead roles in musicals at the local Wharf Theater on Fisherman's Wharf in Monterey. She received kudos for all her performances, which led to her to be chosen to sing the lead role in *The Merry Widow* with MOA in 1996. Three months prior to opening night, she injured her neck at home during an exercise routine, but the show must go on, and she received her usual kudos for all seven of her performances.

After the operetta, her condition was so severely exacerbated it triggered full-blown fibromyalgia, and she became bedridden for two years, and housebound for ten. During this time, she developed a protocol for a lasting cure after deciding to leave the care of the medical profession that offered no hope. Over the following ten years, she developed a cure in alternative medicine while writing her book *Curing Chronic Fibromyalgia – Choosing What Works,* to help others guide their way out of the disease.

After curing herself, she reunited with the love of her musical and spiritual life, great American baritone, James Tippey, in 2011. Through his love and generosity, he retrained her voice, and she set out on her late-life venture, *Viva La Diva – Keeping The Songs Alive*, a concert series to sing in the many retirement homes in her local community. She delighted her older audiences with the beauty of classical songs and arias, and another life-long dream of hers came true.

While James Tippey, AKA Garland Andrews, and Valerie Lumley joyfully studied together and developed a new repertoire for her concert series, much to his surprise, she became the protégé he had been searching for his entire life, and had never found. He became the father figure she never had. For the next five and a half years, they traveled around the world on cultural adventures, and while at home Valerie sang six classical concerts for him before he passed away in her arms in 2016.

It was all a magical experience for them both, and the fulfillment of their karmic destiny. Valerie wrote *The Grand Master And His Protégé - A Memoir Of Love, Courage, Endurance And Devotion,* to honor his life and their relationship that is "always and forever." This book was released on Amazon on Garland's birthday, November 26, 2019.

Valerie then wrote *The Inappropriate Therapist – Surviving The Dysfunctional Family And Learning To Thrive,* to help others who grew up in moderately to severely dysfunctional families. Her aim was to help survivors gain the understanding and tools to free themselves from their childhood adaptations that have become maladaptive as adults, gain some control over their lives, and restore their energy so that they can reach their nearest and fullest potential. She dedicates this book to all survivors of dysfunctional families everywhere.

RESOURCES

American Psychiatric Association. *Diagnostic and Statistical Manual of Mental Disorders*. 4ᵗʰ Edition, Pages 648, 650, 721; 1994.

Aron, E.N. *The Highly Sensitive Person*. New York: Broadway Books Publishing. 1996.

Balch, P. A. ; Balch, J. F. *Prescription for Natural Healing*. Fibromyalgia Syndrome, Page 374; TMJ Syndrome, Page 565; Stress, Page 646; 3ʳᵈ Edition. New York: Penguin Putnam Inc. 2000.

Carnes, P. J. *The Betrayal Bond – Breaking Free of Exploitive Relationships*. Deerfield Beach, FL: Healthy Communications, Inc. 1960.

Cloud, H.; Townsend, J. *Boundaries*. Grand Rapids, MI: Zondervan Publishing House, 1997.

Golomb, E. A. *Trapped In The Mirror – Adult Children of Narcissists In Their Struggle For Self*. New York: Quill Publishing – William Morrow, 1992.

Gray, J. *Men Are from Mars and Women Are from Venus*. New York: Harper-Collins Publishers, 1994.

Institute of Natural Resources. *Stress, Depression, and Pain*. P. 1-32. June 2005

James, M; Jongeward, D. *Born To Win – Transactional Analysis with Gestalt Experiments*. Menlo Park, CA: Addison-Wesley Publishing Company, 1984.

Jeffers, S. *Feel The Fear And Do it Anyway*. New York: Fawcett Columbine Publishing, 1987.

Lumley, V. *Curing Chronic Fibromyalgia - Choosing What Works*. Manassas, VA: Edge Publishing Company, 2010.

Peck, M. S. *The Road Less Traveled*. New York: Touchstone Publishing – Simon and Schuster, 1978.

Peck, M. S. *People of The Lie*. New York: Touchstone Publishing – Simon and Schuster, 1983.

Time Magazine. *How Your Mind Can Heal Your Body*. Special Issue. January 2003.

Whitman, A. *Secret Joys of Solitude*. Readers Digest, April 1983.

www.ingramcontent.com/pod-product-compliance
Lightning Source LLC
Chambersburg PA
CBHW072125270326
41931CB00010B/1672